The Cultural Roots of British Devolution

The Cultural Roots of
British Devolution

Michael Gardiner

Edinburgh University Press

© Michael Gardiner, 2004

Edinburgh University Press Ltd
22 George Square, Edinburgh

Typeset in 11/13 Palatino and Futura
by TechBooks India, and printed and
bound in Great Britain by CPI Group
(UK) Ltd, Croydon, CR0 4YY

A CIP record for this book is available
from the British Library

ISBN 0 7486 1920 8 (hardback)
ISBN 0 7486 1921 6 (paperback)

The right of Michael Gardiner
to be identified as author of this work
has been asserted in accordance with
the Copyright, Designs and Patents Act 1988.

Contents

For Edwin Morgan

Acknowledgements

Parts of this book are based vaguely on arguments made in journals, including *Scottish Studies Review*, *Edinburgh Review*, *Textual Practice*, *Interventions* and *Reconstruction*; thanks to the editors and readers for advice, and to Nicola Carr, Stuart Midgley and Eddie Clark at EUP. I owe a greater debt to my publishers than most. Thanks to Kyoko for various kinds of help. Thanks to my colleagues at Chiba University for maintaining an environment where scholarship is still properly valued. Some of the themes in this book were developed in lectures and seminars at Tsuda College, Meiji University graduate school and the University of Tokyo; thanks to the students who came up with striking ideas in a highly exotic subject, and to Hisaaki Yamanouchi, Graham Bradshaw, Nobuo Kamioka, Ai Tanji, and Toshi Kubota for getting me to the position of having to explain. Parts of this book arose after conversations with the following people, some of whom helped hugely by reading sections, and some of whom allowed me to thieve their ideas: Robert Crawford, Douglas Dunn, Willy Maley, Lindsay Paterson, Andrew Nash, Edwin Morgan, Chris Jones, Alan Riach, Kirsti Wishart, Cairns Craig, Bart Moore-Gilbert, Derrick McClure, Brendan Wilson, Roderick Watson, Maggie Nolan, Robert Young, Sonita Sarkar, and Andrew Murphy. Since none of these correspondents had this 12-inch remix in mind, the book's failings are absolutely mine.

Preface

The UK is a nuclear power with substantial armed forces; it is usually first in line behind the US's remote changes of regime, and was itself the originator of the 'Star Trek convention', where it is accepted that every life-form in the universe probably speaks the dialect of English as we do. It has one of the world's largest economies and has a vast cultural reach from publishing to fashion to pop music. It is also, however, a union which has never behaved like a union, and a state without codified rules or bill of rights, run by an executive which has long given up debating policy. It has a first-past-the-post voting system which deliberately excludes voices from outside the main two, increasingly similar, parties, and a 'national' culture which is lost with no imperial blackboard on which to be written. In this context, devolution is not a Scottish or Welsh process but a British one. It can be described, as I will try to show below, as the *last* British political process. It is a postcolonial process: the United Kingdom was created for imperial aims, and, despite cracking in the twilight of colonialism, still pursues neocolonial economic policy via a polity whose shape has not changed much in the meantime.

The causes and aims of devolution are therefore disputed, in part according to the cultural significance granted to each British nation. This misrecognition represents one of the greatest ironies of contemporary Britain: those in the devolving areas tend to see the changes occurring as national, and bring longstanding and comprehensive national cultures to this viewpoint, whereas the state government goes to great lengths to convince the English public that the process is regional and that there is no national worry. The modern Scottish idea of devolution is constitutional and democratic in stress, and difficult to stop; London's idea still sticks to a Gladstonian imagery of delegation (the original, now outmoded meaning of the term 'devolution'). In this sense, Britain is 'divided' not simply in having more than one national culture – something we already knew, and which has never changed – but in having different ideas of what 'national culture' means. As I try to show, the official idea that devolution means granting some authority to tribal peoples to pursue their own self-interest is one that barely scratches the surface.

This book argues that devolution represents the endgame of a growing ambivalence deep in the British management of culture. Images of the most stable period of Victorian unionism have been fantastically successful in export, but post-British criticism is as old as the British union itself; despite a tendency of critics on both sides of the border to concentrate on party political nationalism, this has been a broad cultural movement. But then so was Britishness itself, which only had any real meaning after unionist intellectuals swung behind it from the 1740s. In this sense, the 'post' in 'post-British' should be seen like the 'post' in 'postcolonial', as having connotations both temporal – a stage of 'hard' politics not yet reached – and epistemological – a stage of secession kicking in about the 1920s. Devolution begs questions of democratic restructuring of each nation within union *and* each nation still affected by Anglophone imperialism; its imperial significance goes deeper than most Scottish nationalists would like to admit. Here there will be little talk of an 'internal colonialism' in the UK; like any attempt to make a sensible contribution to the field today, this book is mindful that Scotland showed enthusiasm for British colonialism disproportionate to its modest population. Yet one major blockage to the properly democratic break-up of this imperial power has been nations' inability to grasp their own complex histories *as colonisers*; nationalists have tended to aim at separation still broadly within the ethnic images given to them in the nineteenth century which had the opposite aim in mind – keeping them in the union. As part of putting the empire state out of its misery, the national specificity of each nation should be recovered in full view of how its national polity has been shaped by its own position as British coloniser. The national cultural revivals which can be discerned in Scotland and Wales and, more problematically, England (and more problematically still, Northern Ireland) preceded devolution just as Britain was supposed to be strengthening its 'national' identity. These revivals are, I argue here, postcolonial insofar as they are post-British; however, this does not instantly render them free of British imperial thinking.

This book draws from Scottish, Welsh, English and Irish contexts but considers the Anglo-Scottish relationship to be key to the union and its break-up. Ireland joined after and left before Scotland, and exerted an extremely strong influence. Northern Ireland represents a special case: there are tensions which closely resemble the sense of the 'national within the nation' described here, and a number of historical Irish parallels will be drawn, but on the other hand these tensions have not since 1922 troubled the whole union. In North-ern Ireland, being a nationalist has so far meant loyalty to a neigh-bouring republic (though Northern Irish nationalism may emerge). There is a perfectly reasonable case for arguing that Northern Ire-land is still a colony. This puts it in a different category from the British nations which took part as Britons and *en masse* in colonial rule. There has been a boom of writing on British–Irish relations over the past few years, and a number of significant studies have added important insights. This is not one of them. This book looks at devolution insofar as it is a process taking place in the three pre-existent nations which became Great Britain in 1603. Then again, the Welsh vote in 1997 was very tight; if the minimum proportion of the overall electorate had been required to reach a certain level as it suddenly was in 1997, there would now be no Welsh Assembly at all. Plaid Cymru, the nationalist party, favours more representation within a British pan-national state, so that the meaning of devolu-tion has not changed, as it has in Scotland, to an alternative form of polity.

Another reason for Scotland's centrality is that, as the break-down of a form of globalisation originally arising from Glasgow and Edinburgh as a Scottish adaptation to Britishness, devolution and other post-British movements could only really have arisen in Scotland. From this over-adaptive Enlightenment moment come modern economics, exportable narratives of civility (and there-fore imperialism), knowledge as a principle of mass arrangement, social anthropology, the subject-self, 'good English', and English Literature. Yet the union unravels as soon as it is conceived; from 1706 there was popular unrest in the cities, and the emergent US and revolutionary France become surrogate republics, taking on what was for many the real meaning of Enlightenment. As each na-tion becomes increasingly bound into a globalised union, a 'Greater Britain', the peripheral nations stiffen their loyalist position, and an unravelling does not take place until imperialism also unravels in the early years of the twentieth century.

The unravelling which ensues is less party political than cultural, but draws political meanings towards it. Here, therefore, after es-tablishing some parameters for Britishness in Chapter 1 (parameters which do not directly correspond to any governmental moment), I try to chart a path from the upsurge of integrated cultural–political nationalism of the late 1920s to later resistances to the evanescent Cool Britannia of the late 1990s, which may prove to have been Britain's last kick. Chapter 2 looks at how a cultural revival in the years immediately following Irish semi-independence also provoked a long search for political voice. The Scottish Renaissance has been so important as a consciousness-raising moment in opposition to a static British polity that the problems surrounding its ethnocentrism are still rarely touched. The third chapter moves onto national differences as concretised on separate education systems; in Scotland, education has taken on a large part of the burden of civic society, and remains resistant to British utilitarianism and economic rationalisation. Chapter 4 extends this to traditions of philosophy, a subject which has occupied a more central curricular place in Scotland than England. In this field as in education, the rift between specialism and generalism can be linked to wider questions of representation, as can be seen by the intimate relationship between education and pro-devolution/pro-independence movements.

Chapter 5 describes one possible form of English nationalism also arising during the pre-devolutionary Britishing years, one which went straight to the most English image of the countryside and precipitated a rift between British and English ideas of the countryside of tradition. Given that Britain has based authority so much on the voice of whoever is already speaking, Chapter 6 looks at the connections between literary writing and constitutional writing, suggesting that, in the absence of a properly written constitution, these forms of representation are intimately linked. The final chapter surveys thinking on the culture of devolution, suggesting that devolutionary questions should be regarded as having democratic significance for the whole of Britain – or whatever Britain becomes – and for those parts of the English-speaking world over which Britain still exerts a direct or indirect force. This book recognises that Britain's key nation, the one with over 80 per cent of the state's population, is also the hardest one to pick out nationally, since three centuries of assumptions over its own centrality have left England in a situation where serious talk of its own sovereignty is slow to appear. One aim, only hinted at below, is to encourage post-British English culture which has been underground for some time.

Chapter One

When Was British Culture?

Britannic Rule

The year 1740 saw the now well-known first performance, in *The Masque of Alfred*, of the song *Rule, Britannia!* by the Scottish poet James Thomson. Voicing a desire to rule the waves appropriated from the Anglo-Saxon King Alfred, a figure with no connection to Britannia as such, the song is typical of contemporary Scottish demands for joint participation in a British 'national' culture after three decades of relative indifference to the union on the part of England. As we know, the song become increasingly associated with the primary expression of British unity – empire – and the imperial Victoriana which later went with it. By the end of the twentieth century it had given its name, via a symptomatically twisted logic, to the short-lived phrase 'Cool Britannia', describing the same cultural impulse, but this time as a defence mechanism of the Anglo-British government, at a time when Britain was well into the process of dispersal via devolution and postcolonialism.

Just as the growth of British Culture signified by 'Rule Britannia' had been based on an increasingly imperialistic Scottish desire to be part of Britain, the withdrawal of Scottish participation has shown the gaps in the culture of state culture in the three decades or so leading up to 1997; since Britain was enabled by and for empire, the long cultural process behind today's sovereignty-minded devolution is definitely postcolonial – though, as we will see, this designation needs careful qualification. On the other hand, the cultural separation of Britannia from the southern British region of England has only just begun. Despite the keenness of some commentators to stress the abundance of St George's crosses at late-'90s soccer matches including Euro '96 and World Cup '98,[1] in 2002, 'Rule,

Britannia!' was still being chanted during the World Cup by English football supporters. This is ironic considering the song's Scottish origins, and the fact that Scotland failed to qualify for the Finals, for the first time since 1974. These fans' songs, in support of the wrong nation altogether, might be the soundtrack to a history of Britain, as it reaches the end credits and the audience sense that they are going to have to provide their own conclusion.

The union of governments between England and Scotland dates from the 1707 Acts of Union. Wales had been swallowed in 1536 with the help of a long-term Tudor pan-British Arthurianism;[2] Scotland required a nominal union, and offered few propaganda opportunities. From 1707 until the time of Thomson's anthem, the British union's stability was still far from certain. It had been decided through a series of bribes and blunders, but had been one of a long line of attempts dating back to the Union of Crowns in 1603, when James VI/I exported foreign policy to London and maintained Edinburgh as a 'secondary capital'.[3] James was a British Scot of a type which would become more familiar in the Enlightenment, representing national interests within Britain to a bemused London bureaucracy. The figure of Britannia was first popularised during the first decade of James's reign, her name symptomatically taken from Celtic tribes. Britannia's earliest known representation was dug up in 1980, in the second year of Margaret Thatcher's rabidly neo-British rule.[4] The monarch's desire for union during this period is seen nowhere better than in Shakespeare's play *Macbeth*, written, like so much of Shakespeare, with a slightly obsequious tone of support for the present monarch's designs, and performed for the king in 1606. *Macbeth*'s polarisation of image-schemes – light, futurity, nature and rightful government (the divine right of kings) versus darkness, untimeliness, unnaturalness and despotic government (the clan system) – makes it one of the most important pieces of unionist propaganda ever written, even coming long before the union as it did. Tellingly, *Macbeth* was performed for British officers before the 1746 Battle of Falkirk, the last Jacobite victory during a 1745–6 campaign which more or less ended resistance to the union.[5] Precisely the same diametric oppositions of light/darkness and civilised/savage were to become familiar in British imperial discourse. There is an abundance of post-union literary comparison between Scottish (and Irish) rebellion and the enemies of the British empire, couched in Shakespearean terms of unnatural evil. *Macbeth* was tellingly revived in an imperialist context by English Romantics, as Britain and France competed for global supremacy during the Napoleonic wars; Coleridge, for example, likened Macbeth's wrongful governance to that of the despot Napoleon.[6]

By 1608 James had already admitted that the project of union was unlikely to win sufficient popularity.[7] But union did not disappear as a political question: further major attempts at governmental union were made by Stuart kings in 1667, 1670 and, after the 1689 Hanoverian revolution, by William in 1690 and Anne in 1702–3. By the end of the seventeenth century, the process had attained a new urgency, since England, always worried about pan-'Celtic' alliances, now faced the possibility of Scotland's proposing a Stuart Catholic successor on the death of Queen Anne. With the Alien Act of 1705, Queen Anne was able to threaten Scotland with a complete trade embargo if union was not completed. After a century or so of trade tariffs, Scotland no longer had an answer to this threat of embargo (which helps to explain Enlightenment Scotland's vehement furtherance of free trade). One imagined escape route had been American colonies, but this required England to unblock its ports, for which union was made a requirement. So, despite a degree of coercion, empire was a motivation on both sides; we should beware of making claims that Scotland or Wales were dragged into imperialism, or assuming that empire was based in any one of Britain's nations. Scotland's own expensive colonial failure in Panama had shown its desire for, and inability to form, an empire under its own state; conversely, England's unwillingness to fight on two fronts showed how global ambition was tied to union. But eighteenth-century Scottish unionism was, as it would again become in the mid-twentieth century, a minority movement. Anti-union demonstrations were common both in and beyond Edinburgh in 1706, and many of Scotland's burghs and counties presented an anti-union petition to the Scottish Parliament in October of that year.[8] In Scotland, the Act only succeeded via a number of coincident chicaneries, as in the 'buying out' of much of the debt-ridden Country Party by the Duke of Argyll.[9] Much of the eighteenth century would be dominated by proto-Secretary of State figures; from 1775 the broker was Henry Dundas. As T. M. Devine has recently noted, the union was also pressured by English manoeuvres in the north of Ireland, which were difficult to read but seemed to signal military intervention.[10] In the midst of an apparent attempt to break up Scottish estates, some nobles felt that assimilation was inevitable, and decided to negotiate for the most proactive deal possible.[11]

As unionist commentators still go to great lengths to point out, Scots were from the start relatively over-represented in British government, as they are today. A London and Edinburgh-unionist Scottish mafia made strong demands for the new British identity, and as Colin Kidd says, '[b]y the middle of the eighteenth century Britishness had become associated with Scottishness, but not with a unified Anglo-Scottish identity'.[12] A fully unified British cultural identity never appeared, but 'British culture' would peak in the nineteenth century in the shape of imperialism. In their desire to participate in the imperial export of Britishness, Scots were taking on the most Whiggish accounts of the Anglo-British 'national' character – 'the classics of the eighteenth century Enlightenment . . . the most brilliant English history of the age, Macauley's . . . [and] standard nineteenth century histories of Scotland by the likes of [Patrick Fraser] Tytler and [John] Hill Burton'.[13] As the rationale of unionist imperialism adapted into populist forms, Scots were often the first to adapt with it: 'just as there was no Old Tory like a Scotch Old Tory, so there would be no Gladstonian liberal like a Scotch one, no Imperialist like the North British variety, and no Labourite like the Glasgow Faithfuls'.[14]

Against early unionism, Jacobitism was a mixed movement which some scholars have attempted to describe as nationalism,[15] and at times representing a pan-British underground politics,[16] but which was also often inflected by religious and clan sectarianism. Armed Jacobite uprisings, intermittently aided by France, occurred as early as 1708, and again in 1715 and 1745. Popular demonstrations were noticeable in 1713 after a rapid rise in salt tax (as in Gandhi's India), in 1724–5 after the imposition of a malt tax, and in the 'Porteus Riot' of 1736, later the subject of Walter Scott's *Heart of Midlothian*, when the Edinburgh Town Guard fired into a crowd watching the execution of a tax-avoider. The Westminster Government was sufficiently alarmed by the riot to propose a punitive crackdown, but, politically at least, this would not come until after 1746, largely because of the intervention of the Duke of Argyll, who skilfully 'brokered' Britain to the natives and occupied a position like later Scottish Secretaries. By the early 1740s, economic benefits to Scotland, largely from the American colonies, were also quietening dissent. In the year *Rule, Britannia!* had its first airing, John Mair's pointedly titled *History of Britain* from 1521, a time at which there was no political entity of Britain at all, was republished. The next year the first volume of David Hume's *Essays, Moral and Political* praised the 'balanced' constitution of the English Parliament.[17] Two years later the British Museum was opened, and two years after that *God Save the King* standardised as a 'national' anthem. The next year Jacobitism was buried by the Disarming Act, which illegalised the symbols of the already devastated rebels and portended the pro-union Scottish Enlightenment. Throughout the decade, 'British' icons such as John Bull were pressed into Gallophobic service in the run-up to the Seven Years' War, as England reluctantly chose Scotland over France.[18] Culturally, *Rule, Britannia!*'s 1740 seems a good time to pitch a starting point for both Britishness and Enlightenment.

Recently in Scottish Studies, and partly in response to Tom Nairn's allegedly 'pessimistic' view, there has arisen a tradition of linking the Enlightenment to an earlier period to show that its advances were part of a longer Scottish continuity.[19] This has precipitated a damaging silence on those aspects of Enlightenment culture which can less confidently be described as advances, particularly the intellectual justification for racist colonialism, largely invented in Edinburgh. Mid-century Edinburgh was in many ways a model of British mercantile individualism, making it odd that so many Scottish critics today seek to claim it as a model of communitarianism. The New Town of Edinburgh, designed more or less in the shape of a union flag and often seen as a symbol of the civility of the high Enlightenment period, actually damaged intellectual production with its architecture of large, separated houses.[20] Via the 1760s Anglo-Edinburgh literati, the term 'culture' itself, sharing an etymological root with 'colony', came to have a thinly disguised racial meaning as 'refined' or 'polished', the cooked rather than the raw, a meaning it retained until the analysis of 'mass culture' in the early twentieth century.[21] The refined was a state that every human could attain, yet was naturally more advanced in some societies. In this sense Adam Smith's linguistic treatises *Lectures on Rhetoric* (from 1748) and his later economic *Wealth of Nations* (1776) are part of the same movement: the civility of the first is narrativised by the second, and progress becomes the story of 'cultivation' – whether of crops or of native minds. Scottish elites therefore worked to turn civility into a universal narrative in which all Britons could take part, while English elites, correctly in the long run, simply continued to view British authority as the English constitution.

The 1746 Disarming Act, a methodical stripping away of the arms and symbols of Scottish statehood, brought, then, a rapid cultural adjustment outwards to British culture. This is not the same as saying that traditions such as national dress were 'invented', as in Hugh Trevor-Roper's now-infamous 1975 essay, which gave its name to the book edited by Eric Hobsbawm.[22] (And Hobsbawm's *NLR* review of Nairn is instructive: Hobsbawm's repetition that Marxism and nationalism are simply not compatible seems to write off the red and black nature of modern Scottish Marxism.)[23] The question of whether tartan 'really' meant national rebellion is now rarely regarded as a sensible one. What is worth noting is how Enlightenment Britain reworked its marginal nations in terms of image and ethnicity within the whole, meaning that each nation could be granted any amount of apparent autonomy without danger to the constitution – a tactic still broadly adhered to in British thinking on devolution.

Enlightenment, Imperialism and America

Perhaps more telling than the banning of Highland dress in the Highlands in 1746 is the way it was still used in the British army to denote fierceness; it was also re-legalised as early as 1782, suggesting its full incorporation into a pan-national family of Britishness. In a débâcle later often cited by Scottish historians, Walter Scott fully confirmed tartan's Britishness when he organised for King George IV's visit to Edinburgh in 1822 a Highland-theme party using fake tartans worn by 'clansmen' who were really British elites. The re-branding of Scotland along British lines proceeded alongside depopulation in an all-round structural adjustment, via which tourists got the emptiness they paid for. The early nineteenth-century draining of the last of Highland dress's political content immediately preceded the emptying of the Highlands and Islands, along lines of laissez-faire economic philosophy which had largely emerged from metropolitan British Scotland itself. In the early nineteenth century, Scotland was indeed necessary as a tourist destination, since the Napoleonic Wars had rendered France (and effectively Europe) off-limits.[24] Initially provocative in a nation where national dress had until recently connoted treason against the state, the royal wearing of tartan to vacation up north turned out a British fashion leader, and kilts are still required equipment for Balmoral hillwalking.[25] The 'short tour' in this increasingly depopulated Highland countryside was made a British institution by Queen Victoria: in the 1840s she and Albert visited three times, and when widowed she cemented this relationship by settling at Balmoral in 1848. The Victorian honeymoon with the Highlands saw the Celtic image posted as ethnic, past, and an increasingly comfortable fit in Britishness.[26] Ironically, access to this self-fulfilling bleakness was aided by travel times reduced by James Watt's pioneering of steam rail.[27] Victorian Celtophilia, as it peaked from the end of the 1840s,[28] allowed for the management of fierceness within state ambition, or, as Christopher Harvie has put it:

coincided with the brief flurry of 1850s nationalism, and effectively produced a docile, Britain-friendly version of it: tartan (mightily strengthened by aniline dyes, invented in that decade), tourism, and the cult of field sports, Highland games, and country dancing, when aristos old and new would fraternize with the less menacing members of the proletariat. In the Highlands the royals could live a life which was 'simple' and Scots, rather than political and English: different from the formality of Windsor and London.[29]

Behind this cultural nationalist politics of course was a union which had come good on its promise of colonial opportunity, beginning with Scots' heavy investment in American trade. Yet a commitment to free trade, in the vein of Adam Smith, had set the American colonies against Britain and put Scots at the centre of settler revolts which split them from Britain in 1783. Although today the US is sometimes held by British liberals to have inherited the 'rights of Englishmen',[30] individualistic Scottish Enlightenment civic thinking was strongly behind the push for independence. William Lyon MacKenzie later led 1830s Canadian rebellions; Andrew Fisher became the world's first Labour leader in Australia,[31] and together Australia and New Zealand produced twelve Scottish premiers.[32] If America was the republican democracy Britain lost, the loss was of each of Britain's nations.

Despite this radical tradition of, as Angus Calder has famously called it, 'revolutionary empire',[33] the kilted Scot, ironically drawing on older Jacobite images, was by the mid-Victorian age empire's most ruthless symbol. (Frantz Fanon would later describe the same process in 'savage-looking' Senegalese mobilised to create an internal self-perpetuating fear in the French empire.)[34] From 1881 all Scottish troops of the British armed forces, even Lowland ones, were *required* to wear Highland dress to show their aggressiveness and, paradoxically, their British loyalty.[35] These soldiers formed an 'indigenous elite', buying their privileged position by providing a role model for other indigenous imperial troops, fighting for a cause beyond their own nation. And although Scottish regiments did disproportionately well in advancement in the armed forces, they also tended to be disproportionately expendable – in the First World War, the death rate amongst enlisted Scottish soldiers was 26.4 per cent, compared with about 11.8 per cent for the British army as a whole (though this also reflects the fact that some 'Celtic' units, such as the

Scots Guards and the Highland Division, were classed as elite and therefore used in conclusive, high-casualty battles).[36] These losses were unusually evenly spread across social classes, suggesting the effective quietening of communitarian traditions.[37] But by the time of devolution, this loyalist 'Scottish soldier' image was being savagely ironised in Irvine Welsh's *Trainspotting*, in which the 'Scottish Soldier' turns out to be a heroin addict who has lost his leg to gangrene, but who uses his injury as an opportunity to beg on a crowded Edinburgh street – where a passing woman who has lost a son in the Royal Scots during the Falklands War represents a typical older working-class Scottish attitude about the misuse of troops ('ah'll hate that Thatcher till ma dyin day') – then fails to grasp the connection between the terms Royal and Scot.[38] Civil society without an imperial mission has shrunk back to the sarcastic bare bones of free trade and individualism.

This was not, of course, exactly the position of Adam Smith. Like most Scottish liberals during the Enlightenment, Smith carefully watched Britain's biggest settler colony, publishing *The Wealth of Nations* in the Declaration year of 1776. His pro-independence stance may indeed have affected British policy towards America.[39] For motivations not entirely unrelated to Edinburgh banking and Glasgow trading interests in America (over half of the whole American tobacco trade), Smith argued for a duty to promote mutual well-being by opening markets to general competition, checked nevertheless by national 'restraints' usually forgotten in New Right accounts (which are satirised in *Trainspotting*). Although for Smith colonies in general could provide rich opportunities – as long as the native inhabitants were forgotten – British American colonies exemplify the dangers of financial wastage through monopolisation. The Americas, the settler colonies, represent the *only* example in Smith's colonial critique:

> The establishment of the European colonies in America arose from no necessity: and though the utility which has resulted from them has been very great, it is not altogether so clear and evident. It was not understood at their first establishment, and was not the motive either of that establishment or of the discoveries which gave occasion to it; and the nature, extent, and limits of that utility are not, perhaps, well understood at this day.[40]

Given this desire to rationalise America in terms of the Scottish conception of free trade, it is not surprising that many of the settler rebels were of Scottish or Scottish-Irish origin. Robert Fulton provided some of the military might;[41] Alexander Hamilton helped force through the Constitution.[42] In the 1770s, Scotland was sending more emigrants to America than was any other part of the UK,[43] taking in both opportunist adventurers and those with dissatisfactions with Britain or who had been made homeless by British policy.[44] Some emigrations were forced, tenants being shifted like virtual serfs; the actual proportion of forced migrations depends on whether we believe nationalist or unionist histories, but once we see the issue as one of wider economic rationalisation, the question, like the contemporary one of the 'emancipation' of slaves, becomes moot – free choice is for those able to stand alone economically. For a small country, the scale of emigration was vast – two-and-three-quarter million people between 1841 and 1931.[45] Unusually for mass migrations, their number contained a sizeable proportion of skilled workers, engineers, bankers and educated people; an entire slice of society had to remake itself in an un-British form.[46] The Scottish Enlightenment's ideas of policy, civil society and history were exported from the British stalemate to much greater success in the revolutionary colony. William Robertson was one of its most widely read historians.[47] Gary Wills' 1978 book *Inventing* argues controversially that the primary influence on the signators of the American Declaration of Independence was not the English constitution, but Scottish Enlightenment free trade.[48]

Here, though, Enlightenment individualism plays its key trick: since Hume and Smith envisaged civilisation as a process undergone equally by every individual and therefore as outside of and prior to existence, the Declaration represents a *backwards* writing towards a standard already set. To borrow a Derridean argument, the American 'people' only arises from the declaration in the document's signature, and so betrays a temporal doubleness in the act of writing a document which seemingly only comes into being after its own signing.[49] The form of the people is already decided before the people's existence. The ideal civil self, confirmed in writing, is always already there before writing can take place. No act of writing then can reach back far enough to disturb the overall narrative – a perfect analogue of the English constitution, which was left untouched even after the English state was dissolved. Individual progress for Enlightenment thinkers is thus underwritten by a knowledge which is universal and there to be discovered. The Scottish Enlightenment was a boom time for apparent certainties about things 'out there', the famously 'Scottish' and eminently imperial habit of classifying and listing in encyclopaedias. The first *Encyclopaedia Britannica*, a bible of British knowledge, was published in Edinburgh in 1768; today, it still bears a thistle as its emblem. As the doubled consciousness of the American Declaration suggests, the knowledge upon which this authority rests places viewer and viewed in a different time: authoritative time is (in Derrida's term) 'future anterior', always past and unreachable by experience. Thus Homi Bhabha has spoken of an 'anterior nation' managing the 'performative' nation during each iterative moment of citizenship.[50] This form of knowledge is primarily visual and 'scientific', sharing a terminology of light and darkness from *Macbeth*: the 'light' of Enlightenment would remain a perfectly serious metaphor for the codification of times of progress in a wide range of fields from agriculture to poetry, as Ronald Beveridge and Craig Turnbull have shown in *Scotland After Enlightenment*.[51] Even today, 'hawkish' American politicians rarely go for ten minutes at a time without using some form of the metaphor of bringing light to dark regions, viewed one way by the viewers of CNN through the lenses of target-seeking missiles.

Enlightenment Scotland then exported a high-British notion of the rational subject-self to the decolonising Americas, who would later readapt the primacy of surveillance of other knowledges to their own version of military-economic globalisation which outstripped even the British empire. Correspondingly, the difference between the victims of violent attacks *on* the USA and those of attacks *by* the USA (and the UK) has been their visibility. The latter, as George W. Bush put it at the outset of the War on Terrorism, hide in the shadows from the light of justice. The critical targeting of Enlightenment is therefore not merely a postmodernist cliché: Enlightenment metaphors continue to have real effects. Even the media technology which displaces imperial violence and delivers it as light to individual families – television – is a product of a very British social context: its pioneer John Logie Baird, like James Watt, was a product of the environs of Industrial Revolution Glasgow. The habit of viewing the control of light as proof of progress within Britain runs deep: in July 1999 at the opening of the Scottish Parliament, Scotland's new First Minister Donald Dewar's inaugural speech attempted to reconfigure British Scotland in association with Enlightenment, 'when Glasgow and Edinburgh were indeed a light to Europe, and the world'.[52] Thankfully, some of the Enlightenment's 'achievements' today make most Scots cringe.

The Rise and Fall of Greater Britain

Smith's objection to the colonisation of the Americas was an economic one – the colonies were being ruled by and for wasteful elites instead of being open to free trade. Even Hume was 'egalitarian' in this sense, although his idea of natural universal progress was candidly racist – 'Of National Characters' is singled out for attention by Henry Louis Gates in *Figures in Black*, and is rightly noted as influencing Kant's 1764 chapter of the same name, and assuming that non-whites are incapable of arts, sciences and even meaningful speech.[53] But even this Hume was anti-colonial in the economic respect, and was one of the first significant British voices supporting American revolt at a time when to do so was a potential career-killer.[54] While praising the English constitution, Hume was aware of how its 'balance' relied on paranoia and factionalism – a criticism which appears prophetic given the inflation of the power of the Parliamentary executive in the twentieth century. But the legacy of Enlightenment Whiggishness served long to blur the boundaries of Britishness, and 'the idea of Britain still hovers between a synonym for a greater England ... and the limited common purpose sought by the Jacobite Britain of multiple kingdoms'.[55]

Britishness is thus a state reliant on continuous cultural effort not to *expose* its divisions. With the high period of Anglo-British nineteenth-century liberalism the economic merits or demerits of colonies become associated with cultural control, rather than territorial occupation. Robert Young has traced this paradoxically postcolonial cultural patrialism back to Jeremy Bentham's 1793 pamphlet 'Emancipate Your Colonies!',[56] which argues that French Enlightenment-revolutionary commitment to 'liberty' ought to extend to the colonies:

> Bentham's pamphlet turned the American Declaration of Independence into a credo for colonial liberation: now that the French themselves had adopted the discourse of universal rights, they could no longer consistently remain agents of colonial domination. [Thomas] Paine's *Rights of Man* (1791–2) was equally applicable not only to women, but also to colonized societies. Henceforth, the concepts of equality, liberty, the rights of man, and national self-determination, would form the justification and very foundation of anti-colonial struggle.[57]

To some extent Bentham's warnings to the National Convention of France over 'national self-determination' proved prophetic with the Haitian Revolution of 1804, when many French liberals did indeed attempt to 'remain agents of colonial domination'.[58] The resultant de-stabilisation of the entire Caribbean was also apparent in British Jamaica, whose tradition of maroon resistance would feed into a rastafarianism tradition which came 'home' via reggae, communitarianism and carnivalesque, to knock a hole in late-British culture.

As Henry W. Meikle documented in his 1912 account (originally written as an Edinburgh University doctorate whose 'main theme [was] the political awakening of Scotland'), Scottish Jacobin letters had begun to appear in number in Edinburgh newspapers from 1782 to 1783, revealing a republican-constitutional desire buried in Smith's free trading.[59] A number of pressure groups demanded reform in policy towards America/the US in the 1780s and 1790s, and the *Edinburgh Review* was revived in 1802 in part to air such arguments.[60] Smith's enlightened free trade was carried in the early nineteenth century by his Whiggish students, including John Millar and Dugald Stewart, who produced an edition of Smith's works in 1811–12 and issued Smith-like warnings about unchecked mercantilism. John Ramsay McCulloch, editor of *The Scotman* and then the economics editor of the *Edinburgh Review* and the first professor of political economy at the University of London, added another important edition in 1828. In turn, quasi-republican free trade would influence English liberals such as Richard Cobden and his followers ('radical Cobdenites') and remain the standard of *fin-de-siècle* liberalism.

Even this anti-colonialism was contained within a wider form of imperialism, at best a kind of proto-commonwealth, and at worst a cut-price empire trained to manage itself. The writing was already on the wall with the New Education Policy of 1835, which encouraged colonists to create a self-managing elite educated and tested in terms of a canon set in place by 'English Literature', itself a largely Scoto-British conception.[61] Even the anti-colonial Liberal Prime Minister William Gladstone, a 'cult figure, with engravings of his head and features adorning many a Scottish home',[62] felt that if the colonies went they would have to be replaced by some other form of bond:

> [p]aradoxically, the fundamental readjustment required was already spelt out by the anti-imperialist Gladstone in 1846, when he redefined the new relation of Britain to its colonies in terms of a commonality of cultural as well as material affiliations, resting 'upon common traditions of the past and hopes of the future . . . '[63]

The perpetual culturalist remaking of Britain as more than the sum of its parts continues today, as devolution is aggressively sold by the Westminster executive against the odds as proof not of dissenting ethical wishes, but of freedom within British cultural diversity.

This emerging 'national' diversity can be generically described as 'Greater Britain'. Now Anglo-British in stress as distinct from the earlier Scoto-British cultural push, it frequently hinged on the sliding of the term 'English' between nation and language. In 1868 the (later) Liberal MP Charles Dilke completed the equation in *Greater Britain*, an influential record of having 'followed England round the world', which concluded that although 'climate, soil, manners of life, and mixture with other peoples had modified the blood', nevertheless 'in essentials the race was always one'.[64] Dilke spells out at great length exactly the sameness-in-difference which marked the move to an ethno-cultural-linguistic idea of empire. He concludes that 'Greater Britain' should be distinguished by its ability to reproduce Anglophone culture across any number of territories: '[i]f two small islands are by courtesy styled 'Great', America, Australia, India, must form a 'Greater Britain'.[65] This magnanimous redefinition of culture as language and 'race' was to prove influential to the imperialist stance of Joseph Chamberlain, to which Gladstone's supporters could not reconcile themselves, and which would split the Liberal Party at the end of the nineteenth century. The ideological strength of the equation of culture and *ethnos* also helps us understand why early Scottish nationalists of the 1920s to 1950s, despite viewing themselves as socialists and modernists, were also irresistibly drawn to the antique metaphor of 'race', particularly when associated with a language. This writing of *ethnos* also contextualises Benedict Anderson's claim in *Imagined Communities* (1983) that nation-states have tended to be built on the integrative codification of print culture.[66] Having hung on to a separate and relatively wide-based educational system, Scotland was already a highly literate society by the peak of nineteenth-century imperialism, but much of its literacy had been pressed into the service of empire. In the newly unionist late-eighteenth century there was a vast growth of printers in Edinburgh, where for 1920s Scotland, ironically following an earlier British method, establishing a 'language' and disseminating it through native resources seemed to have become *the* method of nationalism: the nation had become structured like a language.[67]

John Seeley's *The Expansion of England* similarly stresses the need to cover over the cultural fissure caused by the dispersion of the 'English' 'race'; before the First World War a variety of writers recognise that settler colonies had a disruptive tendency to unilaterally redress the imbalances of Britishness overseas – that imperialism could 'revitalise the used-up atmosphere of British politics'.[68] As well as making the remarkable prediction that the world's two future superpowers would be the US and Russia (thus going one better than Hume, who only foresaw power moving west to America), Seeley also explains here why native nationalisms are liable to overwhelm parts of the empire which cannot demonstrate a shared culture. The culture which would hold together the Anglophone empire would again, of course, be centred on models of civility gleaned from English Literature and the English constitutional 'balance'. Thus Seeley reformulates imperialism as a British cultural duty which looks less colonial than federal, 'a new imperialist dream of a union of English-speaking peoples, a federation governed by an imperial parliament in London',[69] implying a 'doubling' of imperial policy relative to English-speaking colonies and 'foreign' ones.[70] Surprisingly, Seeley is absent from John Kendle's extensive *Federal Britain* (1997); despite the federalist-imperialist terms accompanying Victorian Scottish and Welsh claims for Home Rule, Kendle's chapter on the '"Federation" of the United Kingdom' assumes the Irish question to be *the* problem of British federation.[71] He does not make much, in other words, of the relationship of nations to the state and the possibility that Britain's member nations today have the potential to 'de-federalise'.

Seeley's influential version of Greater Britain rests on the classical idea that *polis*, rather than being specific to location, is something a 'race' takes with it (we imagine a Victorian colonist struggling to disembark from an Indian train with a bulky suitcase). Despite belonging politically to Greater Britain – meaning the Anglophone empire – this portable imperial identity is unfailingly English wherever it goes. And *contra* Kendle's emphasis, Seeley himself seems to view Britain itself as a form of imperial federation, with its own residual troublesome natives:

> The native Australian race is so low in the ethnological scale that it can never give the least trouble, but even here, since we reckon New Zealand in this group, we are to bear in mind that the Maori tribes occupy the Northern island in some force, much as in the last century the Highland Clans gave us trouble in the northern part of our own island...[72]

In rhetoric again remarkably close to the British account of devolution, Seeley stresses that this bond is not a relationship of colonist to 'conquered state', as in 'the old colonial system', but one which implies a kind of regional autonomy.[73] In one of the most telling passages of the book, he indicates that the federalisation of member regions capable of Anglo-British 'national' civilisation is the same both inside and beyond the union:

The tie that holds together the parts of a nation-state ... is analogous to a family bond. The same tie would hold a nation to its colonies, if colonies were regarded as simply an extension of the nation. If Greater Britain in the full sense of the phrase really existed, Canada and Australia would be to us as Kent and Cornwall.[74]

So within a century or so the British stress had moved from Scottish demands to be *included within* Britain, to English assumptions of *standing for* Britain. This is remarkable given that England only really became interested in the idea of Britain when, as Linda Colley and others have described, it offered rich opportunities for counter-French mercantilism. But by the end of the nineteenth century, the Greater British push had an increasing urgency because of the question of Irish Home Rule, for which, as Kendle describes, various federal solutions were suggested. But by the last two decades of the century, 'internal' dissenters to Greater Britain were no longer restricted to Ireland: although a great deal of active sectarianism existed in Scotland, unionism no longer enjoyed a hegemony, even in the apparently 'paternalist' environment of Glasgow. The Highland Crofters' Party gained five seats in the 1885 election, in which a total of only twenty-seven unionist MPs were returned in the whole nation, seemingly in a call for constitutional change.[75] The Scottish Home Rule Association was established in 1886.[76] When there was a revival of radical unionism in the late 1880s, voters in both Scotland and England began to turn to the Independent Labour Party, a party whose founder, Kier Hardie, fought the 1888 Mid Lanark election in a declared alliance with Irish nationalists.[77] The Liberal party rallied in the late 1900s, successfully portraying Scottish Labour as the latest in a series of faddish social pressure groups, but had nevertheless realised that it could no longer persuade the working-class and the young back to outright unionism.[78] The loss of the youth by unionist parties is a direct analogue of pre-devolution culture, in which the disenchanted young vote proved impossible to recapture for any flavour of constitutional conservatism, far less a Greater British kind. On the set-up of the Scottish Parliament, young people showed the greatest optimism for independence and the most proactive stance towards it: in 1999, 43 per cent of eighteen-to twenty-four-year-olds in Scotland favoured full independence as a constitutional option, and two-thirds of them expected independence to come before the end of the 2010s.[79]

So the period from the 1870s to 1920, during which the Irish question dominated British parliamentary business, saw an abrasive mix of new, 'cultural' imperialism and sub-British nationalism.

By the early 1910s there were strong claims for Home Rule within the Scottish Labour Party (SLP), claims which were to some extent a means, as I. C. G. Hutchison says, of 'pre-empting [British] Labour', in a general consensus that Scotland's place in Britain, like Ireland's, was no longer stable.[80] After the 1918 Reform Act and the wartime concentration of class consciousness, especially in Glasgow, where there were also a large number of Irish immigrants, Liberal Party policy was eclipsed. But as in the case of the Liberals, the question of Home Rule caused serious divisions in the Labour Party, the SLP becoming a pro-Home Rule voice within the movement. In January 1919, the 'Red Clydesiders', following a campaign of rent strikes and socialist education, attempted to declare a Scottish republic in George Square. T. C. Smout (a historian not noted for leaning left-wards) quotes the strike leader William Gallacher as claiming '[a] rising was expected. A rising should have taken place. The workers were ready and able to effect it'.[81]

The 1919 rising has doubtless been exaggerated, as one line of historical research has shown.[82] However, to say, in Murray Pittock's words, that Red Clydeside 'passed into the mythology of the left' is no longer to consign it to ideology, given the status of 'myth' amongst Scottish thinkers who have absorbed ideas of myth and tradition developed by Alisdair MacIntyre, concentrating less on the truth or falsehood of national icons than on lived social facts.[83] The 'livedness' of myth is not lost on Pittock, with a dual literary/historical background; he concludes his study by stressing that 'de-mythologisation' of the national story (the 'tradition of the invention of tradition' briefly in the 1970s and '80s)[84] leads to nothing but caricature and blame.[85] The events of 1919 were in any case new to British politics; as T. M. Devine puts it, 'the events of January 1919, set as they were against the background of the Russian Revolution, sent shock waves through the ranks of the middle classes and crystallized their need for a political party that could halt the irresistible march of socialism'.[86] British reaction to these disturbances, coinciding with partial Irish independence in 1922, led to a purging of the Labour Party on the one hand, and on the other to the break-off of discontented Home Rule socialists to set up Plaid Cymru in 1925, and in 1927 the National Party of Scotland, from 1934 today's Scottish National Party.

So despite bourgeois tendencies remaining in place to this day, Scottish party political nationalism has roots, not only in ethno-centrism, but also in socialist anti-imperialism, using Scottish citizenship to counter Greater British culture. The position of national resistance to imperial culture is nevertheless still incomprehensible to much of the first world – where, at least until postcolonialism, most of the theorists of nationhood tended to live – which routinely perceives nationalism as *de facto* racial. (This association has been encouraged in Britain, as Tom Nairn has pointed out, by a broad range of the British media, keen to give nationalism a 'racial' angle.)[87] Similar breaks from Labour from the left have been repeated in Scottish culture and politics, for example after the failed referendum of 1979,[88] *pace* Jim Sillars's famous railing against 'ninety-minute nationalists'.[89] Such breaks have become a check on British power blocs set in place by an over-powerful executive and the 'first-past-the-post' system, and after 1997 provided a vital forum for political debate when the Westminster Parliament had collapsed into an ultra-centrist, management-minded consensus politics. The Scottish Parliament, though much smaller, immediately instated Green and Socialist MSPs, a state of affairs unthinkable in Westminster.

Kendle thus observes that the Irish question reconfigured the way in which *all* British people related to their imperial government, by forcing questions of constitution. Gladstone was promising Home Rule All Round by the 1879 election, but, until at least the sea change of the 1920s, most claims for Home Rule still framed the nation in a wider federal network. The Greater British model now became thoroughly domestic: by the mid-1880s, as Kendle puts it, 'Gladstone had intuitively recognized that only a "federal" scheme would meet "national" aspirations in the United Kingdom and preserve union'.[90] This became the kernel of every subsequent answer to claims for Home Rule: satisfy '"national" aspirations', complete with inverted commas around the epithet national, within the wider framework of a different-but-common Greater national destiny. 'Home Rule within empire' was by 1895 the policy of parliamentary Liberals as a whole,[91] one which increasingly identified attacks on the constitution 'at home' (including Ireland) with those from the colonies. This meant that 'those analysts who examined the interconnection of home rule and imperial union tended to emphasize that a system which simply conferred local government did not diminish the supremacy of the British parliament nor, therefore, work irreparable injury on the empire'.[92] The Irish and other Home Rule questions in other words 'had raised key concerns about the relationship between the Celtic fringe and the centre of power in London and how that linkage could be ameliorated and preserved'.[93] In colonial Ireland, John Maclean and James

Connolly were demonstrating that nationalism and socialism were not incompatible.[94] By 1918, the 1913 Home Rule Bill had become potentially dangerous, and was not revived. By the 1920s, modern nationalism was beginning to set itself against the British ideal of Home Rule as a means of regional-imperial management. As J. A. R. Marriott put it as early as 1911, the British management of peripheral nationalism became 'a centripetal, not a centrifugal, movement'.[95]

Between the Blairs: The Era of 'Good English'

Adam Smith's *Lectures on Rhetoric* were first delivered at the end of the most fatefully British decade (1748–51) at Edinburgh University to an audience of law and divinity students, and then at Glasgow University in a course of Rhetoric and Belles Lettres (1751–63). Despite – or because of – being delivered by a Scot, the *Lectures* represented a huge step towards the discipline known as 'English Literature'.[96] Britain's first chair in English Literature would be established, not in England, but in Edinburgh in 1762, and occupied by Hugh Blair. Like those of Ferdinand de Saussure, Smith's notes did not form a single manuscript, but were gathered and published gradually by his students, who recognised their importance 'in a country where there is no standard of language, or at least one very remote'.[97] They were not written down until 1762–3, when they were already overlapping with Robert Sheridan's *Course of Lectures on Elocution*, which reflected the desire of his candidly titled *British Education* (1756) to correct the 'false tastes' of the northern part of Britain, 'the dialect of this country most imperfect'.[98] Smith's influential lectures mixed examples from Greek antiquity (reflecting Edinburgh's 'Athenian' image) with those of Pope, Milton and the honorary Englishman Swift, and offered students a programmatic guide to avoiding 'vulgarity' by following the best 'standard of Language' – in other words, an English literary canon.[99] Ironically, Smith opens the *Lectures* (or rather, the lectures open in their present written order) with a phraseology which for readers today recalls the literary theory which would later accompany the break-up of that canon two centuries later:

> Perspicuity requires not only that the expressions we use should be free from all ambiguity proceeding from synonymous words, but that the words should be natives (if I may [say] so) of the language we speak in. Foreigners, though they may signify the same thing, never convey the idea with

such strength as those we are acquainted with and whose origin we can trace.[100]

The 'trace' has since become a problematic term, always partaking of an otherness which can never quite be managed. For Smith the prospect of a hybrid English, which he finds himself typifying, is a source of great anxiety, and he sets about (again like a mirror image of literary theory) to correct 'defects' and 'ambiguities' so that language is clear to every 'Englishman', which term already carries the sense of 'Anglophone man'. Smith's lectures were reworked and codified by Hugh Blair, who became, as Thomas P. Miller puts it, 'the first influential professor of English'.[101] Straddling the eighteenth-century tradition of 'rhetoric' and a more modern Eng. Lit. conception of 'style',[102] Blair codified English Literature's function as 'the cultivation of sensibility in modern civic society'.[103] These lessons were pivotal for Scottish students, for whom 'civic society' was what was left when government had gone south. Via Blair's student friend John Witherspoon, this linguistic over-compensation would be exported to the rhetoric of Revolutionary America, while, ironically, propping up an Anglo-British tradition at home.[104] As David Daiches has shown, Blair's work was becoming curricular in American universities by the 1780s, and his rhetorical approach can be directly linked to the Constitution itself.[105]

If the discipline of English Literature did indeed grow from Smith's high-Enlightenment rhetorical standardising, its concomitant method of assessing culture in terms of immanent properties of civility was to remain extraordinarily resilient, surviving up to and through the New Criticism of the mid-twentieth century. English Literature's logic of referring standards to previous standards rather than to social effects – also the logic of English's default in Greater Britain – only began to stagger during the pre-devolutionary half-century. The 'theory' which replaced older 'New' methods of criticism was at base a post-Enlightenment reading of imperial civic standards, of which English Literature remains the prime example. Yet what is still missing from the analysis of specific imperialist discourses in postcolonial criticism – central to the study of 'English' today – is a general account of the state of the union itself. Even in the late 1990s, when devolution was taking apart the union, most postcolonial critics continued to ignore the national makeup of the world's most successful colonising state. Homi Bhabha, key chronicler of English Literature's 'narration' of identities, and then member of staff of one of Britain's most radical universities (Sussex), spent much of the 1990s discussing questions of transnationalism, cultural marginality, and break-up, without reference to the transnational and margin-centred status of Britain itself.[106] Only one essay in the groundbreaking Bhabha-edited 1990 collection *Nation and Narration* mentions Adam Smith, and not in terms of the unification of a national study of humanities, but of the economic idealism of 1800s America.[107] This is not simply to demand that Scotland be given its creative due (which remains the thrust of many nationalist critics), but rather to post a reminder that some contexts of the falling-apart of English Literature can be missed even by postcolonial studies unless 'British culture' is also historicised.

Connections between Scotland and the successors of English Literature have also remained underground: although Scottish universities had by the 1980s become sensitive to an interdisciplinary attack on English Literature, there also existed a more general fear that stressing postcolonial ambivalence or getting bogged down in '-isms' would detract from the nation's settled will.[108] Commentators on 'Celtic' Britain have, at least until very recently, tended to concentrate on the actions of individuals rather than locating these actions within a wider framework of postcolonial action. There has been a general belief that since Scotland had not itself been a colony, it is separable from English Literature without discussion of the colonising responsibility of Scotland in British culture. One of the most disappointing moments in Tom Nairn's 2000 book *After Britain* is when he summarily dismisses the idea that 'we' have self-colonised, then passes on without mention of Scotland's *national* history as coloniser.[109] Other literary historians like Murray Pittock and Cairns Craig have been acutely aware of the need to connect postcolonialism to the passing away of British culture. Yet Craig surprisingly shies away from any mention of Said, Spivak or Bhabha in the body of his book *The Modern Scottish Novel: Narrative and the National Imagination*, despite the book's apparent thematic similarity to *Nation and Narration*. After drawing the first footnote in the form of Timothy Brennan's important paper on the novel as a national 'form' in *Nation and Narration*,[110] the two post-British approaches to English Literature remain separate. Robert Crawford's *Devolving English Literature* is a study to which the above account of 'English' is heavily indebted; it has recently been described by Willy Maley and Ellen Raïssa Jackson (a bit puzzlingly) as an important 'postcolonial' account of Scottish literary history.[111] Yet Crawford's book abruptly stops short of incorporating postcolonial models, and argues for 'an idiom uncontaminated by the limitations and blind-spots of that [postcolonial] discourse'.[112]

The problem with this is that there is no pure tradition; English Literature has been a catalogue of contamination and blind spots, and has tied up a variety of national cultures in Greater British, imperial standards from which the national is not that easily separated. The Scotland that participated in British Culture, exemplified by Crawford's intricate survey of English Literature, does not lose its Britishness through mere volition, but requires a vigilant process of re-contextualisation relative to British empire. As Frantz Fanon stressed in *The Wretched of the Earth*, submerged national cultures cannot be 'remembered', they have to be 'recovered' in a form which jettisons any simple claims to continuity (or cleanness).[113] Thus when the nationalist hero Winnifred Ewing stated in her 1999 Scottish Parliament inaugural speech that the Parliament is 'hereby reconvened', questions over the 're-' are begged: is the people represented in 1999 the people represented in 1707? Has the Greater British Eng. Lit. model of culture as ethnocentric continuation been swallowed whole, and if so, is the nation 're-' made likely to be more democratic and inclusive than Britain? And if not, why bother talking about national traditions at all?

If we do engage with the 'contaminated' discourse of postcolonial studies, we find that the passage from Fanon's 'second' to 'third' phases of nationalism, from 'remembering' to 'remaking', is a remarkably close description of the passage from 1920s/'30s Scottish and Welsh cultural nationalism and political nationalism, to the more eloquently democratic demands being made throughout the UK in devolutionary times. If the '20s/'30s 'second phase' – discussed in the next chapter – saw the reconstruction of an imagined 'us' with a fixed language, equating, as did New Criticism, past written authorities and present speech, then more recently, nationalism has put itself in a position to question the methods of British Culture more fundamentally. Correspondingly, Homi Bhabha's Fanonian inside attack on English Literature *is* highly applicable, as some scholars have noted.[114] Although Bhabha's Derridean readings of an Enlightenment tradition centred on Kant do not properly account for the influence on Kant of the paring down of experience in Humean scepticism, the universalist ethics Bhabha zones in on are also common to the Scottish Enlightenment. For Bhabha, those anterior aspects of the nation which are founded on such a universal ethics prior to any social action are relegated to an ideal narrative beyond all history, and conversely, the performative nation is dispersed in contingent enunciations (as in radical aesthetic practice) which perpetually undercut anterior wholeness.

Where the anterior nation flattens out the ambivalent movement that people experience as nationality, in Fanonian terms, their *expérience vécue*, action is described in equally post-English Literature terms as a 'double narrative movement'.[115] National experience and national democracy depend, in this model, on the negotiation in speech and writing of the image of an imagined past nation, typically interpolated by state authority:

> We then have a contested conceptual territory where the nation's people must be thought in double-time; the people are the historical 'objects' of nationalist pedagogy, giving the discourse an authority that is based on the pre-given or constituted historical origin *in the past*; the people are also the 'subjects' of a process of signification that must erase any prior or originary presence of the nation-people to demonstrate the prodigious, living principles of the people as contemporaneity: as that sign of the *present* through which national life is redeemed and iterated as a reproductive process.[116]

So the present of the people's history involves an insistence on lived-experience which 'has its own ambivalent narrative', and which replaces the ideal English of 'English' Literature.[117] Where in Benedict Anderson's imagined community 'sociological solidity' is repeated across plural objects in bounded social space, produced in a 'meanwhile' space *prior to* signification, for Bhabha this solidity is interrupted by a 'supplementary movement' which we can understand as sub-British national representation buried within the British discipline of 'English'.[118] This is a powerful model of how the present-ness of speech is connected to action and then to political change; postcolonial approaches nevertheless have frequently been criticised for over-stressing textuality, for imagining that texual criticism is *de facto* a political act with consequences in the world.[119] But a stress on language is perhaps easier, rather than harder, to understand in a region which has taught itself to associate civility with an outside standard dialect, nebulously known as 'English', and which made itself central to empire by inventing ways to adapt to and even invent this form.

The first attempt against English Literature to represent a Scottish national people – an interruptive writing directed at state culture – corresponds to the opening phase of modern sub-British nationalism. The 'Scottish Renaissance', born with mid-1920s cultural nationalism but only building up popular influence in the mid-1950s, represented a moment at which Greater British culture was turned upside down, and 'economic reversals and literary revivals animated "orthodox" nationalism'.[120] Coming at almost exactly the same time as Irish semi-independence, this movement represents *the* founding moment of post-British culture on the mainland. Ironically though, its aggressive reversals often left English Literature's linguistic authority intact by escaping to another, ideal language. The movement also solidified the idea that the traditions of British member nations were fixed and untouchable, by repeating Greater Britain's association of language and ethnicity. Everywhere the Renaissance collapses Scotland into an 'anterior' nation. Yet its explicit nationalisation of culture would prove central to ideas of the centrality of writing to democracy which would emerge in the 1970s and '80s as even more pressing questions of representation.

Notes

1. For example, Keith Robbins, *Great Britain: Identities, Institutions, and the Idea of Britishness* (Harlow: Longman, 1998), p. 341.
2. See Murray G. H. Pittock, *Celtic Identity and the British Image* (Manchester: Manchester University Press, 1999), pp. 16–17; Krishan Kumar, *The Making of English National Identity* (Cambridge: Cambridge University Press, 2003), pp. 136–45.
3. Murray G. H. Pittock, *Inventing and Resisting Britain: Cultural Identities in Britain and Ireland, 1685–1789* (Basingstoke: Penguin, 1997), p. 8.
4. Madge Dresser, 'Britannia', in Raphael Samuel (ed.), *Patriotism: The Making and Unmaking of British National Identity, Vol. III: National Fictions* (London: Routledge, 1989), pp. 26–49.
5. A. R. Braunmuller in William Shakespeare, ed. Braunmuller, *Macbeth* (Cambridge: Cambridge University Press, 1997), p. 4.
6. Samuel Taylor Coleridge, 'From "Lectures on the Characteristics of Shakespear"', in Jonathan Bate (ed.), *The Romantics on Shakespeare* (Harmondsworth: Penguin, 1992), pp. 129–47.
7. See T. M. Devine, *The Scottish Nation* (London: Penguin, 1999), p. 3; John Kendle, *Federal Britain: A History* (London: Routledge, 1997), p. 5; Pittock, *Inventing and Resisting Britain*, p. 8.
8. Devine, *The Scottish Nation*, p. 9.
9. Ibid. pp. 13–14; Christopher Harvie, *Scotland and Nationalism: Scottish Society and Politics 1707–1994* (London: Routledge, 1994), p. 37.
10. Devine, *The Scottish Nation*, p. 16.
11. Harvie, *Scotland and Nationalism*, p. 39.
12. Kidd, *Subverting Scotland's Past: Scottish Whig Historians and the Creation of an Anglo-British Identity, 1689–c. 1830* (Cambridge: Cambridge University Press, 1993), p. 205.
13. Ibid. p. 274.
14. Tom Nairn, *The Break-up of Britain: Crisis and Neo-nationalism* (London: NLB, 1977), p. 152.

15. See Murray G. H. Pittock, *The Invention of Scotland* (London: Routledge, 1991), pp. 21–61.
16. S. J. Connolly, 'Varieties of Britishness: Ireland, Scotland, and Wales in the Hanoverian State', in Alexander Grant and Keith Stringer (eds), *Uniting the Kingdom?: The Making of British History* (London: Routledge, 1995), p. 197.
17. In Knud Haakonssen (ed.), *David Hume: Political Essays* (Cambridge: Cambridge University Press, 1994), pp. 1–77.
18. Raphael Samuel, 'Introduction: The figures of national myth', in Samuel (ed.), *Patriotism: The Making and Unmaking of British National Identity, Vol. III: National Fictions* (London: Routledge, 1989), pp. xi–xxxvi: xxv–xxvi.
19. For example, Craig Beveridge and Ronald Turnbull, *The Eclipse of Scottish Culture: Inferiorism and the Intellectuals* (Edinburgh: Polygon, 1989).
20. Cf. Murray G. H. Pittock, *A New History of Scotland* (Stroud: Sutton, 2003), pp. 231–2.
21. See Robert Young, *Colonial Desire* (London: Routledge, 1995), pp. 30–6.
22. Hugh Trevor-Roper, 'The Invention of Tradition: The Highland Tradition of Scotland', in Hobsbawm and Ranger (eds), *The Invention of Tradition* (Cambridge: Cambridge University Press, 1983), pp. 15–42.
23. Eric Hobsbawm, 'Some Reflections on The Break-up of Britain', *New Left Review*, 15, September–October 1977, pp. 2–23.
24. Pittock, *A New History of Scotland*, p. 245.
25. Devine, *The Scottish Nation*, p. 235; Pittock, *Celtic Identity and the British Image*, pp. 37–8; cf. the discussion of Edwin Muir in Nairn, *The Break-up of Britain*, p. 121.
26. Cf. Malcolm Chapman, *The Gaelic Vision in Scottish Culture* (London: Croom Helm, 1978).
27. Harvie, *Scotland and Nationalism*, pp. 54–5.
28. Graham Morton, *Unionist Nationalism: Governing Urban Scotland 1830–1860* (East Linton: Tuckwell, 1999), pp. 4–5.
29. Christopher Harvie, *Scotland: A Short History* (Oxford: Oxford University Press, 2002), p. 175.
30. Stephen Haseler, *The English Tribe: Identity, Nation and Europe* (London: Macmillan, 1996), p. 33.
31. Harvie, *Scotland: A Short History*, p. 163.
32. Harvie, *Scotland and Nationalism*, p. 64.
33. Angus Calder, *Revolutionary Empire* (London: Cape, 1980).
34. Frantz Fanon, *Black Skin, White Masks*, trans. Charles Lam Markmann (London: Pluto, 1986), pp. 146–7, 166; Frantz Fanon, *The Wretched of the Earth*, trans. Constance Farrington (Harmondsworth: Penguin, 1967), pp. 130–1.
35. Devine, *The Scottish Nation*, pp. 240–1.
36. Ibid. p. 309.
37. Pittock, *A New History of Scotland*, p. 266.
38. Irvine Welsh, *Trainspotting* (London: Minerva, 1993), pp. 318–21.
39. Alexander Broadie, *The Scottish Enlightenment* (Edinburgh: Birlinn, 2001), p. 22.
40. Adam Smith, *An Inquiry into the Nature and Causes of the Wealth of Nations* (New York: Collier and Son, 1909), p. 416.

41. Cf. Andrew Hook, *From Goosecreek to Gandercleugh: Studies in Scottish-American Literary and Cultural History* (East Linton: Tuckwell, 1999).
42. Christopher Harvie, *Scotland: A Short History*, p. 136.
43. Here 'UK' means the United Kingdom of Britain, formed in 1707.
44. See Devine, *The Scottish Nation*, p. 89; T. M. Devine, *Scottish Emigration and Scottish Sovereignty* (Edinburgh: John Donald, 1992).
45. Pittock, *A New History of Scotland*, p. 252.
46. See Devine, *The Scottish Nation*, p. 471; Ned C. Landsman, 'Introduction: The Context and Functions of Scottish Involvement with the Americas', in Landsman (ed.), *Nation and Province in the First British Empire: Scotland and the Americas* (Lewisberg, PA: Bucknell University Press, 2001), pp. 15–35.
47. Broadie, *The Scottish Enlightenment*, p. 49.
48. Andrew Hook, *Scotland and America: A Study of Cultural Relations 1750–1835* (Glasgow: Blackie, 1975); Gary Wills, *Inventing America: Jefferson's Declaration of Independence* (Garden City, NY: Doubleday, 1978).
49. Jacques Derrida, *Otobiographies: l'enseignement de Nietzsche et la politique du nom propre* (Paris: Éditions Galilée, 1984), pp. 22–3.
50. Homi K. Bhabha, 'DissemiNation: Time, narrative, and the margins of the modern nation', in Bhabha, *The Location of Culture* (London: Routledge, 1994), pp. 139–70.
51. See Beveridge and Turnbull, *The Eclipse of Scottish Culture*.
52. Donald Dewar, address to the opening of the Scottish Parliament, quoted from *Reporting Scotland*, BBC Scotland, 1 July 1999.
53. David Hume, 'Of National Characters', in Knud Haakonssen (ed.), *David Hume: Political Essays* (Cambridge: Cambridge University Press, 1994), pp. 78–92; Henry Louis Gates, Jr, *Figures in Black: Words, Signs, and the 'Racial' Self* (New York: Oxford University Press, 1989), pp. 17–18.
54. See Donald W. Livingstone, 'Hume, Barbarism and American Independence', in Richard B. Sher and Jeffrey M. Smitten (eds), *Scotland and America in the Age of the Enlightenment* (Edinburgh: Edinburgh University Press, 1990); also Robert Young, *Postcolonialism: An Historical Introduction* (Oxford: Blackwell, 2001), p. 85; on Hume's frowned-upon radicalism, see Thomas Docherty, *Criticism and Modernity: Aesthetics, Literature, and Nations in Europe and Its Academies* (Oxford: Oxford University Press, 1999), pp. 116–60.
55. Pittock, *Resisting and Inventing Britain*, p. 58.
56. Young, *Postcolonialism*, pp. 85–6; cf. Richard Gott, 'Little Englanders', in Samuel (ed.), *Patriotism, Vol. I: History and Politics*, pp. 90–102: 94.
57. Young, *Postcolonialism*, p. 86.
58. Cf. C. L. R. James, *The Black Jacobins: Toussaint L'Ouverture and the San Domingo Revolution* (London: Allison and Busby, 1980).
59. Henry W. Meikle, *Scotland and the French Revolution* (Glasgow: James Maclehose and Sons, 1912), p. vii.
60. See Andrew Hook, 'Scottish academia and the invention of American Studies', in Robert Crawford (ed.), *The Scottish Invention of English Literature* (Cambridge: Cambridge University Press, 1998), pp. 164–79.
61. See Chris Baldick, *The Social Mission of English Criticism 1848–1932* (Oxford: Clarendon, 1983), pp. 70–1; Gauri Visnawathan, *Masks of*

Conquest: Literary Study and British Rule in India (New York: Columbia University Press, 1989).

62. Devine, *The Scottish Nation*, p. 282.
63. Young, *Postcolonialism*, p. 93; the interrupted quotation is taken from Kenneth N. Bell and W. P. Morrell, *Select Documents on British Colonial Policy 1830–1860* (Oxford: Clarendon, 1928). This quotation has been left in to stress the temporality of the nations conceived.
64. Charles Wentworth Dilke, 'Preface to the First Original Edition [1868]', in *Greater Britain: A Record of Travel in English-Speaking Countries* (London: Macmillan, 1894).
65. Dilke, *Greater Britain*, p. viii.
66. Benedict Anderson, *Imagined Communities: Reflections on the Origin and Spread of Nationalism* (London: Verso, 1983).
67. Cf. Young, *Postcolonialism*, p. 172.
68. Alfred Milner, 'Introduction', in *The Nation and the Empire* (London: Routledge, 1998 [1913]), pp. xi–xlviii: xxxi; cf. George Parkin, *Imperial Federation: The Problem of National Unity* (London: Macmillan, 1892); Robbins, *Great Britain*, p. 214.
69. Young, *Postcolonialism*, p. 39.
70. Ibid. p. 40.
71. John Kendle, *Federal Britain: A History* (London: Routledge, 1997).
72. John Seeley, *The Expansion of England* (London: Macmillan, 1895), p. 47.
73. Ibid. p. 65.
74. Ibid. p. 63.
75. I. C. G. Hutchison, *A Political History of Scotland* (Edinburgh: John Donald, 1985), p. 154; see also T. C. Smout, *A Century of the Scottish People* (London: Fontana, 1997), p. 253.
76. Harvie, *Scotland and Nationalism*, p. 17.
77. Hutchison, *A Political History of Scotland*, p. 181.
78. Ibid. p. 223.
79. Lindsay Paterson et al. (eds), *New Scotland, New Politics?* (Edinburgh: Polygon, 2001), pp. 89–90.
80. Hutchison, *A Political History of Scotland*, p. 242.
81. Quoted in Smout, *A Century of the Scottish People*, p. 259.
82. Ian McLean, *The Legend of Red Clydeside* (Edinburgh: John Donald, 1983).
83. Pittock, *A New History of Scotland*, pp. 266, 268, 301; cf. Alisdair MacIntyre, *After Virtue* (Notre Dame: University of Notre Dame Press, 1984), pp. 204–25; Cairns Craig, *The Modern Scottish Novel: Narrative and the National Imagination* (Edinburgh: Edinburgh University Press, 1999), pp. 22–33.
84. The phrase comes from an informal talk by Bruce Robbins.
85. Pittock, *A New History of Scotland*, pp. 301–3.
86. Devine, *The Scottish Nation*, p. 315.
87. See Tom Nairn, *Faces of Nationalism: Janus Revisited* (London: Verso, 1997), pp. 57–67, 194–221.
88. Cf. Pittock, *A New History of Scotland*, p. 283.
89. Devine, *The Scottish Nation*, pp. 600–2.
90. Kendle, *Federal Britain*, p. 60.
91. Young, *Postcolonialism*, p. 41.

92. Kendle, *Federal Britain*, p. 63.
93. Ibid. p. 78.
94. Pittock, *A New History of Scotland*, p. 267.
95. Quoted in Kendle, *Federal Britain*, p. 69.
96. Cf. Robert Crawford, 'Introduction', *The Scottish Invention of English Literature*, pp. 1–21.
97. Alexander Wedderburn, quoted in Robert Crawford, *Devolving English Literature* (Edinburgh: Edinburgh University Press, 2000), p. 28.
98. Quoted in introduction to Adam Smith, *Lectures on Rhetoric and Belles Lettres*, ed. John M. Lothian (Carbondale and Edwardsville: University of Southern Illinois Press, 1971), pp. xi–xl: xxxv.
99. Adam Smith, *Lectures On Rhetoric and Belles Lettres* (Indianapolis: Liberty Fund, 1985) (reprint of *The Glasgow Edition of the Works and Correspondence of Adam Smith Vol. IV*), p. 4. This edition is the one quoted hereafter.
100. Ibid. p. 3.
101. Thomas P. Miller, 'Witherspoon, Blair and the Rhetoric of Civic Humanism', in Sher and Smitten (eds), *Scotland and America in the Age of the Enlightenment*, p. 100.
102. Cf. Franklin E. Court, *Institutionalizing English Literature: The Culture and Politics of Literary Study, 1750–1900* (Stanford, CA: Stanford University Press, 1992), pp. 17–38.
103. Ian Duncan, 'Adam Smith, Samuel Johnson and the Institutions of English', in Crawford, *The Scottish Invention of English Literature*, p. 37.
104. Miller, 'Witherspoon, Blair and Civic Humanism', pp. 108–9.
105. David Daiches, 'Style Périodique and Style Coupé: Hugh Blair and the Scottish Rhetoric of American Independence', in Sher and Smitten (eds), *Scotland and America in the Age of Enlightenment*, pp. 209–26.
106. See, for example, Crawford, *Devolving English Literature*, p. 309.
107. David Simpson, 'Destiny Made Manifest: The Styles of Whitman's Poetry', in Homi Bhabha (ed.), *Nation and Narration* (London: Routledge, 1990), pp. 187–8.
108. Cf. Michael Gardiner, 'Interdisciplinarity After Davie: Postcolonial Theory and Crises of Terminology in Scottish Cultural Studies', *Scottish Studies Review*, 2.1, spring 2001, pp. 24–38.
109. Tom Nairn, *After Britain* (London: Granta, 2000), pp. 227–30.
110. Craig, *The Modern Scottish Novel*, p. 9.
111. Ellen Raïssa Jackson and Willy Maley, 'Celtic Connections: Colonialism and Culture in Irish-Scottish Modernism', *Interventions*, 4.1, 2002, pp. 68–78.
112. Crawford, *Devolving English Literature*, p. 310.
113. Fanon, *The Wretched of the Earth*, pp. 167–73.
114. See Willy Maley, 'Cultural Devolution? Representing Scotland in the 1970s', in Bart Moore-Gilbert (ed.), *The Arts in the 1970s: Cultural Closure?* (London: Routledge, 1994), pp. 78–98; Roderick Watson, 'Postcolonial Subjects?: Language, Narrative Authority and Class in Contemporary Scottish Culture', *European English Messenger*, 7.1, 1998, pp. 21–31; Ronald Beveridge and Turnbull, *The Eclipse of Scottish Culture: Inferiorism and the Intellectuals*.

115. Bhabha, 'DissemiNation', p. 145.
116. Ibid. p. 145.
117. Ibid. p. 153.
118. Ibid. p. 154.
119. See Aijaz Ahmad, *In Theory: Classes, Nations, Literatures* (London and New York: Verso, 1992); Steven Slemon, 'The Scramble for Postcolonialism', in Chris Tiffin and Alan Lawson (eds), *De-Scribing Empire: Postcolonialism and Textuality* (New York: Routledge, 1994), pp. 15–32.
120. Harvie, *Scotland and Nationalism*, p. 36.

Chapter Two

The First Scottish Renaissance

Language and Nation

This chapter concerns one of the first important instances of post-British culture outside of Ireland, one arising at the time of Irish separation, from about 1921. It holds that, although the embryonic modern cultural nationalist movement, centred on the Scottish Renaissance's key iconoclast Hugh MacDiarmid, moved Scottish national culture towards an international modernist stream of thought, its stance was nevertheless closer to the high-British ideas of T. S. Eliot and New Criticism than is usually admitted.[1] In particular, its rightly applauded stance towards Scots language nevertheless tended to standardise language and fix this standard to a historically static nation. Here I see the 1920s Renaissance as an important *First* Renaissance, containing some of the seeds of a post-British culture, but inevitably drawn into types of ethnocentrism which would still have to be broken down as calls for democratic separation strengthened.

We have seen how a post-colonial imperialism in the 1860s and '70s increasingly attempted to redefine the body of the Anglophone empire as a culturalist 'Greater Britain', and that territorial colonial expansion stalled. Colonies' financial worthiness increasingly came into question during this period, one in which the question of Irish independence was frequently on the agenda of the British Parliament. A Welsh political class also began to pull away from the English one into which it had been absorbed, and the fabric of Britain became strained at the same time as the fabric of empire.[2] 'Greater Britain' had allowed for a framework in which British empire was based less on the possession of colonial land than on the franchising of 'English' culture in each locality, a replicable cultural standard which was placeless and morally universal. This reduced the need for costly colonial government possessions – though there would be a second and more frantic colonising phase before the turn of the century – and made maintenance of empire seem reasonable even to anti-colonials within the Liberal Party. Empire, with its silent centre of an unclearly defined Englishness, had come to be understood as a shared bond transcending local autonomies. In practice, this shared bond was often seen as a common behaviour carried by English language. The Anglophone empire, with its Anglo-Saxon roots and its potential for civility, was not the feverish tropical empire, which largely dated from the end of the nineteenth century; it was a reliable and familiar federation. The Anglophone empire was still in the 1920s a *de facto* greater nation, or, to use a term by that time already outdated, a race.

Thus the taken-for-granted tone of Charles Dilke's influential 1868 description of 'follow[ing] English round the world', describing his own imperial voyage, can help us understand why even in the 1920s, Scottish cultural nationalists were prone to collapse claims for a separate language into claims for a separate 'race'. Under Greater British conditions, language had come to signify the cultural competence of a 'people', and so had conversely become a primary term for the empire's various cultural nationalisms. In terms of Benedict Anderson's claim that European nations were built on integrative print cultures,[3] for the majority of the people of Greater Britain, whose speech did not correspond to the written standards handed down to them educationally, establishing a written language could stand for recovering experience. Founding a language was to be the central nationalist project of the First Scottish Renaissance, though this foundation has left a legacy which in some ways hampers devolution, conceived in its 1990s form.

The growing Irish Home Rule question had from the late nineteenth century to the 1910s also crystallised Home Rule questions in Scotland and Wales, particularly after the First World War discredited empire in the eyes of working-class communities while it extended the reach of state.[4] The years 1917–19 saw a rapid growth in class consciousness in parts of Britain *contra* the British war effort, for example in Glasgow, which had previously been integral to imperialism.[5] It was against this background of constitutional and class disturbance that the Anglophone version of modernism peaked in the early 1920s; yet literary modernism, seen in its traditionally Eng. Lit. Eliot–Bloomsbury sense, is curiously un-modern, working through chaos to find a buried Greater British tradition of civility (ironically beholden to the Scottish Enlightenment). The adaptations of 'English' culture, where English is understood in its nebulous ethno-linguistic sense, to its waning grip over Greater Britain, form the background to T. S. Eliot's 1922 poem *The Waste Land*, perhaps the single most recognisable text of Anglo-British modernism, and written by a Greater Briton showing a symptomatic over-adaptation to imperial standards, as had many post-union Scots. Eliot belongs near the end of an Anglican, seafaring, imperialist aesthetics which had slid under Greater Britain. In *The Waves*, Virginia Woolf exaggerates the 'colonial' defensiveness of her Eliot-like character Louis by having him Australian rather than American, intensely jealous of the cricketing hero Percival, and constantly conscious of the need to Anglicise his speech.[6] But after the pressures of war, anti-colonialism and socialism, by 1922 Greater British culture was clearly dysfunctional. Thus *The Waste Land*'s dry, barren, infertile London has lost not an England, but an image of a borderless England, or rather this image's centrality to a Dilke-like Greater British Anglophone culture. Eliot attempts to reassert such a default, listening for a traditional order of 'English', and finding it in the now-faint canonical echoes which each individual poet must work to hear under the dust. In this sense, *The Waste Land* is one moment in a long cultural rearguard action which takes in the Victorian and Georgian rural nostalgia which Eliot so despises; if it represents the flagship text of modernism, then modernism is the end of an era, not the beginning of one.

The success of this rearguard standardisation is seen in the way that by 1932, F. R. Leavis's *New Bearings in English Poetry* – the seminal New Critical account – had already historicised Eliot's discernment of cultural loss as a canonical fact on the level of Shakespeare, Milton and Shelley. The New Criticism which accompanied Eliot went back to the future in shuffling an English canon and presenting it as new and radical – a scheme not unlike the Blairite conception of devolution, which is still, in the sense of hanging on to confederation, imperial. The early-twentieth-century English 'home', used paradoxically not by Little Englanders but by residual imperialists, the England of Rider Haggard, had been ideally rural, endless and untouchable, and *de facto* ethnocentric, as against a real ongoing urbanisation, change, cosmopolitanism and (though they rarely put it in these terms) miscegenation.[7] The English modernist 're-duced aesthetic' similarly protects 'traditional' ideas of high literature from a hostile mass society by concentrating on images with perfect form – in one version indebted to Ezra Pound, imagism.

Small and perfectly formed but taking no chances by engaging with the social, the image of imagism works somewhat like the proposition in logical positivism, limiting any damage to the pre-given order, and electing individual cultural gatekeepers to manage this limitation.

Correspondingly, although *The Waste Land* has often been seen as inaugurating an aesthetics of interruption and disturbance, a look at contemporary criticism – for example, that by Edmund Wilson in December 1922 in *Dial*, a magazine which awarded Eliot a prize of $2,000 –[8] shows how Eliot on the contrary triggered a desire for cultural discreteness or 'understanding', the reconstruction of an Anglo-British interpretive order. In maritime metaphors that would not be lost on critics like Paul Gilroy,[9] *The Waste Land* associates cultural death with the loss of control over water (the international space), with drought, and with infertility:

Here is no water but only rock
Rock and no water and the sandy road
The road winding above among the mountains
Which are mountains of rock without water
If there were water we should stop and drink
Amongst the rock one cannot stop or think
Sweat is dry and feet are in the sand
If there were only water amongst the rock
Dead mountain mouth of carious teeth that cannot spit
Here one can neither stand nor lie nor sit
There is not even silence in the mountains
But dry sterile thunder without rain
There is not even solitude in the mountains
But red sullen faces sneer and snarl
From doors of mudcracked houses.[10]

This slipping away of water in *The Waste Land*'s scheme of civilisation thus strongly recalls the loss of a sea-bound empire based on the Thames, an 'Oceana', as another Greater British account put it.[11] The metaphor of water as grand politics remains today, when a shift in political paradigms is still described as a 'sea change'. The withering of Greater Britain's Anglophone standards coincides with Britain's ability to 'rule the waves' from the Thames, a river worried about having lost its status as a slipway for global culture. Wilson took up the water metaphor early to suggest that Eliot had not only rippled the surface but also stained the 'sea' of modern poetry, which would, in the Anglophone reduced aesthetic, become obsessed with protection against cultural loss.[12] Wilson's 'explanatory' reaction to the poem, as that of other 1920s critics (or at least sympathetic ones), had already been provided with a model in the poem itself, which foot-noted its own allusions, thus simultaneously occupying poetic and critical ground. The author circumscribes his own social function with the same logical manoeuvre by which Enlightenment thinkers knew the goals of civility before any civilising process; grand nar-ratives required occupation of a prior time of authority.

For this individualistic Eliot, the metaphor of the 'crowd' who re-ceive civilisation reflects an Anglo-British, Hobbesian anxiety over an originary 'state of anarchy' avoided by sovereignty and consti-tution. Neo-Enlightenment, Spenglerian models of the progress of societies allow Eliot to see the London crowd around him as alto-gether anonymous unless returned to a non-specific civility common to all great cultures. The immediate model is the Scot J. G. Frazer's *The Golden Bough*, an attempt to write the same narrative over many societies, which inherits its universalism and knowledge-arranging stance direct from the Enlightenment. In Eliot's Spengler, civilisa-tion actually corresponds to the phase of decay which great Euro-pean cities have reached, a phase which follows directly after full maturity.[13] On the other hand in MacDiarmid's Spengler, civilisa-tion is to be saved by the revitalisation of the small nation – an ar-gument looking ahead to today's pro-independence argument that post-imperial democracy will be returned to the former UK by its nations. MacDiarmid indeed indicates in *Lucky Poet* that it was the combination of nationalist and socialist aims which made Scotland ripe for revolution.[14] MacDiarmid's reading of the grand narrative is in many ways a post-British one, Eliot's a Greater British one. Leavis's *The Great Tradition* (1946), not so far from Quiller-Couch Georgianism as it claimed, similarly pushed a conception of the modern which was strongly Anglo-American, or, Greater British.[15] Despite the vague Anglocentrism of New Criticism and Blooms-bury, the nationally specific literary presence of England itself is still left largely unaccounted for; it is perhaps only with the genera-tion of poets surrounding J. H. Prynne and 'anglo langpo' (Geoffrey Hill is a distinguished exception) that 'anglo' returns.

For Eliotic modernism, the position of the cultural legislator re-mains that of the discrete, chosen individual. Three years earlier his *Tradition and the Individual Talent* had stressed the responsibilities of all poets to an 'inner voice' arising from a sense of ethnic belonging.[16] The artist's responsibility is to maintain and help critical tradition 'adjust' to threatening circumstances, rather than entering into an open-ended dialogue: '[t]he existing order is complete before the new work arrives; for order to persist after the supervention of novelty, the *whole* existing order must be, if ever so slightly, altered'.[17] The duty of the leader of a race is to continuously re-order culture so as to keep it protected within an overall continuity. Protection is certainly afforded for example by the reduced aesthetic of imagism, which is concerned to re-arrange existing fragments in such a way as to protect their form. Similarly, occupying something like the position that logic would occupy for Wittgenstein, musical tone was for Eliot a metaphysical form which ordered content, yet remained free of content itself. In Platonic style, no human language directly interferes with a tone which remains, like the image of England for imperial export, beyond history. In *The Waste Land*, any such voice as appears is merely as 'singing out of empty cisterns and exhausted wells'.[18]

Perhaps most marked by Hugh MacDiarmid's move in 1921–2 to Synthetic Scots,[19] the Scottish Renaissance should, like Eliotic modernism, be seen within this matrix of partial Irish independence, Welsh revival, the socialist upsurge and the crisis of Greater British maintenance of linguistic standards. Indeed one explanation for MacDiarmid's seeking a new aesthetics of 'Scots language' is that, apart from polite hybrid forms like those of W. B. Yeats, there were few answers to the literary invention of 'good English' which had centred English Literature in England. MacDiarmid was able to take advantage of a vague but growing post-kailyard desire for a national Scottish literary language, and to link that language to nationhood. At this point however, Scots were still strongly involved in Greater British culture in its 'good English' sense. Following in the standardising North British footsteps of Adam Smith, J. A. H. Murray had been the first major editor of *The Oxford English Dictionary* (1879–84).[20] At the height of the MacDiarmid revolt in 1924, another Scot, John Reith, took up a Received Pronunciation form of Standard English for the new BBC, which even today, as he had hoped, speaks for 'Britain' when many other cultural organisations have abandoned it.[21] In 1921, the Newbolt Report on *The Teaching of English in England* was still describing the Standard as a pedagogical necessity and a timeless inheritance even when it is changed or moves location.[22] The report aimed to 'destory evil habits of speech' in order to instil 'the right kind of national pride' – though in *which* nation, England or Britain, remains symptomatically unclear.[23] A similar kind of Anglo-British linguistic fundamentalism, *contra* the actual speech of British or even English people, was again one of the factors behind the cultural revolt of devolution, when Norman Tebbit would link an imagined decline in Standard English to rising crime.[24] (And W. N. Herbert has interestingly taken the argument forward to show that some of Edwin Morgan's most influential work can be seen as a cultural defence against the silent standardisations of the Cox Report of 1989.)[25] Broadly within this context, MacDiarmid attempted to reverse Anglo-British standardisation, and whether or not with direct attention to Newbolt, pushed for a national post-British language.

This Renaissance was thus born in fertile ground: in his introduction to MacDiarmid's *Sangschaw* (1925), John Buchan noted MacDiarmid's alternative modernist aesthetic of an artificial literary vernacular:

> Since there is no canon of the vernacular, he makes his own, as Burns did ... [and] selects where he pleases between Aberdeen and the Cheviots. This audacity ... is a proof that a new spirit is to-day abroad in the North, which ... is both conservative and radical – a determination to keep Scotland in the main march of the world's interests, and at the same time to forgo no part of her ancient heritage.[26]

This 'audacity' is strongly tempered here: the movement is taking place 'in the North' ('North Britain' remaining a common Victorian term for Scotland), and is painted as retaining a unionist commitment to visible difference within the union. Its 'both conservative and radical' tendency strongly recalls both the antiquarian unionist nationalism of figures like Walter Scott and indeed Buchan himself, and the subsequent British conception of devolution as allowing a 'distinct' character for Scotland within the union's ongoing place 'in the march of the world's interests'. Moreover the search for speech within written literary canons, the idea of the vernacular itself, had a British Romantic heritage, being traceable to a time when Britain was furiously developing an Anglocentric 'native' identity.[27] This 'native' Anglo-British voice was naturalised in Wordsworth's *Prelude*, and survived through to Eliot's neo-Romantic wish for 'the ordinary, everyday language which we use and hear'.[28] Popular English vernacular poetry and folk music were revived in Greater Britain, as well as a Seeleyesque interest in the apparent ambition and prosperity of Elizabethan England, echoes of whose poets are to be heard in *The Waste Land*.[29] Anthologies like *The Oxford Book of English Verse* (1900) and *Georgian Poetry* (1911) had already centralised the English Vernacular,[30] and Eliot joined this increasingly 'Englished' British tradition just as Britain's imperial *raison d'état* was beginning to desert it. What is less often suggested though is that the Scottish Renaissance 'answer' to Eliot, despite its sensitivity to Anglocentrism, relied on a similar aesthetics of ethno-linguistic authority in the form of Synthetic Scots.

A more familiar definition of the movement had come in Alexander McGill's 1924 'Towards a Scottish Renaissance', in part intended to ready the audience of the *Scottish Educational Journal* for MacDiarmid's attacks on the ignorance of his fellow Scots.[31] McGill described 'a new spirit … evident in the land':

> This group, to which has been given the nickname of the Scottish Renaissance Group by Professor Denis Saurat, in an article he wrote for the *Revue Anglo-Americaine*, has formed itself gradually in the last few years round the personality of a young Scottish journalist, C. M. Grieve [Hugh MacDiarmid].[32]

Alan Riach, later editor of the definitive multi-volume edition of MacDiarmid describes how the Renaissance aesthetic challenged the possibility of the Greater British agenda: '[a]t the heart of the debate in Scottish intellectual life in the period between the wars are the questions of identity defined by language, nation, and class'.[33] The Renaissance is perhaps more accurately described as stemming from the 1895 suggestion of Patrick Geddes, another figure enjoying a revival today.[34] What MacDiarmid grasped though was that in Scotland, unlike in England, literary modernism had to remake itself after the long habit of going south in English Literature. The bereft kailyard tradition which was left behind had already become opaque with George Douglas Brown's more barbed *The House With the Green Shutters* (1901);[35] MacDiarmid's *A Drunk Man Looks at the Thistle* was aimed *both* at kailyard ideas of national identity and at *The Waste Land*. Alan Bold describes the voice of *A Drunk Man* as 'Scotland's aggressive answer to the defeatist mood of Eliot's *The Waste Land*'.[36] Of course, the single most striking aspect of this long poem (at least at that time) was its claim to adopt an entirely new language, albeit in the neo-Romantic terms of the vernacular. In 1927 in 'A Theory of Scots Letters', MacDiarmid makes a vehement case for the centrality of the vernacular as 'a vast storehouse of just the very peculiar and subtle effects which modern European literature in general is assiduously seeking'.[37] Elsewhere he points to 'the huge extent to which dialect is entering into the stuff of modern literature in every country' – an early description of how, *contra* Eliotic authority, modernism was often based on non-standard diction.[38] *A Drunk*

Man shares its interest in artificial lexicons with other canonised modernist classics like *The Cantos* and *Finnegans Wake*, yet moves its distinctiveness to the level of language – the nation being structured like a language.

Given the difficulty of fitting nations into the socialist movement (a problematic which describes much twentieth-century Scottish culture), and against the infertile dryness of Eliot's London – '[t]he wasted seam that dries like stairch/And pooders aff'[39] – MacDiarmid employs a dialectical progress of wild opposites, imaged as drunkenness, allowing for the perpetual recreation and destruction of standards (and here we could compare the trope of inebriated dialectic to James Kelman's Booker Prize anti-hero who has drunk himself into amnesia at the outset of the story, and whose havering is not heard by the British authorities).[40] MacDiarmid's dialectic has roots not only in Marxism but also in G. Gregory Smith's now famous 1919 description of how cultural opposites unite in Scottish culture in an 'antisyzygy'.[41] In 1926, just before publication, the dialectical concern with experience was underlined in the addition of a section on the General Strike (and indeed it may have been the failure of the strike that finally took MacDiarmid to party political Nationalism).[42] Just as in the pre-devolutionary 1980s, British economic management of the 1920s took a disproportionate toll on Scotland, prompting a conjoined black and red cultural attack; the task of the Renaissance was to orchestrate the crossover of socialist and nationalist critiques. Living in a nation not nationally represented, again in the 1920s as in the 1980s, also allowed for the insight into how ideal and experience are never quite harmonious. Thus *A Drunk Man* moves restlessly between experience and image:

> To prove my saul is Scots I maun begin
> Wi' what's still deemed Scots and the folk expect,
> And spire up syne by visible degrees
> To heichts whereo' the fules ha'e never recked.[43]

Drink is a hyperbolic contrary to the 'drought' of *The Waste Land*, 'fu' (full, or drunk) in opposition to empty, or dry. 'Drouth' can mean both dryness in terms of desire for human contact, and, more colloquially, desire for alcohol. Drunkenness also triggers a rambling discussion of sexuality and childbirth, to challenge Eliot's visions of (cultural) infertility and waste. Drunkenness moves us between what 'seems' and what is experienced, prompting inclusion rather than despair. The poem's speaker does not, like Eliot's, help tradition to 'adjust' to protect itself, but forces a clash of experience with received images of society, in order to:

> begin
> Wi what's still deemed Scots and the folk expect,
> And spire up syne by visible degrees
> To heichts whereo the fules hae never recked.

> But aince I get them there I'll whummle them
> And souse the craturs in the nether deeps[44]

The poetic voice here arises from the apparently incommensurate opposites of 'heichts' and 'deeps' (high culture and experience), and does not finally occupy either. Thus the growth of the poetic voice is 'A mongrel growth, jumble o disproportions,/Whirlin in its incredible contortions'.[45] Where Eliot maps the definite city of London onto a fantasy of a sterile desert, MacDiarmid throws together 'illusion' and 'conclusion' so that the two can never finally be reconciled:

> Hauf his soul a Scot maun use
> Indulgin in illusions,
> And hauf in gettin rid o them
> And comin to conclusions
> Wi the demoralisin dearth
> O onything worth while on Earth.[46]

The most sophisticated claims for the politics of this process of dialectic have come from Alan Riach, whose account shows a productive fluctuation in MacDiarmid's narrative 'I'.[47] For G. E. Davie, MacDiarmid's poetic voice requires an alienation of 'familiarity', a process of writing through perspectives of nation and family not one's own, and continuously re-creating the self, rather than re-adjusting.[48] Within the context of 1920s nationalisms, this modernism's engagement with the social is in a sense more 'modern' than that of Eliot, in the sense of a quest for newness. One co-founder with MacDiarmid of the National Party of Scotland (NPS), R. B. Cunninghame Graham, also a co-founder of the Scottish Labour Party (SLP) in 1888, and someone who grasped the doubleness of the national and the social, was also a key native informant for 'English' modernist Joseph Conrad, whose *Heart of Darkness*'s Thames reappears in more elegiac form in *The Waste Land*.[49] Indeed, a case could be made that many of the themes of *The Waste Land* are a toned-down version of insights already present in Conrad. Conrad had in his Scottish friend a telling indicator of the class and nation fix which would eventually conjoin in the 1990s.

Party and Cultural Politics

Recent accounts which stress the Britishness of the labour movement perhaps overestimate the parliamentary impasse which met popular nationalist claims in the early twentieth century.[50] The Irish socialists needed a War of Independence to overcome the absorptive power of the British constitution; the Red Clydesiders had been Home Rulers with no parliamentary option. The Scottish Home Rule Association (SHRA) had been formed as long ago as 1886, but in its post-1918 had a more leftist membership, in part showing a Scottish disillusionment with Greater Britain which would lead to the '20s Renaissance. Since Greater Britain had extended both within and outwith the union, its fall can be linked to the SHRA's dramatic growth between 1918 and 1923.[51] A Scottish National Convention met between 1924 and 1927, its claims for Home Rule summarily rejected by British MPs in Westminster. Scotland's residual pre-war unionism had largely disappeared, leaving a cultural malaise: the nation looked back over the last century of culture and found kailyard, canniness and imperial Anglophilia. Where the 1900s and 1910s had seen a bolstering of the English canon Quiller-Couch-style amidst some panic over urbanisation and imperial decline, there was no separate recognisable Scottish canon – which is in a sense what MacDiarmid later set out to create. Pessimistic accounts of Scotland's inability to create a national culture, accounts barely thinkable in the sunshine of pre-war unionism, came in 1926 with George Malcolm Thomson's *Caledonia* and, more famously, Edwin Muir's *Scottish Journey* (1927), intended in part as a reply to MacDiarmid's *Albyn*.[52]

This is where the Renaissance conjoins cultural and political nationalism. Its most defining point was perhaps MacDiarmid's *Contemporary Scottish Studies*, published in the *Scottish Educational Journal* between 1925 and 1927 (thus the importance of education as a marker of sub-British cultural difference in the mid-'20s as in the late '90s). MacDiarmid's now well-known articles attack educationalists' lack of knowledge of a native Scottish literary tradition, as well as castigating teachers for 'correcting' their pupils' speech (a practice which nevertheless remained virtually intact at least until the 1980s, when a grimly conservative Lallans appeared as an optional extra). *Contemporary Scottish Studies* belong exclusively to the realm of neither the cultural nor the political, and indeed ignore the generic boundaries which could keep sub-British nations merely cultural. A striking feature of this moment is the crossover of cultural and political roles; Yeats joined the Dáil even as a new-age hippy, and Cunninghame Graham headed *two* parties. (In Scotland, the obvious precursor is the Enlightenment, when the *literati* had serious power; the nadir would be the immediately pre-devolution period, when the semi-literate John Major was Prime Minister.) MacDiarmid was involved in the foundation of the NPS in 1926–8, created via an alliance of the SHRA, the activist Scottish National League (SNL) and the Scottish National Movement. The early party attracted many members of the Independent Labour Party; the Irish Free State was sometimes cited as a model, as were socialists like James Connolly and John Maclean.[53] Many socialists however had tended to view Home Rule as a low priority until the Renaissance linked it to socialism in the literary imagination.[54] Plaid Cymru (PC), already established, was also perceived along cultural and communitarian lines, but PC has never exerted a fully pro-independence, post-British pressure, and nor do they today, concentrating on the Welsh Executive as a parliamentary pressure group. Wales still has very few separate civic institutions upon which to base a state.[55] Arthurian and Tudor mythscapes have weighed heavily on Wales's sense of separateness, and the Welsh Renaissance, which pre-dated the Scottish one, had trouble collapsing culture and politics. Christopher Harvie has pointed out that early PC's established heritage hamstrung it as a party:

> Both [PC and the NPS] mobilised students and intellectuals; both stressed linguistic distinctiveness and a native tradition of decentralised democracy, currently under threat. But the *Blaid* followed a nationalist renaissance in Wales which had lasted for some sixty years. Its career was to be bedevilled by its association with forces – the Welsh language, nonconformist radicalism and temperance – now waning but still able to frustrate any consensus in favour of home rule. In Scotland the *absence* of an effective nationalist tradition was, paradoxically, a source of strength. In the eyes of its younger and more radical supporters, the new movement was a catalyst; its consequences unprecedented and unpredictable.[56]

In Scotland's 'native tradition of decentralised democracy' the older form of independence struggle joins the more recent push for a democratic form of devolution. The way in which a new type of nationalist politics directly follows a major attempt at cultural rebuilding anticipates the separatist sympathies which were culturally driven in the 1980s and '90s. Indeed one problem with cultural renaissance in Scottish and Welsh forms was that it overshot party politics altogether – again, as in the 1980s and '90s process of new-style devolution.[57] Cultural and political processes would gradually merge throughout the century – in the dialectical way for which MacDiarmid had hoped – and 1980s nationalist culture had a clearer idea of its political aims.

The NPS, with its apparently unrealistic leftist bias, did not last. The Renaissance novelist Neil Gunn, though lauded by MacDiarmid in *Contemporary Scottish Studies*,[58] was one figure involved in secret merger talks with the much more conservative Scottish Party in 1933, a merger which would involve compromises including the expulsion of MacDiarmid himself.[59] In preparation for the merger of 1934 which created the SNP, the NPS moved to a soft Home Rule position, a move marking the end of this phase of sub-British national culture, since the diluted form of devolution represented an imperial federalism, or regional membership of a Greater Britain. The idea of devolution which emerged later in the twentieth century, *contra* Westminster's increasingly frantic claims to have final control, can be figured as a gradualist move towards independence working largely through cultural difference. That this has not been fully realised by New Labour is probably a sign of how deeply embedded British imperial images still are in English culture, as some recent analysts of Englishness have recognised. Yet the vaporising of the left of the NPS in 1933 was perhaps an outcome of MacDiarmid's iconoclasm – his inability to shake off Enlightenment individualism – as much as any impractical socialism. MacDiarmid as politican became increasingly isolated between the mid-'20s and mid-'30s, leading to a period of despair.[60] His editorship of, and contribution to, various journals with various party leanings from the early '30s shows an increasingly desperate search for a political solution via an existing cultural nationalism. In the early 1930s, political power moved from independence-seekers to middle-class federal devolutionists, and to the setting up of 'heritage' societies such as the National Trust for Scotland and the Saltire Society (and this would be continued post-war to some extent, in a slightly more populist vein, in the Edinburgh Festival from 1947 and STV from 1955).[61] Conversely, the early SNP, in attacking the cultural left, came to be seen as anti-intellectual. Although the party line would change again around the start of World War II, the inability to translate between the realms of culture and politics, which had been separated by British ideology, became the limit of the First Renaissance. By 1936 Edwin Muir could proclaim that Scottish letters no longer had an international influence.[62] Muir's *Scottish Journey* (1935) echoes J. B. Priestley's 1934 *English Journey*, in seeing a tradition dangerously compromised by urbanisation and modernity.[63] Muir's own solution, as he puts it in *Scott and Scotland* (1936), is to recover a lost 'homogeneous' culture (and here I hardly need quote Frantz Fanon to illustrate the pitfalls of such ideas of recovery). In this sense of rejecting homogeneity MacDiarmid was certainly groundbreaking; this however still leaves the problems of the archaic linguistic 'standard' and his tendency to see Glasgow and Edinburgh, *pace* Eliot's and Priestley's London, as inauthentically Scottish, as unreal cities. (This last would be addressed at great length by Edwin Morgan, who has been more than happy to see Glasgow experience as authentic.)

In terms of its ambition as a thoroughgoing national cultural and political re-structuring, the scale of MacDiarmid's project was only popularised again in the late 1950s, in a Second Renaissance which would soon metamorphose into something more contemporary, to the umbrage of MacDiarmid himself. His own *Contemporary Scottish Studies* was reprinted in 1976 into a very different cultural and linguistic scene. His *To Circumjack Cencrastus* gave its name to the magazine *Cencrastus*, from the early 1980s a major forum for the political–cultural discussions which would immediately precede devolution. Significantly, a multi-volume edition of MacDiarmid's works only began publication in 1992, spanning the period of devolution. What changed between the 1920s and the 1990s was, I suggest, the gradual realisation of the extent to which sub-British emergence had to be a post-imperial project. Nationalists' relation to imperialism had begun in some confusion:

> Ideologically, the NPS had its own antisyzygy. During World War I, nationalism had taken on a new meaning: liberation from imperialism. Muirhead [leader of the SHRA] approved, equating Scotland with the exploited colonies, but the nation of Home Rule *qua* imperial federation was still important to those who longed for the pre-war balance.[64]

For Richard Finlay, the question of Scotland's place in empire was *the* major division between Scottish nationalists between the wars.[65] Whereas the SNL was from 1920 anti-colonial and backed Irish independence, the NPS always had problems reconciling imperialists and anti-imperialists; when the major parties began noticing Scottish Nationalism in 1932 with the possibility of the Scottish Party merger, the NPS jettisoned its anti-imperialists in favour of 'Empire Free Trade'.[66] Until the 1930s, when the significance of socialist nationalism was felt, participation in British empire could still connote a specifically Scottish, Whiggish and neo-Enlightenment conception of advancement. As Michael Fry has recently put it (from a position broadly sympathetic to empire):

> Scots believed they possessed better ideas about Empire than the English, who notoriously had acquired it in a fit of absence of mind. An idea about Empire, a modern evolution of the kind sought by all progressive Scotsmen, was how pioneers of Home Rule conceived of their project. So Scottish Nationalism grew up compatible with Empire.[67]

In the beginning the SNP was still behind the imperialist civilising mission, resolving that 'Scotland shall share with England the rights and responsibilities they, as mother nations, have jointly created and incurred within the British Empire'.[68] After the merger with the Scottish Party, the SNP's model became Northern Ireland rather than Ireland, stressing the loyalist tendencies in Scottish identity. By 1938–9, though, the SNP had rethought imperialism, and by 1942 explicitly rejected any Scottish identity 'bound up with any notions of the imperial past'.[69] This may have been a party political step forward (albeit one which attempts to jettison all Scottish imperial history, as many nationalists still do), but imperialist nationalist sentiment would remain latent, at least until the 1960s. At this point, Fry has argued, the nationalism which had once been imperial was in a position to present itself as unrelated to imperialism, yet without any change in the mindset of improvement; he shrewdly notes that Margaret Ewing's celebrated victory at Hamilton in 1967 occurred in the last month of British rule at Aden, an outpost defended by the Argylls.[70] In this sense the cultural and political movement of Renaissance was certainly behind later devolutionary movements, yet this legacy must be read against the grain.

The 1920s MacDiarmid similarly, despite his own Marxism, was not anti-imperialist, and amidst the praise for his pioneering work his nationalism should be seen as problematic in this context. Empire is still civilising, in this weighted reading of the Marxist claim that all societies must pass through 'modernity' (a left version of Eliot's coffee-table collection of savageries). In 1926, at the peak of the nationalist Renaissance, MacDiarmid's *Albyn* called for Scotland's continued centrality to empire:

> The Empire not only stands in no danger from Scotland coming into line with the other component parts of it, but it will give Scotland for the first time an effective share and say in

Imperial affairs. Scotland has contributed far too much to the upbringing of the Empire to want to withdraw from it. It is, indeed, the very opposite motive that is at work. It is the recognition of how grossly anomalous it is that Scotland, which has contributed so preponderantly to Imperial development, which should be relegated to so inferior and ineffective a place in it, and have no voice in determining and disposing its future . . . A concern with Scottish domestic welfare is just as much an Imperial consideration as preoccupation with the affairs of any other part of the Empire.[71]

At times the ethnocentrism at the heart of this imperial sentiment was manifest: one 1923 article in *The Scottish Nation* sees MacDiarmid lament that '[t]aking other foreign elements into account, it is appalling to find that there is one non-Scot in every nine of Edinburgh's population and one in eight in Glasgow's'.[72] He also frequently lapses into discussion of the nation's 'distinctive psychology'.[73] What such outbursts show are not simply racism (splitting people into distinct groups with distinct characteristics, sometimes mapped onto nations), but racism's concomitant muddling of terms: without any such fixed citizenship as Scottish (such qualities belong to states, not mere nations), how do we identify a non-Scot, unless using ethnocentric measurements of genetic similarity, or the type of equally ethnocentric images of unchanging tradition then popular amongst English literary elites? Critics like Tom Nairn are still struggling to deal with the effects of this muddling: the idea that Britain's outer nations customarily see themselves as 'races' and are congenitally anti-English is a difficult one to shift, while many of these nations' spokespersons, Nairn included, have long encouraged the emergence of an English democracy which has been mangled by Britain. In other words, even had party politics gone its way, the inter-war Renaissance would have found it difficult to imagine a non-ethnic Scottish citizenship to back an independent nation. Thus the adduction of postcolonial literatures in relation to MacDiarmid in Riach's introduction to *Contemporary Scottish Studies* is not quite convincing, unless we identify the Renaissance with the very first ethnocentric rumblings of postcolonialism, as in *négritude*.[74] Precisely what is missing from Renaissance thinking is the ability to get beyond a racial 'we' continuing to civilise the empire; in that form it is probably as well it never led to independence. This exclusionist sense of national identity, reliant on race, was already late, not early.[75] The time lag it pointed to in Scottish culture – the endless attempt to catch up with the 'mainstream' cultures of imperialism – would concur with Nairn's description of how Scotland's lateness blocked effective nationalist Romanticism in the nineteenth century. The same indeed goes for England, since 'English Romanticism' was always peculiarly Anglo-British, failing in its project of an English nationalism. In the decades before devolution, these gaps between ethnicity and nationhood became popularly visible in Scotland; in the context of England, despite a larger immigrant population, they are even more difficult to shift.

Ethnicity and Authenticity

So the Renaissance, a period central to sub-British national culture which would grow in the second half of the century, also carries key contradictions which to some extent return it to Britishness, and are not easily described as post-British. For one thing, that the figure of MacDiarmid should have been so central until so recently is partly due to his strong-ego (Poundian) stance which, as I have suggested, remains intact from the Enlightenment's exhortation to the individual to grasp civility (and MacDiarmid describes David Hume as 'the greatest Scotsman who has ever lived').[76] Like Eliot and Pound, MacDiarmid increasingly became the man behind the poetry, the individual talent gathering disparate voices and arranging them into a tradition, in this case enabled by Synthetic Scots. This was amplified in the Second Renaissance: Duncan Glen's 1964 study *Hugh MacDiarmid and the Scottish Renaissance* shows something like a New Critical unpacking of embedded reading under an individual authority; in the same year the survey *Hugh MacDiarmid: a festschrift* reads like a roll-call of the second wave.[77] Glen's magazine *Akros* reached a peak of MacDiarmid-centredness in a special double number in 1970, which contained a sixty-three-page interview featuring full-page close-ups of the man himself, living-room ornaments and thistle door-knocker.[78] A 1980 study confirmed that the age had been 'The Age of MacDiarmid'.[79] What is problematic about biographical criticism is not so much any problem of personal politics, as how close it remains to the ideals of high-British English Literature, which accorded linguistic authority to chosen individuals within a limited canon of Great Men, largely for imperial purposes. This history of worthy individuals has also fed into a Scottish national defeatism leading from the Enlightenment's Anglocentric Britishness through Carlyle's great English writers to the kailyard left at home. As Cairns Craig puts it:

Scottish culture has cowered in the consciousness of its own inadequacy, recognising the achievements of individual Scots simply as proof of the failure of the culture as a whole. Succeed, and you are no longer Scottish (not really Scottish) – you are like David Hume or Muriel Spark, someone who has leapt beyond the bounds set by Scottishness.[80]

Increasingly for Renaissance writing, there exists a world in view of, but not touching, this strong subject-self – close to Humean knowledge but far from the dialectic which opens *A Drunk Man*. The later MacDiarmid can be cast in the position of the Enlightenment and Victorian British encyclopaedists, seeing and arranging various knowledges under his expert eye. Of previous Scottish poets, what he values most is their ability to 'assimilate and utilize' knowledges.[81] The phrase 'assimilate and utilize' also appears in the mid-period poem *The Kind of Poetry I Want*, where the nation is to be a race of scientists, technicians and encyclopaedists, looking for totalisation of the information available:

A poetry concerned with all that is needed
Of the sum of human knowledge and expression,
The sustaining consciousness,
The reasonable will of our race,
To produce this super-individuality, Man
[…]
                    the specific man in us
Has the power to assimilate, utilize, override, and fuse
All our individual divergencies[82]

If this position is specifically Scottish, we run into a problem of epistemological authority which also appears in Robert Crawford's reading of MacDiarmid and others in *Devolving English Literature*; despite its suasive description of modernism as provincial, this study tends to imply that viewing and arranging a number of objects is the same as entering into a productive (or dialectical) relationship with them.[83] What links Crawford's key modernists (Eliot, Pound, Joyce, Lewis) is the strength of surveying ego which arranges fragments from a stable centre. But arrangement of knowledge is not the same as allowing knowledge *into* the strong subject-self, either for the Edinburghers who made the first *Encyclopaedia Britannica*, or for modernists like MacDiarmid. In neither MacDiarmid nor Crawford's reading do we get a sense of the extent to which Scottish identity is built on the imperial violence of collecting and arranging knowledges. Scotland may have been provincial in British terms; but precisely because of this, it has been exaggeratedly central in global-imperial terms (and ironically an account of this exaggerated centralisation is exactly what makes Crawford's account so groundbreaking). Rather than breaking down the speaking subject to allow a shifting knowledge touched by otherness, the kind of poetry MacDiarmid's speaker wants is a 'poetry with the power of assimilating foreign influences'[84] into a self unspoilt and untroubled by otherness, and capable of viewing 'the whole':

> poems concerned with technical matters
> [...]
> And all the other manifestations
> Of *cultismo* and *concettista* through the ages[85]

As I have hinted above, this authoritative position is in many ways similar to that of the Anglo-British movement of New Criticism.[86] Riach elsewhere admits that the Anglo-British modernism which sought to evade Victorian Romanticism by presenting an impersonal series of fragments in practice often reinstated the brilliant individual (author or critic) as a measure of value in synthesising them.[87] However, soon after, the Second Renaissance was challenged by other strains, viewed *tout court* by MacDiarmid as illiterate and lazy. Ian Hamilton Finlay's *Glasgow Beasts* refused the 'Synthetic Scots' model for a comic bestiary accompanied by papercut pictures and poems in un-synthetic Glasgow English.[88] Finlay went on to produce concrete poetry in the early 1960s, and sculpture from around 1966. Much of Finlay's work is a biting critique of Enlightenment civility, mixing images of nature and artifice, respectability and cruelty; the method of concrete poetry also disrupts the stable viewed object-image, forming speech into definite shapes to ironically image the way national languages become 'imaged'.[89] In the 1960s, Edwin Morgan, Scotland's first pioneer in concrete poetry, drew heavily from MacDiarmid, but also moved Synthetic Scots onwards to a less standardised model. MacDiarmid vented his frustration at abuses of Synthetic Scots during 'Writers' Conference' of the Edinburgh Festival in 1962, where he harangued as feckless bohemians a collection of writers including Alexander Trocchi (who later collaborated with R. D. Laing)[90] and William Burroughs.[91] The criticism of Finlay would be intensified in *The ugly birds without wings* and in MacDiarmid's refusal to be anthologised alongside him.[92] Mark Scroggins quotes a defence of the Synthetic Scots experiment at all costs, now with a highly standardising turn: '[Finlay's *Glasgow*

Beasts is] not the kind of Scots in which high poetry can be written, and what can be done to it . . . is qualitatively little, if at all, above Kailyard level'.[93]

The question then is when the Renaissance really escapes Arnoldian-Eliotic Romanticism in its ideas of linguistic authority. Renaissance literature even showed reverence for Standard English by using apostrophes to note deviations; one example is the substitution of '-in" for '-ing', ending in the accidental use of 'pidgin", in the 1926 first edition of *A Drunk Man*, a contraction for a phantom gerund 'pidging'.[94] Normally words do not use apostrophes to show where they differ from cognate words in foreign languages; in this sense, did the Renaissance really believe it had a separate language at all? 'A Theory of Scots Letters' moreover, pitching the difference between authentic vernacular and inauthentic doggerel as an 'educated knowledge', corresponds to the *class* difference between what A. J. Aitken has called Standard Scottish English (SSE) and Educated Standard Scottish English (ESSE).[95] Linguistic authenticity is still in this sense as important to MacDiarmid as it was to the Eliot of *Tradition and the Individual Talent*, and it is still difficult to escape class hierarchies. Regardless of the avowed Marxism of some Renaissance writers, this now looks like a highly exclusionist idea of a language; it is far away, for example, from the recent diction of James Kelman or Janice Galloway, which looks for a way to write out the linguistic building blocks of southern Scottish speech – without apostrophes. So it is difficult to accept Herbert's assertion that MacDiarmid 'anticipates with surprising accuracy' the French situationists of the 1960s, employing a radically obstructive form of anarchist mischief in a linguistic 'drifting' through dictionaries, and in deliberately overlong poems.[96] If MacDiarmid's pronouncements have an irony, it is less the playful radicalism of situationism than the egotism of a James Bond villain: 'If I write in a language I invent wholly myself and insist upon calling it Scots in defiance of all precedents, nothing you can do can prevent my ultimate success'.[97] Even allowing for humour, this is not the language of communality or even communism, but a return to the British moment of individual cultural guardianship.

The question of how Synthetic Scots relates to speech is still often confused today, by equating Scots, Synthetic Scots, and the dialect of English which most Scottish people speak. There arises, as with all 'folk'-influenced culture, the possibility that a language may have to be pushed back out of history altogether before it becomes really authentic. MacDiarmid does put a historical frame on his Scots – 'Dunbar, not Burns' (Burns being largely to blame for kailyard culture by *not* revitalising Scots language, and thus laying it open to British images of Scotch kitsch); but many more have assumed that Synthetic Scots is somehow naturally related to the people, whereas it demands an elite education and is reliant on archaic printed authorities. Like Eliot, MacDiarmid turns to a dialect which favours its relationship to prior sources over everyday speech more describable as 'English'. Another way to describe this is as a disavowal: it separates off a fixed language so authoritatively native that it is not spoken by anyone, avoiding the fact that non-Standard dialect speakers are constantly being presented with grammatical choices *within* a language. Indeed, diglossic (bidialectical) speakers are required to be particularly adept at phrase-choice to survive socially.[98] The tendency to replace speech with an authoritative language fits over the Enlightenment subject, gaining civility by acquiring and organising – an encyclopaedic tradition which we have seen legislating *against* political nationalism.

In this sense of protection of a standard language adduced to a 'people' but guarded by an individual, the MacDiarmid-inspired mid-century version of the Scottish Renaissance was indeed triggered in a similar way to that in which the classically canonised Eliot–I. A. Richards line triggered New Criticism. Both movements were late-British – although at least one had a reasonably clear vision of which nation it was trying to speak for. Both left long critical hangovers of unpacking allusions embedded in poetry. And both turn to the 'reduced aesthetic' of poetry as protection from the mongrelised crowds around them. In Eliot's case, this had rendered the crowds of Britain's biggest city a faceless mass; in MacDiarmid's case, Glasgow and Edinburgh are like 'ploomen [ploughmen] in a pub,/ They want to hear o naething/ But their ain foul bubbub'.[99] This criticism is ironic given Glasgow's willingness to stir up a communist revolution after World War I. And despite the dialectical promise, *A Drunk Man* is both assimilationist towards foreignness and denunciative of 'inauthentic' Scottish ideas in export. The drunk speaker is insightful about the abuses of native culture, but joins them to a defence of nationality conceived as pre-modern, authentic, anterior and pure:

> You canna gang to a Burns supper even
> Wi'oot some wizened scrunt o' a knock-knee
> Chinee turns roon to say, 'Him Haggis – velly goot!'
> And ten to wan the piper is a Cockney.

No' wan in fifty kens a wurd Burns wrote
But misapplied is a'body's property,
And gin there was his like alive the day
They'd be the last a kennin' haund to gi'e –

Croose London Scotties wi' their braw shirt fronts
And a' their fancy freen's, rejoicin'
That similah gatherings in Timbuctoo,
Bagdad – and Hell, nae doot – are voicin'

Burns' sentiments o' universal love,
In pidgin' English or in wild-fowl Scots,
And toastin' ane wha's nocht to them but an
Excuse for faitherin' Genius wi' *their* thochts.[100]

Perhaps this ethnocentrism is the dialectical drink talking, but its strong-authentic-man position was common in the Renaissance. In a late interview, MacDiarmid describes the Scots as 'a hard drinking, woman loving race of people'.[101] Not only is MacDiarmid returning here to the discredited terminology of turn-of-the-century British imperialism he is also further entrenching the ethnic visibility which had frozen the Celtic image in Britain. If today's Scots were really the speech of those living in or born in Scotland (the only measures of national belonging for a stateless nation), it would not only partake of English, ancient Scots and Gaelic, but also a wide range of languages whose speakers many nationalists are still unwilling to accept as real Scots. Though it has left a problematic and popular legacy, this form of nationalism waned after the second wave: in the special *Chapman* on Edwin Morgan in 1991, Robert Crawford points out that the Renaissance's indispensibility to Scottish culture had already been thoroughly historicised:

> Where 18th-century Scots strove to create a British (as distinct from English) literature, 20th-century Scottish writers aim, on the whole, for a post-British identity that is particularly Scottish in a new way. MacDiarmid's way was Anglophobic, a strident rewriting of the story of Scotland as encyclopaedic and fierce, internationally-oriented and chauvinistically macho. MacDiarmid's Scotland now appears curiously antique, its anachronistic nature highlighted in his eulogy of authentically 'Scottish' pubs which are 'men only', as opposed to 'meretricious deScotticised' bars where 'Men (if you can call them that) even take their wives and daughters along with them'.[102]

The products of the First and Second Scottish Renaissances are paradoxical, both opposing Eliot's Anglo-British will to order and imagining a post-British form of the nation, yet replacing British standards with shadow-standards which hold them in place. This tendency to become entrapped within the very boundaries of 'English' which the movement sought to escape makes more sense seen in terms of the 'Greater Britain' context in which national language fell under imperial culture. What the postcolonial unpacking of this context opens up is the extent to which linguistic variants were already catered for within an empire redefined *as* shared Anglophone culture. Post-British forms taking forward a dialectical struggle to get free of this imperial background altogether would belong to the Third Renaissance, which immediately preceded devolution.

Notes

1. Cf. Robert Crawford, 'Hugh MacDiarmid's Poetry of Knowledge', *Proceedings of the British Academy*, 87, 1994, pp. 174–6.
2. See Krishan Kumar, *The Making of English National Identity* (Cambridge: Cambridge University Press, 2003), pp. 196–202.
3. Benedict Anderson, *Imagined Communities: Reflections on the Origins and Spread of Nationalism* (London: Verso, 1983).
4. Tom Nairn, *The Break-up of Britain: Crisis and Neo-nationalism* (London: NLB, 1977), p. 47; Hugh MacDiarmid, 'Albyn: Scotland and the Future', in Alan Riach (ed.), *Albyn: Shorter Books and Monographs* (Manchester: Carcanet, 1996), pp. 1–39: 1–12.
5. T. M. Devine, *The Scottish Nation* (London: Penguin, 1999), p. 315.
6. Virginia Woolf, *The Waves* (London: Penguin, 1992).
7. Henry Rider Haggard, *A Farmer's Year* (London: Longman Green, 1899); see also Alun Howkins, 'The Discovery of Rural England', in Robert Colls and Phillip Dodd (eds), *Englishness: Politics and Culture 1880–1920* (London: Croom Helm, 1986), pp. 62–88.
8. Edmund Wilson, 'The Poetry of Drouth', in Michael Grant (ed.), *T. S. Eliot: The Critical Heritage* (London: Routledge and Kegan Paul, 1982), pp. 138–44.
9. See Paul Gilroy, *The Black Atlantic: Modernity and Double Consciousness* (London: Verso, 1993).
10. T. S. Eliot, 'The Waste Land', in *The Complete Poems and Plays* (New York: Harcourt Brace, 1950), p. 47.
11. James Anthony Froude, *Oceana, or England and her Colonies* (London: Longmans, 1886).
12. Wilson, 'The Poetry of Drouth', p. 139.
13. See Oswald Spengler, *Decline of the West: form and actuality*, trans. Francis Atkinson (London: Allen and Unwin, 1992).
14. See Hugh MacDiarmid, *Lucky Poet: A Self-Study in Literary and Political Ideas* (Manchester: Carcanet, 1994), p. 144.
15. F. R. Leavis, *The Great Tradition: George Eliot, Henry James, Joseph Conrad* (Harmondsworth: Penguin, 1972).

16. T. S. Eliot, *Selected Prose* (London: Faber and Faber, 1975), p. 39.
17. Ibid. p. 38.
18. Eliot, 'The Waste Land', p. 48.
19. See Robert Crawford, 'Hugh MacDiarmid's Poetry of Knowledge', pp. 169–87.
20. http://www.oed.com/public/inside/editors.htm, consulted 2003; on Scottish abandonment of 'language', see David Daiches, *The Paradox of Scottish Culture: the eighteenth-century experience* (London: Oxford University Press, 1964), pp. 22–3.
21. See J. C. W. Reith, *Broadcast Over Britain* (London: Hodder and Stoughton, 1924), pp. 157–62; Andrew Marr, *The Day Britain Died* (London: Profile, 2000), pp. 36–9.
22. See Chris Baldick, *The Social Mission of English Criticism 1848–1932* (Oxford: Clarendon, 1983), pp. 92–8; Francis Mulhern, *The Moment of Scrutiny* (London: NLB, 1979), p. 121; also George Sampson, *English For The English: A Chapter on National Education* (Cambridge: Cambridge University Press, 1921), pp. 40–8.
23. Quoted in Lynda Mugglestone, '"Proper English" and the Politics of Standard Speech', in David Morley and Kevin Robins (eds), *British Cultural Studies: Geography, Nationality, and Identity* (Oxford: Oxford University Press, 2001), pp. 180–94.
24. Mugglestone, '"Proper English"', p. 192.
25. W. N. Herbert, 'Morgan's Words', in Robert Crawford and Hamish Whyte (eds), *About Edwin Morgan* (Edinburgh: Edinburgh University Press, 1990), pp. 65–74; cf. Colin McCabe, 'Language, Literature, Identity: Reflections on the Cox Report', *Critical Quarterly*, 32–4, 1990, pp. 1–13.
26. Quoted in *Agenda*, 1969, p. 42.
27. Cf. Edward Said, 'Jane Austen and Empire', in Said, *Culture and Imperialism* (New York: Vintage, 1994), pp. 80–97.
28. William Wordsworth, *The Prelude*, ed. Mark L. Reed (Ithaca: Cornell University Press, 1991); T. S. Eliot, 'The Music of Poetry', in *On Poetry and Poets* (New York: Noonday Press, 1957), pp. 26–38.
29. See Kumar, *The Making of English National Identity*, pp. 114–20.
30. Arthur Quiller-Couch, *The Oxford Book of English Verse, 1250–1900* (Oxford: Clarendon, 1900); E. H. Marsh (ed.), *Georgian Poetry* (London: Poetry Bookshop, 1912–22).
31. Alan Riach, 'Introduction to Hugh MacDiarmid', in Riach (ed.), *Contemporary Scottish Studies* (Manchester: Carcanet, 1995), p. xi.
32. Alexander McGill, 'Towards a Scottish Renaissance', in Alan Riach (ed.), *Hugh MacDiarmid: Contemporary Scottish Studies* (Manchester: Carcanet with Mid Northumberland Arts Group, 1995).
33. Hugh MacDiarmid, *Collected Prose*, ed. with an introduction by Alan Riach (Manchester: Carcanet, 1996), p. xiv.
34. Murray G. H. Pittock, *A New History of Scotland* (Stroud: Sutton, 2003), p. 271; see various essays in *Edinburgh Review*, 88, 1992.
35. George Douglas Brown, *The House With the Green Shutters* (Edinburgh: Canongate, 1996).

36. Alan Bold, *MacDiarmid: The Terrible Crystal* (London: Routledge Kegan Paul, 1983), p. 85.
37. Hugh MacDiarmid, 'A Theory of Scots Letters', in Alan Riach (ed.), *Hugh MacDiarmid: Selected Prose* (Manchester: Carcanet, 1992), pp. 16–33: 22.
38. Hugh MacDiarmid, 'This Scottish Strain', from *Albyn*, in MacDiarmid, ed. Bold, *The Thistle Rises* (London: Hamilton, 1984), pp. 142–8: 144.
39. MacDiarmid, *Complete Poems Vol. 1*, eds Michael Grieve and W. R. Aitken (Manchester: Carcanet, 1993), p. 120.
40. James Kelman, *How Late It Was, How Late* (London: Secker and Warburg, 1994).
41. G. Gregory Smith, *Scottish Literature: Character and Influence* (London: Macmillan, 1919); similar comparisons of bilingualism/diglossia and dialectic resound throughout the twentieth century: Edwin Morgan's 'Scottish Poetry in English', in *Crossing the Border* (Manchester: Carcanet, 1990), pp. 14–15; Robert Crawford's and Roderick Watson's uses of Mikhail Bakhtin in various places; and Cairns Craig, *The Modern Scottish Novel* (Edinburgh: Edinburgh University Press, 1999), pp. 30–1: 89.
42. Angus Calder, 'Introduction' to Angus Calder, Glen Murray and Alan Riach (eds), *The Raucle Tongue: Hitherto Uncollected Prose* (Manchester: Carcanet, 1996), pp. 3–7: 7.
43. Hugh MacDiarmid, *A Drunk Man Looks at the Thistle*, ed. Kenneth Buthlay (Edinburgh: Scottish Academic Press, 1987), p. 6.
44. MacDiarmid, *Complete Poems Vol. 1*, p. 83.
45. Ibid. p. 116.
46. Ibid. p. 157.
47. Alan Riach, *Hugh MacDiarmid's Epic Poetry* (Edinburgh: Edinburgh University Press, 1991).
48. George Elder Davie, *The Democratic Intellect: Scotland and her Universities in the Nineteenth Century* (Edinburgh: Edinburgh University Press, 1961).
49. Cf. Robert Crawford, *Devolving English Literature* (Edinburgh: Edinburgh University Press, 2000), p. 240.
50. See Kumar, *The Making of English National Identity*, p. 169; Stephen Haseler, *The English Tribe: Identity, Nation and Europe* (London: Macmillan, 1996), p. 159.
51. Peter Lynch, *SNP: A History of the Scottish National Party* (Cardiff: Welsh Academic Press, 2002), p. 29.
52. George Malcolm Thomson, *Caledonia, or the Future of the Scots* (London: Kegan Paul, 1927); Edwin Muir, *Scottish Journey* (London: William Heinemann, 1935), pp. 213–50.
53. Christopher Harvie, *Scotland and Nationalism: Scottish Society and Politics 1707 to the Present* (London: Routledge, 2000), p. 25.
54. Cf. Pittock, *A New History of Scotland*, p. 267.
55. See Marr, *The Day Britain Died*, p. 77.
56. Harvie, *Scotland and Nationalism*, p. 24.
57. See ibid. p. 155.

58. MacDiarmid, in Riach (ed.), *Contemporary Scottish Studies*, pp. 308–13.
59. Richard Finlay, *Independent and Free – Scottish Politics and the Origins of the Scottish National Party, 1918–1945* (Edinburgh: John Donald, 1994), p. 128.
60. See Harvie, *Scotland and Nationalism*, p. 106.
61. Harvie, *Scotland and Nationalism*, p. 28; Pittock, *A New History of Scotland*, pp. 273, 294.
62. Edwin Muir, *Scott and Scotland: The Predicament of the Scottish Writer* (Edinburgh: Polygon, 1982), pp. 110–14.
63. Edwin Muir, *Scottish Journey* (London: Fontana, 1934).
64. Harvie, *Scotland and Nationalism*, p. 27.
65. Richard J. Finlay, '"For or Against?": Scottish Nationalists and the British Empire, 1919–1939', *Scottish Historical Review* LXXI, 1–2, October 1992, pp. 184–206.
66. Finlay, '"For or Against?"', p. 197.
67. Michael Fry, *The Scottish Empire* (Edinburgh: Birlinn, 2001), p. 496.
68. Quoted in Lynch, *SNP*, p. 41.
69. Finlay, '"For or Against?"', p. 206.
70. Fry, *The Scottish Empire*, pp. 490–1.
71. Hugh MacDiarmid, 'Albyn: or Scotland and the Future', in Alan Riach (ed.), *Albyn: Shorter Books and Monographs* (Manchester: Carcanet, 1996), pp. 1–39: 24–5.
72. Hugh MacDiarmid, 'English Invasion of Scotland', in Riach (ed.), *Contemporary Scottish Studies*, pp. 115–16.
73. Quoted in Riach, introduction to MacDiarmid, *Contemporary Scottish Studies*, p. xxii; cf. Hugh MacDiarmid, 'Plea for a Scottish Fascism', in Calder, Murray and Riach (eds), *The Raucle Tongue* (Manchester: Carcanet, 1998), pp. 82–7; 'Programme for a Scottish Fascism', in Alan Riach (ed.), *Selected Prose* (Manchester: Carcanet, 1992), pp. 34–8.
74. Riach, introduction to MacDiarmid, Riach (ed.), *Contemporary Scottish Studies*, pp. xxx–xxxi.
75. Cf. Eric Hobsbawm, *Nations and Nationalism Since 1780: Programme, Myth, Reality* (Cambridge: Cambridge University Press, 1992); Kumar, *The Making of English National Identity*, pp. 175–225.
76. Hugh MacDiarmid, 'David Hume: Scotland's Greatest Son', in Alan Riach (ed.), *Albyn*, pp. 297–310.
77. Duncan Glen, *Hugh MacDiarmid and the Scottish Renaissance* (Edinburgh: Chambers, 1964); K. D. Duval and Sydney Goodsir Smith (eds), *Hugh MacDiarmid: a festschrift* (Edinburgh: Duval, 1962).
78. 'A Conversation – Hugh MacDiarmid and Duncan Glen', *Akros*, 5–13, April 1970, pp. 7–72: 62, 70.
79. P. H. Scott and A. C. Davis (eds), *The Age of MacDiarmid: Hugh MacDiarmid and his influence on contemporary Scotland* (Edinburgh: Mainstream, 1992).
80. Cairns Craig, *Out of History: Narrative Paradigms in Scottish and British Culture* (Edinburgh: Polygon, 1996), p. 1.

81. Hugh MacDiarmid quoted in Maurice Lindsay (ed.), *John Davidson: A Selection of his Poems, with Preface by T. S. Eliot and Essay by Hugh MacDiarmid* (London: Hutchinson, 1961), p. 50.
82. MacDiarmid, 'The Kind of Poetry I Want', in W. R. Aitken and Michael Grieve, *Complete Poems Vol. II*, pp. 1003–35: 1004–05.
83. Robert Crawford, *Devolving English Literature*, pp. 216–70.
84. MacDiarmid, 'The Kind of Poetry I Want', p. 1011.
85. Ibid. p. 1005.
86. For a discussion of the simultaneous creation of and obedience to 'prior' standards in New Criticism, see Mulhern, *The Moment of Scrutiny*.
87. Alan Riach, 'Towards a Poetics of Hugh MacDiarmid', in Herbert and Richard Price (eds), *Gairfish Shibbo-Lithos* (Dundee: Gairfish, 1992), pp. 22–9: 24.
88. Ian Hamilton Finlay, 'Glasgow Beasts', in *The Dancers Inherit the Party, and Glasgow Beasts, an a Burd* (Edinburgh: Polygon, 1996).
89. Cf. Michael Gardiner, 'Towards a Post-British Theory of Modernism', *Pretexts*, 11–2, 2002, pp. 133–46.
90. '[Laing's "sigma"] project was launched by Alexander Trocchi's brochure, "The Invisible Insurrection of a Million Minds", to which Laing contributed an enthusiastic note of sponsorship' – Peter Sedgwick, *Psycho Politics* (London: Harper and Row, 1982), p. 264; Edwin Morgan has indicated to me that 'Laing featured on Trocchi's Sigma Portfolios (1964–7), and they collaborated on various antiuniversity and similar projects' – private correspondence, 1 August 1999.
91. Described by Andrew Murray Scott, 'Mr. MacDairmid and Mr. Trocchi: Where Extremists Meet', in *Chapman*, 83, 1996, pp. 36–9, and by Edwin Morgan, 'The Fold-in Conference', in *Gambit*, autumn 1962, reproduced in *Edinburgh Review*, 97, spring 1997, pp. 94–102.
92. Hugh MacDiarmid, '*The ugly birds without wings*', in Alan Riach (ed.), *Albyn*, pp. 318–31.
93. Hugh MacDiarmid, *Letters*, ed. Alan Bold (London: Hamish Hamilton, 1984), p. 687, quoted in Mark Scroggins, 'The Piety of Terror: Ian Hamilton Finlay, the Modernist Fragment, and the neo-classical sublime', Flashpoint Web Issue 1, 1997: http://webdelsol.com/FLASHPOINT/ihfinlay.htm. Consulted 2000.
94. MacDiarmid, *A Drunk Man*, ed. Buthlay, p. 8; differences from the 1926 edition are given on pp. 201–3.
95. MacDiarmid, 'A Theory of Scots Letters', p. 23; cf. A. J. Aitken, 'Scottish Speech: a historical view with special reference to the Standard English of Scotland', in A. J. Aitken and Tom McArthur (eds), *Languages of Scotland* (London: Chambers, 1979), pp. 85–118.
96. W. N. Herbert, 'Sciffies Across the Shibboloch', in Herbert and Price (eds), *Gairfish: Shibbo-Lithos*, p. 6.
97. Quoted in J. G. Outterstone Buglass, 'Arne Garborg, Mr. Joyce, and Mr. M'Diarmid', September 1924, in Calder, Murray and Riach (eds), *The Raucle Tongue*, pp. 233–8: 238.

 98. See Nairn, *The Break-up of Britain*; Peter Trudgill, *Sociolinguistics: An Introduction* (London: Penguin, 2000), p. 102.
 99. MacDiarmid, *Complete Poems Vol. 1*, p. 108.
100. MacDiarmid, *A Drunk Man*, ed. Buthlay, pp. 6–8 (lines 21–52), but my orthography here follows Buthlay's rendering of the 1926 edition.
101. Hugh MacDiarmid, 'Valedictory', 'Kaleidoscope' radio interview with Tom Vernon, 25 September 1977, in *The Thistle Rises*, pp. 286–94: 294.
102. Robert Crawford, 'Morgan's Critical Position', *Chapman*, 64, spring/summer 1991, pp. 32–7: 32.

Chapter Three

The Question of General Education

Davie's Counter-Attack

The educational systems of England and Wales on one hand, and Scotland on the other, have never been unified, except for certain aspects of higher education entry and overall funding. The Acts of Union guaranteed in principle the autonomy of each system, underscoring the importance of separate educational traditions; however there have always been debates over conceptual and curricular autonomy, coming into sharper focus in the 1960s. Education has assumed a primary significance in stateless Scotland, where education is viewed as fundamental to national identity. By 1707 there were already twice as many universities in Scotland than in England, served by a parish school system dating back to James IV, whose breadth fed into the (inevitably exaggerated) ideal of inclusion of rural and working-class communities. This inclusiveness would by the second half of the nineteenth century be concretised in a significant advantage in general literacy.[1] Scottish ideas of education have remained index-linked to ideas of nationhood, quietening when ideals of inclusion and applied generalism seem to be served, and becoming conflictual at other times, as in post-1979 privatisation. In one reading of the Scottish generalist tradition, a role of education is to 'attack...the false conception of the State as a directing ethical force'.[2] There is by comparison a notable lack of literature on specific English (or English and Welsh) education, and less sense of a danger of the English system being either 'subsumed' by a British one, or left over after it. As in most aspects of civic and cultural life, post-union England was left with a sense in 1707 that it was able to continue as before, whereas in Scotland concentration was on remaining areas of civic distinctiveness.

The unifying point for modern British systems of education is usually taken as the 1872 Education Act, which standardised the traditional Scottish parish school system by making schooling compulsory and bringing the voluntary and public sectors together under a single system of elected school boards funded by the Scotch Education Department. For some, the move of administration to London (eventually; at first it was temporarily taken care of in Edinburgh) and the eclipse of universal parish schooling represented an intellectual annexation; R. D. Anderson for example cites the rage of the rector of Edinburgh High School.[3] The older system of the humanities which had developed in Scotland as part of a 'generalist' approach to education was, in one interpretation, 'assailed'.[4] The new system allowed for a form of negotiated sovereignty whereby working-class members of the community were drawn into school administration and the Labour movement gradually allowed to dilute Christian zeal. This form of autonomy did produce a relatively inclusive national education, and stayed any nationalist socialist attack.[5] In the 1910s and 1920s, however, the main teachers' union, the Educational Institute of Scotland, became increasingly militant, going on strike in 1911 – though they would make few inroads between 1872 and 1918.[6] MacDiarmid's highly influential *Contemporary Scottish Studies* were published in the mid-1920s in an *educational* journal; MacDiarmid stressed many of the educational qualities which would later be viewed as part of an un-British tradition, such as low university entry and leaving ages,[7] and pushed A. S. Neill's 'child-centred' approach, which would not come into vogue until much later.[8] In the mid-1980s this state of affairs would almost be repeated, with educationalists playing a central role in the push for devolution, and a specifically Scottish 'general' education returning with a gradual interdisciplinarity and wide-viewed publishing projects like Polygon's *Determinations*, recalling, in a post-British context, how Enlightenment thinkers used to communicate across fields.[9] Between these two moments an explicit and provocative re-reading of educational history had been undergone by G. E. Davie. Although the phrase which forms the title of Davie's 1961 *The Democratic Intellect* was actually coined by Walter Elliot as early as 1932 (and in *Akros* MacDiarmid claims joint credit with Davie for marketing the idea), the concept of a distinctive sense of the civic role of education was popularised and politicised by Davie in the early '60s.[10]

Davie's claim that educational freedom was being undermined was not original– he sets out to account for the academics who during the century between the 1820s and the 1920s had worked towards 'traditional' inclusiveness and interdisciplinarity. It is significant that the book was published when the literary–political upheavals of the 1920s were being rediscovered, yet another round of educational Britishisation was widely perceived to be taking place. Davie argues that from the late nineteenth century, moves to adapt the Scottish university system to the English one were not only an Anglo-British overstepping of union, but more importantly were also classist as well as classicist, threatening the goal of a general education for a wide student body. Scotland had in this sense long 'neglected' the classics, in the sense of refusing to place primary importance on Greek and Latin grammar, with the dubious parallels which could be drawn between ancient civilisation and British Empire; thus Matthew Arnold's mid-Victorian description of Scottish education as simply un-cultural.[11] The story Davie tells is of a nineteenth-century battle to maintain philosophy as a connective discipline in the face of classical training, which he sees as hampering youthful intellectual curiosity.[12] The general enquiry which had developed in Scotland from ancient times (with an ear towards France often impossible in England) had been based a range of subjects on a first-principles philosophical approach; student essays were largely peer-tested rather than being corrected from above by the teacher – thus the 'democratic' intellect.[13] Defence of this tradition had led as early as 1836 to a threat to sue the crown over the scope of Scottish education, a turf battle which would be replayed in arguments between Edinburgh and Westminster in 2000 over university fees. The twin pillars of this remarkably resilient tradition can be seen as generalism – the interconnectedness of disciplines via some form of applied theory, and inclusiveness – the ideal of drawing students from as wide a range of backgrounds as possible. This is not to say that either of these aims has been completely successful, or even universally accepted, in Scotland; rather, the tradition itself helped shape ideas of nationhood, and encouraged separation from Britain.

Davie was writing in a situation in which the Robbins committee was about to report (1963) and in which Scottish education had long (1872–1957) fallen under the Secretary of State via the Scottish Education Department, which had moved back to Edinburgh in 1930, but remained British.[14] The Murray Report of 1957 had required scientists to come up with practical applications rather than pure research.[15] At the moment of *The Democratic Intellect* there was also a general belief that Scottish-educated professors had been surreptitiously replaced by Oxbridge-educated ones. This requires qualification: even if alma mater were an index of 'national' beliefs, this was probably less significant than their class bias; besides which, if there had been a period of replacement, it was the late nineteenth century.[16] More serious was Davie's claim that interdisciplinarity was being chipped away in favour of Anglo-British classicism, a taste reflected in funding. Despite the imperialist legacy of the Enlightenment, Scottish education was neither easily anchored to the epistemological supremacy of imperial knowledge entered via the gateway of Plato, nor to the internalisation of Latin which encouraged parallels between the Roman empire and the British one in so many English Victorian public schools.[17] On the other hand, by 1872 the Scottish system had already adapted to British norms within empire, and for Anderson by the turn of the century it was broadly imperial-loyalist.[18] But after the shocks of the 1920s, reread in the late '50s, the misfit of state and educational ideals was for Davie a crisis of civic integrity.

For Davie, public attitudes to general, open-access university education in Scotland are national beyond party political or even class loyalty – a situation which still holds today, as commentators such as Lindsay Paterson and David McCrone show with extensive field work.[19] The process Davie describes in terms of the maintenance of national education is of maintaining the interdisciplinary Ordinary (three-year) degree in the face of encroaching specialisation. (This stress has not aged well: the three-year non-Honours degree's popularity has plummeted.) Generalist thinking would retain a 'staged' system rather than a 'tiered' one, meaning that students could continue to gradually specialise, rather than being weeded out early for specific specialisations or jobs. The four-year, Honours degree was ideally a combination of generalisation and specialisation (in the same way that universities and other more specialised tertiary education systems now interrelate).[20] This tradition, as Davie would stress in his follow-up *The Crisis of the Democratic Intellect* (1981), had again been threatened by Ordinance 70 in 1919 – the year of the Clydeside disturbances. Ordinance 70, a blueprint for university entry tests, put relatively more stress on 'English', paradoxically sparking a Scottish mini-revival in philosophy by retaining philosophy's place – as it does today, in 'theory'. Yet Ordinance 70 also systematised university testing along British lines, and Davie describes the cultural crisis arising from criticism as the continuation of a 200-year struggle in education. He also sees MacDiarmid's *A Drunk Man Looks at the Thistle* as contributing directly to the debates, and assuring a counter-cultural renaissance in Scottish philosophical education.[21] He notes a range of poets rallying against Ordinance 70 in the First Scottish Renaissance – MacDiarmid and Edwin Muir in the 1920s, and Sorley Maclean and Robert Garioch in the 1930s.

So what was the 'distinctive' answer of Scottish education? In Davie's description, Scotland's ancient educational principles were, firstly, continentalist in nature, following from the times of medieval links between Scottish universities, initially largely St Andrews and the University of Paris, and maintaining strong connections to the later French philosophers who digested the educational ideas of *la philosophie écossaise*.[22] Even the Germanicism with which Coleridge is credited as having introduced into early-nineteenth-century England already existed in the post-Enlightenment common sense tradition, which saw its job as 'to elucidate by analysis [philosophical principles] obscure foundations'.[23] This continentalism, largely un-reliant on Oxbridge as a stepping-block for ideas, should be remembered when we look at Scotland's relation to the body of thought later known as theory. Secondly, for Davie Scottish universities from early times used a peer-based approach to university classes in which 'decisions as to the order of rank in the class often lay not with the professor but with the vote of the class'.[24] This student-centredness prefigured the sense of a need for a student voice in student unions (from the 1880s), and indeed even the more utilitarian and market-oriented twentieth-century tendency to see the student as a client. Ideally, this meant that rather than a top-down system of authoritative knowledge, conclusions would arise from class discussion, which took up a large amount of time compared to lectures. Thirdly, Davie stresses interdisciplinarity – a resistance to over-specialisation in university courses which turned into a running battle throughout the nineteenth century. Specifically (and again, this is important to the origins of 'theory'), Scottish professors struggled to keep philosophy on the curriculum, against the largely philological training in Greek language believed to help discipline the imperial mind. This underlined entirely different ways of thinking about education: for Anglo-British educators Scots were backward in the classics, and for Scottish educators grammar-learning blocked philosophy as a first port of entry into other, related disciplines. Davie narrates the ways in which many Scottish generalist thinkers resisted the recommendations of a series of Commissions between the 1820s and the 1890s – approximately the period of the imperial civilising mission – to modernise university education in favour of competitive knowledge of the classics.

From the English side though, analysts have tended to see this Anglo-British education within a class *rather than* a national context, as an instrumental 'streaming' of children from an early age. Hilary Sheedman, in charting the rise of the 'great' English secondary school – schools which struggled to adapt to a testable version of the classics to send a high proportion of students to Oxbridge – has noted that the systematisation and pressuring of schools bolstered a British class system already in place, representing 'the conversion of social hierarchies *into* academic hierarchies'.[25] Nevertheless, this is not to collapse English education into an apparently culturally representative public school system: many accounts of Englishness, some of which I will note in Chapter 7, tend to take the English public school education which boomed during the decades preceding World War I as representative of English education as a whole, anachronistically and revealing an unexamined class bias. The resultant atrophied or 'unsystematic' nature of 'British education' (as it was presented) was, according to James Scotland, a source of embarrassment at the second Paris exhibition in 1878.[26] For Harold Silver, over-specialisation in general in English and Welsh education was in the first half of the twentieth century becoming problematic, but was always supported by the British state.[27] Or as David Reeder puts it, in the late nineteenth and early twentieth century, the re-structuring of English schools was intended to move them towards a more 'differentiated system' by functioning to 'select . . . children and allocating them to different occupational levels in the economy'.[28] In this reading the Anglo-Welsh-British system was dual but one-staged, separating students into different tertiary streams, while Scottish university education was singular but two-staged, leaving a general, pre-specialised period of education.[29]

The new 'Academies' on the other hand, while arising from an equally national context, prepared children for more specialised university courses, and effectively raised the traditionally early entry age (though today it remains a year earlier: Scottish Highers are usually taken at 17, A levels at 18, and Scottish universities offer a broader base in their first two years to offset the pre-A-level gap, meaning that a 'general' early tertiary period remains). *The Democratic Intellect* represents the beginning of a period of insistence on a national duty to make this pre-specialisation period widely available; its Victorian focus hints at the relationship of British education and imperial civility. Davie is concerned to reinstate a tradition of socially applied thought which he himself calls 'theory'.[30] Later Davie would describe how this kept the awkward

Enlightenment conception of a separate civil society within the union alive in nineteenth-century Scotland: 'Despite the new interpretation of the Union which saw Scotland's contribution in practical or moral terms as consisting of soldiers or ships' engineers rather than philosophers, Adam Smith's ideas about the country's intellectual role within the Union . . . remained alive.[31] This re-telling of democratic intellectualism gained widespread currency from the 1960s, and fed into a conscious idea of breaking away from a long-ingrained habit of extrinsic adjustment.

The Legacy of the Democratic Intellect

Two strong qualifications to Davie's identification of a democratic intellectual tradition have arisen. Firstly, the Scottish Education Department has been pragmatically compliant with British norms; commentators such as Lindsay Paterson, James Kellas and David McCrone have shown how, even amidst the despair of the Thatcher administration, a Scottish 'national interest' was often negotiated within British institutions – Kellas's 'official nationalism'.[32] A pragmatic, 'pluralistic' model has been taken up specific to education by McLennan (1989), Jordan and Richardson (1987) and McPherson and Raab (1988), who, also mid-Thatcher, came to see Scottish education as corporatist and bureaucratically entrenched, and Scotland's educational voice as one effective pressure group within the UK.[33] Walter Humes has (1986) condemned the narrowness of the 'leadership class' in early-twentieth-century Scottish education, their mercantile drive, and the way in which they used now-discredited assumptions about intelligence, especially to promote the supposedly classless status of the 'lad o' pairts', many of whom became school inspectors, perpetuating the suffocating system.[34] Thus for Anderson, 'the creation through education of "modern" mentalities – loyalty to the British state, particularly in written culture, religious devotion based on rationality rather than superstititon – was all largely complete before the state came on the scene'.[35] Post-1872 panics are thus a red herring, and we look in vain for social identities imposed by British education. To an extent Humes exemplifies the trope of 'de-mythologising' the democratic intellectual tradition, a popular one in the early Thatcher years following the tradition of the invention of tradition. This cultural scorched earth policy has in turn rightly been criticised by commentators who recognise it as necessitating a retro-unionist defeatism underestimating the extent to which education can shape the polity passing through it.[36]

The second qualification of Davie's stance was that the ideal of wide inclusion of students from varying social backgrounds was just that: an ideal, which rarely corresponded to practice. In James Scotland's 1969 *History of Scottish Education*, Davie's 'tradition' is characterised as pietistic, sectarian, anti-English, conservative, superstitious and over-canny, hardly an ideal of democratic generalism.[37] Similarly for H. M. Paterson writing in 1983, the lad o' pairts, scoring educational successes beyond his station, represented a tiny minority magnified beyond all meaningfulness, boys who had to fight through a favouritist and deeply classist system.[38] In his celebrated *History of the Scottish People* T. C. Smout similarly describes the prevailing educational ethos as conformist, the 'democratic' of 'democratic intellect' as a 'depressing' narrow meritocracy.[39] Carter and Withrington (1992) more frankly challenge the paucity of Davie's sources,[40] while Gray et al. (1983) denounce the 'myth' of Scottish openness, pointing out that when student numbers rose dramatically in the 1960s, the proportion of working-class entrants actually went down.[41] R. D. Anderson has stressed that much more opportunity in Scottish education has been given to the middle classes, and the lad o' pairts was drawn from an extremely narrow upper-working-class band.[42] Gray et al. also argue that the Ordinary degree, rapidly losing popularity, was becoming a 'ghettoised' route into schoolteaching, rather than an accessible refuge from specialisation.[43] Lindsay Paterson and Andrew McPherson use Pierre Bourdieu to show that that children acquire 'cultural capital' from their parents, meaning that certain types of household are far more likely to produce university students, even given a perfectly inclusive system.[44] In any case, Anderson argues, English universities were never as conservative and over-specialised as portrayed by Davie.[45] Anderson does also, however, note that the democratic myth, although often unsubtly deployed, has acted as a definite 'creative force', a point also argued by Paterson in post-Hobsbawm vein.[46] The democratic intellectual idea, as it impacted in the 1960s, was claimed by many groups for various uses, which cannot all necessarily be judged by simple claims to validity.[47]

The point is that despite the justified criticisms, Davie did unify a community of thought. Even James Scotland, in his unflattering history of Scottish education, agrees that the Ordinary degree was decimated in the first half of the twentieth century by a narrowing of options for undergraduates and the removal of much of the importance of philosophy.[48] This raises a controversial point about whether – even if philosophy is 'a privileged subject' to be maintained at all costs – 'Anglicisation' necessarily closes the subject down; generalism may indeed have strengthened in the early twentieth century.[49] Moreover since, as Scotland notes, the 'rights of the student' became increasingly important post-1945 (and more famously, post-1968), it would seem that a renaissance of the older system of peer-judgement was on the cards, and required a post-British rethinking of the 'modernising' impulse. The place of the student in society was traditionally a more influential one in Scotland than in England (and a glance at Blair's 1997 government shows that it remained so, packed as the executive it was with Scots who started out in student activism, like Gordon Brown). Since 1496 and the planting of parish schools, the lad o' pairts – sparse though his numbers may have been – was a key export.[50] Until the establishment of the University of London in 1836, Scotland had four universities (briefly five) as opposed to its neighbour's two, and those four were distributed around the country, rather than being only in the south-east. This is not to make any assertion about the relative qualities of the two educational systems, but to bear in mind that distinctive educational systems create their own ideas of civil society, and that an era of re-historicisation, such as the post-Davie one, will reorientate the relationship of civil society to political change.

As in the civic/political upheavals of the Enlightenment which concretised Britishness, so with the pre-devolutionary upheavals which shook Britishness, communication across disciplines is instrumental. While MacDiarmid rose to fame in the 1920s, partly via an educational journal and attempting a dramatic interdisciplinarity in which poetry and culture cohabited with science and technology, John Burnet, Professor of Greek at St Andrews, described how the SED was killing off generalism, to be given another voice in the 1960s by Davie.[51] John Anderson was also vocal about the conflict between the traditional Scottish curriculum and, as Davie tellingly puts it, the 'neo-utilitarian' British reorganisation taking place.[52] For Anderson, philosophy and the increasingly popular and government-sponsored sciences should meet in dialogue rather than in hierarchy, as was implied by the erosion of Scottish arts at the time.[53] Elsewhere Davie even suggests in his reading of the Enlightenment that arts and theoretical sciences should power economic growth.[54] This interdisciplinary response would certainly resemble a radically new form of Enlightenment, helping to explain an ongoing blindness over the imperialistic tendencies of the eighteenth century, but one which pulled away from British standards rather than rushing towards them. There is a new interdisciplinarity behind the twentieth century sub-British cultural revivals, ironically growing from Ordinance 70's skewing the 'English' of 'English Literature' by giving the field a privileged place alongside mathematics, Latin, literature and philosophy. 'English' was progressively rethought, as it would be in pre-devolutionary times, with something like the opposite impulse to an Adam Smith or a Hugh Blair. Eventually it came to merge with critical thinking which for many commentators spearheaded a post-British counter-culture.[55] Indeed English Literature's shading into theory in its appreciation of textuality would be vital once Scottish philosophy departments passed through their brief renaissance of the 1920s into a period of relative silence, during which British logical positivism tried to encourage them to occupy secondary positions by being more 'useful' to other subjects.[56] 'English' was in some sense the paradoxically natural home of generalism.

The new English met the old English on its way back from the Empire: this would never again be the subject which had been behind the Indian Civil Service exams and had ironically been pioneered in Glasgow and Edinburgh. Paterson points out that a non-New Critical version of English Literature was becoming popular from the 1930s, and was becoming a thorn in the side of the Anglo-British, gradualist, Eliotic 'tradition':

> Although these views could be seen as resembling the emerging idea in England that 'the great tradition' of English literature was the main instrument of cultural transmission – the idea which such writers as F. R. Leavis and T. S. Eliot developed from Matthew Arnold – the Scottish version was more thoroughly democratic, perhaps rather more resembling Raymond Williams's reinterpretation of the Leavisite approach (Williams 1963 [*Culture and Society, 1780–1950*]). This was not the initiation into a priesthood of literary taste, but a modernised expression of the tenets of Scottish common sense philosophy: good-quality works of imaginative literature 'enlarge the discipline of life by supplementing, refining, and correcting it' [Scottish Council for Research in Education, *Curriculum for Pupils of Twelve to Fifteen Years*, 1931].[57]

If we lay this telling argument end to end with Robert Crawford's *Devolving English Literature* (1992),[58] we get a good perspective on the evolution and devolution of 'English' in Scotland – at first, there is a pragmatic Enlightenment demand to be at the centre of global Britishness (best dated from the 1740s rather than from 1707), then a high period of Carlyle-esque individual successes mixed with the loss of national politics, then, from the 1920s, a much more divergent desire to put 'English' into historical, communitarian, local, and national frames. Eventually this leads to a thorough rethinking of Scots' place within 'English Literature', and of what English Literature was all about – as in Crawford – along with a desire to give specifically English national meaning back to the epithet 'English', and, as Paterson provocatively hints, the dropping of the generic border with early Cultural Studies.

When writing *The Crisis of the Democratic Intellect* in the mid-1980s, Davie did in some sense imagine such an interdisciplinary renaissance, and its centrality to apparently pure political questions.[59] Education was gradually seen to have a control role in constitutional reform. Surveys in Brown et al.'s *New Scotland, New Politics?* (2001) show that most Scottish residents placed a high emphasis on education, were more enthusiastic about the expansion of Higher education – especially those who identified themselves as 'feeling Scottish' – and were willing to pay higher taxes for better education.[60] Trust in education as a civic institution was ranked second only to trust in banks.[61] Indeed we can add to the national differences recounted by Davie the fact that educational plans have always figured large in the building of new constitutional assemblies:

> Precisely because education is linked to renewing the national culture, to investing in the national economy and to maintaining the civic institutions which embodied the nation in the absence of national independence, it has always occupied the attention of new legislators in newly autonomous national parliaments.[62]

Interdisciplinarity and Devolution

Generalism, reworked with an eye to its own power as myth (in the MacIntyre sense), can thus be seen as pulling away from specialised training, for example for imperial civil service tests, and aiming at an educated and less stratified national community, one which cannot remain indefinitely under a British umbrella. Generalism also offers the possibility of breaking up ossified forms of study, the most obvious of which is 'English Literature', now being given new disciplinary designations. An interdisciplinary curriculum, joining questions across a range of subjects and to an extent working from generalist images, is also likely to be a more civic curriculum, one which parents and educators will expect to happen in a public space with little in common with the individualistic mercantile Britain in which society ended up having no society. Perhaps one of the most marked differences between Scotland and Britain as emphasised in the past few decades has been the former's interest in the public nature of education.

Even before the advent of comprehensive schools, from the 1940s 'omnibus schools' were widely tried out – schools offering a 'two-stage' education, junior and senior, and aiming to allow pupils the opportunity to go on to the advanced stage of secondary education (though they only occupied a maximum of 38 per cent of the school population).[63] From 1962, O grades formed a 'bridge' to higher education or employment. By the mid-1970s, only 5 per cent of Scottish children were outside the comprehensive system, a preference which was seemingly unrelated to the cost of private schooling.[64] While there was still a great deal of 'wastage' (children not finishing the secondary higher course), the number of students staying on through their fourth year was dramatically increased from the 1930s to the 1970s.[65] By this time, Department of Education grants had increased, making university attendance possible for more working-class children.[66] The establishment of comprehensives in the 1950s and '60s fed into a general Scottish welfare statist suspicion of private schools, and, in immediately pre-devolutionary times, of 'opting out'. According to most commentators, the British state has in general worked to fragment the two-stage ladder, while a primary aim of the Scottish Parliament is to re-establish the two-stage system beyond the reach of tiered selection processes.[67] In this sense as in many others, Scots have come to strongly defend a particular, and decreasingly British, version of the welfare state; Paterson has described the welfare state as a modernised and active form of rationality operating *particularly* in education.[68]

For Paterson and others, whereas pre-devolutionary Scotland was able to present itself as one interest group within the British welfare state, and thus negotiate certain forms of 'autonomy',[69] and while Conservative governments of the 1980s and '90s had a policy which looked from some angles like educational generalism, privatisation and opting out remained unpopular in a Scotland which still had a strong emotional stake in the welfare state. Although Thatcher's policy of privatising education continued apace in England and Wales, she sensibly eased off in her third term in Scotland, by which time it was of course too late.[70] Here also Scotland found itself, mid-privatisation, 'taking back into its own hands the key institutions of its national identity', of which education was possibly the key institution.[71] Educationalists came to the fore in calling for the constitutional changes behind the modern form of devolution,[72] and '[t]he growing confrontation has left a legacy of mistrust, and so has continued in the slow decay of the United Kingdom state in Scotland'.[73]

Educationalists then have often been representative of popular views on constitutional change as they are inflected in civic life.[74] Scottish teachers, teachers' unions and academics, while often realising the degree of fiction in democratic intellectualism, nevertheless understand that education has a higher priority in Scotland than in Britain, and this understanding is public and political. The belief that a Parliament would be good for education was one of the single most significant factors behind devolution, and educationalists themselves took an active part:

> As the Union began to decay in the 1980s and 1990s, the civic leaders of Scottish education played a prominent role in campaigning for a parliament: for example, the main teachers' trade union, the Educational Institute of Scotland, supported and helped to finance the Scotland Forward organisation advocating 'Yes' in the 1997 referendum.[75]

Lack of representation by unwanted inter-referendum governments had merely been the final straw here; 'the argument that a Scottish Parliament is needed to democratise the Scottish Office long predates the Conservative government'.[76] Unlike in 1979, a number of prominent university figures backed a Yes vote in the 1997 referendum – though the official stance remained one of scepticism.[77] In contrast to the earlier 'negotiated autonomy' model, the absolute independence of education was now reckoned to be instrumental.[78] This was not just an academic view: the Scottish Referendum Survey of 1997 shows that 71 per cent of those asked believed that a Scottish Parliament would increase the quality of education in Scotland.[79] Paterson points out even more strikingly that in 1997 only one person in twenty-five believed that education would actually get worse under the new Parliament, most being sure that it would bring a new governmental accountability.[80] Thus in his 1995 *Education and the Scottish People* R. D. Anderson makes the argument that Scotland shows how national education systems serve to consolidate nation-states – that educational coherence is behind state coherence. For

Paterson similarly, democratisation is an ongoing process arising through the reform of institutions, with education squarely behind ideas of the 'public domain'.[81] Thus as Britain's northernmost nation's ideas of how it defined itself forayed beyond the state representation in the 1980s, the result was a corresponding desire for change in the polity. A major reason for the movement towards devolution was the desire to safeguard education.[82] Indeed, the issue of guaranteeing educational standards and access can be seen as a new national politics, since it is meant to create a democratically responsible people. Polity and education have been joined in the post-British mind: '[c]laims that Scottish independence depended on its education system – at least in part – have been intimately bound up in the debate over self-government in the last three decades'.[83] Paterson's 2003 account even defines democracy *as* the difficult question of access to a quality general education:

> Giving access to common types of educational institution, but continuing to define real education in general academic terms, has been Scotland's attempt to answer the conundrum of all mass systems of education: how to reconcile democracy with the necessity of selection, both selection of culture in the maintenance of excellence, and selection of people, allocating individuals to differentiated occupations while also preparing them for life as equal citizens in the common culture of the community.[84]

This returns us to the enabling power of the myth of democratic intellectualism, as pointed up in 1995 by R. D. Anderson. Referring to some of the more anti-Davie moments in W. Humes and H. M. Paterson's *Scottish Culture and Scottish Education* (1983),[85] Paterson re-historicises the idea of myth in a context in which literature and philosophy have re-coalesced to blur the limits of fictionality, and in which important philosophers have been reassessed. Paterson's reading of myth (via Raymond Williams, a figure rightly taken to task by Paul Gilroy for the ongoing ethnocentrism of his pioneering conception of 'British Cultural Studies')[86] partakes of MacIntyre's proactive definition, rather than the more classical 'ideological' definition of myth:

> Alasdair MacIntyre has summed up a similar argument [to Williams] very neatly: 'traditions, when vital, embody continuities of conflict . . . Looking back over the century, the striking feature about the myth [of the democratic intellect] is its mobilising capacity – precisely the capacity of human beings to select parts of it into programmes for shaping the present and the future.[87]

The idea that myth is something inhabited and enabled by action, *contra* the model of myth as ideology, in part explains the way in which one of philosophical generalism's inheritors was English Literature, which has always been concerned with the real effects of written fictions. Cairns Craig uses MacIntyre in a similar way in the introduction to his *The Modern Scottish Novel*, in search of a conception of tradition which is lived rather than being pinned down to proofs of truth or falsehood.[88] This form of myth functions as a strongly shared sense of national purpose, not simply reducible to governmental concessions or fixed images; nor is it like the neo-liberal Blairite sense of 'community'. This Scottish educational mythscape weakened during the high-British nineteenth century[89] but dramatically returns with Davie, and Davie as he was rediscovered in the 1980s and '90s. This re-awakening for Paterson pushes Adam Ferguson's ideas of education for citizenship two centuries forward to the Constitutional Convention, which resulted in direct demands for devolution.[90]

Given the expanded role of the democratic intellectual myth in Scottish polity, as well as the fact that a higher proportion of people go through higher education in Scotland than in Britain, it is not surprising that the first serious boundary dispute between the Edinburgh and Westminster Parliaments arose over education, specifically over university student fees, which Edinburgh did not want imposed. This argument over jurisdiction led to the Independent Committee of Inquiry into Student Finance in 1999, and the conclusion that students in Scotland should be exempted from fees from autumn 2000.[91] (However, in a way which is very revealing about the nations' relative democracies, 1997 surveys show both the Scots and the English agreeing in about equal proportion that fees should be free to the student; it was just that Westminster could do nothing about it.)[92] With a large proportion of Scots in 1999 prioritising more equal access to education, the question of universal free education began to look like a concrete issue linked to separatism.[93] This would mark Scotland as a typical emergent nation-state, or as the authors of *New Scotland, New Politics?* put it:

> Precisely because education is linked to renewing the national economy and to maintaining the civic institutions which embodied the nation in the absence of national independence, it has always occupied the attention of the new legislators in newly autonomous national parliaments.[94]

In other words, education and autonomy operate in a relationship of mutual influence. This mutual push has been in part guided by the failure of national democracy which delivered unwanted state governments in the 1980s and '90s. It is in this broad sense that tertiary education has again become political with the debates over devolution, perhaps even more so than in the time of the early Davie.[95] As Paterson argues, this is a popular debate, being pushed by participants rather than led 'from above' by politicians, who actually remain quite silent over matters of curriculum.[96] Moreover, following MacIntyre, where 'tradition' is an ever-changing environment to be occupied, there is a sense of perpetual revolution in educating sub-British nations to question their own traditions and challenging them to mature cultural revivals.[97] A good 'general' education in this sense prevents an all-out technocracy and encourages knowledge about governance, not a priority of British education.[98] And since the products of non-selective, government, schools tend to be even more anti-selection,[99] there has been a growing civil statism opposing British education since the 1960s.

Moreover, what has recently been interestingly proposed is that, despite the inevitable dip in expectations for the Scottish Parliament between 1997 and 2001, not only is the myth of democratic intellectualism still active in Scotland, but also in England there is increased concern about the inclusive function education should have in shaping wider society.[100] Since Scotland has for so long been carefully defining its own educational traditions, the 'wider society' defined in England would also have to be a post-British one – perhaps in some difficult sense an 'English and Welsh' one. One difference in the re-shaping of civil society between Scotland and England and Wales is that Proportional Representation mitigates against a British stance of cautious bureaucratic reform, and introduces more critical 'minority' voices. So in Paterson's words, 'Scottish politics is becoming normal' in that a productive civic/parliamentary tension is 'now contained within Scotland's own polity'.[101]

It is difficult to imagine that the process of rethinking educational tradition outside of Britain will not be reproduced in England and Wales – that while Scottish polity redevelops itself in tandem with education, English education will remain fixed to imperial standards of specialised learning and reduced access. What is missing, as I suggested at the head of the chapter, are accounts of specifically English educational traditions; as the arguments surrounding Davie show, these accounts need not be entirely coherent, positive, or even in agreement, but they do need to be attempted so as not to lose all sense of accountability. The new national educations will be successful insofar as they draw the widest section of the populace possible in terms of class and ethnicity. Scotland in this sense currently has an advantage on being able to draw on a tradition of interconnection by a 'general' form of thought – one formerly commonly housed in the discipline of philosophy, but perhaps equally inflected through 'theory' and housed within whatever Eng. Lit. departments decide to call themselves next. The creation of a democratic post-British polity is indissoluble from the re-creation of a post-British tradition of thought working via education. The next chapter correspondingly moves to the way in which traditions of philosophy-then-Eng. Lit., Anglo-British and post-British, have themselves been separating for the past half-century or so.

Notes

1. Lindsay Paterson, *Education and the Scottish Parliament* (Edinburgh: Dunedin, 2000), p. 11; R. D. Anderson, *Scottish Education Since the Reformation* (Glasgow: Economic and Social History Society of Scotland, 1997), pp. 8–9; Murray G. H. Pittock, *A New History of Scotland* (Stroud: Sutton, 2003), p. 235.
2. Paterson, *Education and the Scottish Parliament*, p. 221.
3. R. D. Anderson, *Education and the Scottish People, 1750–1918* (Oxford: Clarendon, 1995), p. 70.
4. James Scotland, *The History of Scottish Education, Volume II* (London: University of London Press, 1969), p. 148.
5. See Lindsay Paterson, *Scottish Education in the Twentieth Century* (Edinburgh: Edinburgh University Press, 2003), pp. 38–9.
6. Anderson, *Scottish Education Since the Reformation*, p. 26.
7. See G. E. Davie, *The Crisis of the Democratic Intellect* (Edinburgh: Polygon, 1986), p. 148.
8. See Paterson, *Education and the Scottish Parliament*, p. 21; cf. Hugh MacDiarmid, 'A. S. Neill and our Education System', in Alan Riach (ed.), *Contemporary Scottish Studies* (Manchester: Carcanet, 1995), pp. 289–97.
9. Davie, *The Crisis of the Democratic Intellect*, p. 183.
10. See Walter Elliot, 'The Scottish heritage in politics', in John George Stewart Murray et al. (eds), *A Scotsman's Heritage* (London: Alexander Maclehose and Co., 1932), pp. 53–65: 64; G. E. Davie, *The Democratic Intellect: Scotland and her Universities in the Nineteenth Century* (Edinburgh: Edinburgh University Press, 1981); Duncan Glen, 'A Conversation – Hugh MacDiarmid and Duncan Glen', *Akros*, V–13, 1970, pp. 9–72.
11. Davie, *The Crisis of the Democratic Intellect*, pp. xix, 210.
12. Ibid. p. 12.
13. Ibid. pp. 17, 22–3, 127; cf. Eugene Kamenka, 'Anderson on Education and Academic Freedom', in D. Z. Phillips (ed.), *Education and Inquiry* (Oxford: Blackwell, 1980), pp. 18–39: 27.

14. Scotland, *The History of Scottish Education, Volume II*, p. 363; Paterson, *Scottish Education in the Twentieth Century*, pp. 17–19.
15. Paterson, *Education and the Scottish Parliament*, p. 215.
16. Davie, *The Crisis of the Democratic Intellect*, p. 164; for a complaint on the continued Anglicisation of staff, see Andrew Lockhart Walker, *The Revival of the Democratic Intellect* (Edinburgh: Polygon, 1994), pp. 215–32; on the social make-up of pre-war Scottish academia, see R. D. Anderson, 'Scottish university professors, 1800–1939; profile of an elite', *Scottish Economic and Social History*, 7, 1987, pp. 27–54.
17. Cf. Robert Young, *Postcolonialism: An Historical Introduction* (Oxford: Blackwell, 2001), p. 33.
18. R. D. Anderson, *Education and the Scottish People, 1750–1918* (Oxford: Clarendon, 1995), pp. 193–200.
19. Davie, *The Crisis of the Democratic Intellect*, p. 39.
20. Ibid. p. 101; cf. Paterson, *Education and the Scottish Parliament*, pp. 52–6.
21. Davie, *The Crisis of the Democratic Intellect*, pp. 123, 129.
22. Ibid. pp. 151–2.
23. Ibid. p. 264.
24. Ibid. p. 15.
25. Hilary Sheedman, 'Defining institutions: the endowed grammar schools and the systematisation of English secondary education', in Detlef K. Müller, Fritz Ringer and Brian Simon (eds), *The Rise of the Modern Educational System: Structural chance and social reproduction, 1870–1920* (Cambridge: Cambridge University Press, 1987), pp. 113–34.
26. Scotland, *The History of Scottish Education, Volume II*, p. 136.
27. Silver, *Education as History: Interpreting Nineteenth Century and Twentieth Century Education* (London: Methuen, 1983), pp. 157–8.
28. David Reeder, 'The Reconstruction of secondary education in England, 1869–1920', in Müller, Ringer and Simon (eds), *The Rise of the Modern Educational System*, pp. 135–50.
29. Scotland, *The History of Scottish Education, Volume II*, p. 274.
30. Davie, *The Crisis of the Democratic Intellect*, p. 108.
31. G. E. Davie, *The Scottish Enlightenment and Other Essays* (Edinburgh: Polygon, 1991), p. 41.
32. Most famously David McCrone, *Understanding Scotland: Sociology of a Stateless Nation* (London: Routledge, 1992).
33. A. G. Jordan and J. J. Richardson, *British Politics and the Policy Process: An Arena Process* (London: Allen and Unwin, 1987); A. McPherson and C. D. Raab, *Governing Education* (Edinburgh: Edinburgh University Press, 1988); cf. Tom Nairn's analysis of Scotland as bureaucracy within the British state in *Faces of Nationalism: Janus Revisited* (London: Verso, 1997).
34. Walter Humes, *The Leadership Class in Scottish Education* (Edinburgh: John Donald, 1986); see also the account of 'display nationalism' in H. M. Paterson, 'Incubus and Ideology: The Development of Secondary Schooling in Scotland, 1900–1939', in Walter M. Humes and Hamish M. Paterson (eds), *Scottish Culture and Scottish Education, 1800–1980* (Edinburgh: John Donald, 1983), pp. 197–215.
35. Anderson, *Education and the Scottish People*, p. 299.

36. Craig Beveridge and Ronald Turnbull, *The Eclipse of Scottish Culture: Inferiorism and the Intellectuals* (Edinburgh: Polygon, 1989), pp. 58–61.
37. See Scotland, *The History of Scottish Education, Volume II*, pp. 257–74; on post-1745 acceptance of loyalism, compare Anderson, *Scottish Education Since the Reformation*, pp. 7, 14.
38. See H. M. Paterson, 'Incubus and Ideology'.
39. T. C. Smout, *A History of the Scottish People 1560–1830* (London: Fontana, 1972), pp. 421–50.
40. R. D. Anderson, 'The Scottish University Tradition: Past and Future', in Jennifer J. Carter and Donald J. Withrington (eds), *Scottish Universities: Distinctiveness and Diversity* (Edinburgh: John Donald, 1992), pp. 67–78: 71–2.
41. J. Gray, A. McPherson and D. Raffe, *Reconstructions of Secondary Education: Theory, Myth, and Practice Since the War* (London: Routledge and Kegan Paul, 1983), pp. 153, 158.
42. Anderson, *Scottish Education Since the Reformation*, p. 19.
43. Gray, McPherson and Raffe, *Reconstructions of Secondary Education*, pp. 161–3.
44. Paterson, *Scottish Education in the Twentieth Century*, p. 18; A. McPherson, 'An Angle on the Geist: Persistence and Change in the Scottish Educational Tradition', in W. Humes and H. M. Paterson (eds), *Scottish Culture and Education* (Edinburgh: John Donald, 1983), pp. 216–43.
45. See Anderson, *Scottish Education Since the Reformation*, p. 32.
46. Anderson, *Education and the Scottish People*, p. 297.
47. See, for example, Lindsay Paterson, 'Policy-Making in Scottish Education: A Case of Pragmatic Nationalism', in Margaret M. Clark and Pamela Munn (eds), *Education in Scotland: Policy and Practice from Pre-School to Secondary* (London: Routledge, 1997), pp. 138–55.
48. Scotland, *The History of Scottish Education, Volume II*, p. 148; on John Anderson's generalism see, for example, P. H. Partridge, 'Anderson as Educator', in Phillips (ed.), *Education and Inquiry*, pp. 3–10: 3–4; J. Mackie, 'Anderson's Theory of Education', in Phillips (ed.), *Education and Inquiry*, pp. 11–17: 12.
49. See R. D. Anderson, *Education and Opportunity in Victorian Scotland* (Edinburgh: Edinburgh University Press, 1983), appendix; Paterson, *Scottish Education in the Twentieth Century*, pp. 73–87.
50. Scotland, *The History of Scottish Education, Volume II*, p. 144.
51. Davie, *The Crisis of the Democratic Intellect*, p. 23.
52. Ibid. p. 61.
53. Quoted in Davie, *The Crisis of the Democratic Intellect*, p. 199; on government support in Britain as a whole, see Harold Silver, *Education as History: Interpreting Nineteenth- and Twentieth-Century Education* (London: Methuen, 1983), p. 189.
54. Davie, *The Scottish Enlightenment*, p. 16.
55. Davie, *The Crisis of the Democratic Intellect*, p. 63.
56. Ibid. pp. 159, 191.
57. Paterson, *Scottish Education in the Twentieth Century*, p. 69.
58. Robert Crawford, *Devolving English Literature* (Edinburgh: Edinburgh University Press, 2000).

59. Davie, *The Crisis of the Democratic Intellect*, p. 183.
60. Alice Brown, Lindsay Paterson, John Curtice, Kerstin Hinds, David McCrone, Alison Park, Kerry Sproston and Paula Surridge, *New Scotland, New Politics?* (Edinburgh: Polygon, 2001), pp. 153, 147–8.
61. Ibid. p. 151.
62. Ibid. pp. 146.
63. Paterson, *Scottish Education in the Twentieth Century*, p. 135; J. Gray, A. McPherson and D. Raffe, *Reconstructions of Secondary Education: Theory, Myth and Practice Since the War* (London: Routledge and Kegan Paul, 1983).
64. Paterson, *Education and the Scottish Parliament*, pp. 23, 26; Paterson, *Scottish Education in the Twentieth Century*, p. 129.
65. Scotland, *The History of Scottish Education, Volume II*, p. 133.
66. Ibid. pp. 34–41.
67. Paterson, *Education and the Scottish Parliament*, p. 34.
68. Paterson, 'Policy-Making in Scottish Education', p. 140.
69. See Lindsay Paterson, *The Autonomy of Modern Scotland* (Edinburgh: Edinburgh University Press, 1994); Lindsay Paterson, 'Policy-Making in Scottish Education'; Clark and Munn (eds), *Education in Scotland*, pp. 138–55.
70. See Paterson, 'Policy-Making in Scottish Education', p. 147.
71. Paterson, *Education and the Scottish Parliament*, p. 27.
72. See Paterson, 'Policy-Making in Scottish Education', p. 149.
73. Ibid. p.150.
74. Cf. Lindsay Paterson (ed.), *A Diverse Assembly: The Debate on a Scottish Parliament* (Edinburgh: Edinburgh University Press, 1998); Paterson, *Education and the Scottish Parliament*, p. 26.
75. Brown et al., *New Scotland, New Politics?*, p. 145.
76. Paterson, 'Policy-Making in Scottish Education', p. 151.
77. Lindsay Paterson, 'Scottish higher education and the Scottish parliament: the consequences of mistaken national identity', *European Review*, 6, 1998, pp. 459–74.
78. See Paterson, *Education and the Scottish Parliament*, p. 29.
79. Brown et al., *New Scotland, New Politics?*, p. 95.
80. Paterson, *Education and the Scottish Parliament*, pp. 1, 29.
81. Paterson, *Scottish Education in the Twentieth Century*, pp. 25, 29.
82. Ibid. p. 29.
83. Paterson, *Education and the Scottish Parliament*, p. 2.
84. Paterson, *Scottish Education in the Twentieth Century*, p. 5.
85. A. McPherson, 'An Angle on the Geist', pp. 216–43.
86. Paul Gilroy, *Black Atlantic: Modernity and Double Consciousness* (London: Verso, 1993), pp. 10–14.
87. Paterson, *Scottish Education in the Twentieth Century*, p. 6.
88. Cairns Craig, *The Modern Scottish Novel* (Edinburgh: Edinburgh University Press, 1999), pp. 22–33.
89. Paterson, *Education and the Scottish Parliament*, p. 35.
90. Ibid. p. 37.
91. Brown et al., *New Scotland, New Politics?*, p. 146.
92. Ibid. p. 148.

93. Ibid. p. 149.

94. Ibid. p. 146.

95. Paterson, *Scottish Education in the Twentieth Century*, pp. 172–3.

96. Ibid. pp. 197–8; see also Paterson's description of a 'policy community' in 'Liberation or Control: What are the Scottish Education Traditions of the Twentieth Century?', in T. M. Devine and R. J. Finlay (eds), *Scotland in the Twentieth Century* (Edinburgh: Edinburgh University Press, 1996), pp. 230–49, and his warning of an eclipse of populism in the Parliament in *Education and the Scottish Parliament*, pp. 65, 67.

97. Paterson, *Scottish Education in the Twentieth Century*, pp. 199–200; *Education and the Scottish Parliament*, pp. 69–70.

98. Paterson, *Education and the Scottish Parliament*, p. 38.

99. Ibid. p. 25.

100. Lindsay Paterson, 'The Survival of the Democratic Intellect: Academic Values in Scotland and England', *Higher Education Quarterly*, 2003, pp. 57–61.

101. Paterson, *Education and the Scottish Parliament*, p. 77.

Chapter Four

Before Theory

Before Theory, After Enlightenment

The interdisciplinary mode of interpretation which became central to the study of Humanities in the 1970s and '80s, and was generically known as theory, has frequently been identified as a post-Enlightenment critique. But what has so far been avoided, and to some extent has been blocked by many working in Scottish Studies, has been the way in which twentieth-century Scottish thought was quietly proactive in criticism of its own Enlightenment tradition, which had helped fix the nation's place in the British union. Although the 1979 referendum failure is often seen as a watershed jolting Scotland into activity, long before this the seeds of a cultural revival had been sown in a post-Enlightenment tradition of thought, which stands in a remarkably similar relation to British imperialism as do deconstruction and postcolonialism to French imperialism. Both of these post-Enlightenment, post-imperial bodies of thought have chipped away at the centred subject-self viewing and arranging knowledge. Both have attempted to show how the universalisation of history around an ideally separate subject-self closes down experience of otherness. Where theory in its Francophone sense relied heavily on the experience of writers from ex-colonies with access to the metropolis, Anglophone theory has also relied heavily on thinkers linked to ex-colonies. However these writers have at times tended to assume that the British Enlightenment and British imperialism originated somewhere between London and Oxbridge, whereas it was in large part an effect of Scotland's, and especially Edinburgh's, exaggerated attempts to re-create itself within the new British union from about the 1740s. Here I suggest that another, sub-British, form of theory has acted as, to borrow Homi Bhabha's phrase, a 'counter-modernity' within imperial Britain.

A post-Enlightenment theoretical tradition has been difficult to look at squarely in the face from a contemporary perspective; questioning the fixed subject has seemed to raise the spectre of an undecided or split self, looking too much like denying political self-determination. G. E. Davie and Alexander Broadie, whose influence on Scottish thought it would be difficult to overestimate, have carefully related the Enlightenment to earlier and later periods of Scottish philosophy to avoid at all costs a reading of English benefits brought to a backward nation. This is perhaps a necessary corrective to the older story of pre-Enlightenment Scottish thought as a perpetual dark age (and Broadie neatly glosses dark and light as meaning a move away from authority, rather than towards civility),[1] but it also denotes a wider area of silence as to where Scottish philosophy relates to high Britishness and the postcolonial. Figures like David Hume relied on candidly racist assumptions to support their moral sense, passed on via Romanticism to nationalism.[2] And the narrativised civility in Hume, Ferguson and Robertson, for whom change is usually one-way, passing from barbarity to refinement along a single universal path enabled a unionist, Whiggish, pragmatic, strategic and globalising historiography only recently challenged by writers like Marinell Ash and Colin Kidd.[3] In Smith's 'stadial theory' of development, the commercial, that is, imperial, stage is always highest; we are already there, they have still to catch up.[4] Union stood for progress, and unmediated Scottish history became an embarrassment; as Murray Pittock has put it, '[a]s the [eighteenth] century progressed, Scottish readings of history in a British context became more and more interlinked with English ideas of Germanic progress towards liberty, the Norman yoke and the overthrow of absolutism in 1689'.[5] Thus famously for Hume, 'the history of England is the history of liberty'; although not all of his peers were so certain about this location of progress,[6] Hume provided an important northern refurbishment of English Whig history, later refracted through Walter Scott's tartan-clad unionism. However much we stress Enlightenment thought on concern for the nation, carefully blurring the nation in question, Hume's historical nation was Britain not Scotland.[7] The Edinburgh *philosophes*, as Nairn has put it, 'belonged to a unique, pre-nationalist stage of socio-economic expression'.[8] Despite their liberalism they were reactionary in the truest sense of the word; most 'could subscribe to some or all of the old [Anglo-British] beliefs concerning the matchless constitution, French slavery etc.'[9]

Broadie has also pointed out though how serious criticisms of Humean scepticism came first not from Kant, but from Thomas

Reid's common sense philosophy, which preceded that of Kant by forty years.[10] In Hume's interpretation of mental freedom, liberty was causal, even Newtonian: a 'science of human nature'. Broadie has pointed out how Hume remained reliant on metaphors of space in which to 'place' ideas in terms of resemblence or contiguity.[11] Hume 'mentalises space', or renders ideas as objects in a spatial field.[12] The visual and the spatial thoroughly underscore Humean thought, and would live on in observation-based scientific advancement in both Edinburgh and Glasgow. But *contra* Hume, for Reid mind was an agent of thought rather than a container of it.[13] Ideas for Reid were mental acts rather than objects, and having ideas also meant giving assent to a community of common sense via action. Thus for Broadie sociality overcomes individuality as a sign of Enlightenment, despite the insistence by figures like Hume on the special place of private property.[14] Action becomes primary and communitarian, as it would be again for twentieth-century Scottish philosophers – Hume, Scotland's most influential thinker, is nevertheless thus for Broadie 'against the grain' of a Scottish tradition of philosophy which has prioritised action over subjectivity.[15]

Post-Enlightenment thought from Reid to the surprisingly theory-like John Macmurray would work to recover this action. One chapter of *After Virtue* by Alisdair MacIntyre (1981), entitled 'Why the Enlightenment Project of Justifying Morality Had to Fail', is oriented against teleology – the process of civility which supersedes history – in a way very similar in some senses to continental thought. Recently there has been a rebirth of interest in MacIntyre; Cairns Craig has noted that *After Virtue*'s analysis of Jane Austin's high-British centring of Englishness shows how 'modern societies have shaped the argument about the "goods" of their tradition and therefore about the very nature of the tradition of which they are a part'.[16] Craig's powerful wider point about MacIntyre is that he frees up the idea of 'tradition' as something which is neither false and therefore dispensable, nor true and therefore ethnic and limiting. Craig however could have gone a step further and compared this MacIntyre to the very similar and influential account of Austin's fixing of 'home' by Edward Said.[17] This comparison would also fit with Craig's concern with the interaction between the Scottish narration of a national 'home' and the British standards which problematised it: 'Scots is not at home in the novel; English is not at home in Scotland'.[18] Said had demonstrated that *Mansfield Park*'s heroine Fanny is located in a form of home culturally and economically centred within fields of significance reliant on the Americas, an arena of imperial rivalry between Britain and France almost exactly from the start (1750s) to the end (1810s) of the Enlightenment. The Americas had of course also been a primary colonial target of Scotland's modest colonial effort, and were indeed one reason for agreement to union. Yet if England represents a situation in which cultural tradition worked successfully in Britain to 'sell national goods' in the neo-Enlightenment high-colonial phase, Scotland represents one in which, precisely because of Enlightenment over-adaptation to union away from national experience, 'home' was never properly centred. As Craig realises, when MacIntyre speaks of a tradition which is both historically grounded and yet not reducible to explicatory statements about what a society is 'like', he is describing a way of linking each enunciation to the effects it has on the world – a position we might associate with Michel Foucault's epistemology in *The Archaeology of Knowledge*.[19] Since Scots since Adam Smith were central to the extrinsic fixing of linguistic standards, it is not surprising that a post-British recovery of language should see Scots worrying at language's material effects. It is equally unsurprising that linking language and the social is exactly what British philosophy has tended to avoid; the aim of much of the most influential British philosophy of the mid-twentieth century was to avoid the pollution of philosophical language by the social. The world as the sum of all true propositions, a discursive adaptation to a neo-Enlightenment supra-history reaches its height in mid-twentieth century Britain as logical positivism.

A. J. Ayer and Gilbert Ryle were influenced by both the English empiricism of G. E. Moore and Bertrand Russell, and the continental positivism of Moritz Shlick and Rudolf Carnap. Carnap's 'radical new objectivity' ended in the famous Wittgensteinian formulation that logic was truthful but need not be factual.[20] Russell had by 1914 asserted in *Our Knowledge of the External World* that the 'outside' of the subject consisted of a purely logical construction of sense-data.[21] The verifiable object, as in Hume, stands over against action in the structuring of knowledge. Ayer's ground-breaking *Language, Truth and Logic* (1934) took leads straight from Hume, expanding Hume's distinction between 'relations of ideas' and 'matters of fact' further to a position from which all statements are either tautological (and therefore verifiable) or contradictory.[22] Contradictory statements are made subject to a Humean stance of scepticism, 'a process of elimination'.[23] Although experience is still the only source of knowledge, logic divides statements into the verifiable and unverifiable (meaning that its quest to destroy metaphysics is actually hampered, since one can say nothing logical without taking a position beyond language itself, as Russell himself had pointed out in his introduction to Wittgenstein's *Tractatus*).[24] Logical judgements require a special position of authority outside the text under examination.

For Ayer the new linguistic rigour arose 'in England' with the work of Moore, suggesting the absorption of Scoto-British into English philosophy.[25] Ayer identifies the line from Hume to Mill, one emblematic of Scottish over-adaptation to Britain, as typical of a tradition of 'English empiricism'.[26] The 'English state' meanwhile is exemplified as 'a logical construction out of individual people'.[27] The point here is that the 'English state' was precisely what was lost, the specificity of England unstatable. As in the example of the unicorn – something which can be imagined yet is not worth speaking about, since fictitious objects have no existence –[28] so the 'English state' can be imagined (though logical positivists never dreamed of doing so), but represents a bad example of a certainty, showing how statements judged as self-evident can fail to translate into social meaning. 'Certainty' is underwritten by scepticism's power over objects. For Ayer the primacy of sense experience implies the separation of substances into separate objects understood as logical constructions, and since no sense-content can ever be an element of more than one material thing, these objects are discrete.[29] Russell's 'theory of types' had already made the distinction between real, singular objects and the logical meta-language which could be used to make statements about them.[30] Similarly, following Russell and Ayer, Ryle attempted in *The Concept of Mind* (1949) to delineate 'significant' statements constituting the first step of philosophical enquiry.[31] All these systems of thought preserve the objecthood of the object while assuming that objects are 'given' by logic.[32] Although philosophy can only ever be legitimately based on logic, logical truths remain strictly ahistorical, heirs to Enlightenment universalism.

Logical positivism, then, in contrast to generalism, is still at base an exact science based on observation of objects whose data feed outwards; it 'is virtually empty without sciences'.[33] And as part of the process of educational reform, during the high period of logical positivism philosophy departments throughout Britain were being strongly encouraged to become more 'useful' by specialising relative to other subjects.[34] G. E. Davie thus portrays Ryle as turning philosophy into a kind of service industry, by leasing its logical rigour to 'hard' subjects.[35] In this sense logical positivism represents a watershed between British and post-British ideas of the function and institutional place of ideas. Anglo-British logical positivism's origins, albeit by that time markedly Anglo-British, belong to a Scottish unionist adaptive context which was no longer sustainable. Its lack of generalism becomes reactive, as in the 'empirical culture' pushed by Thatcher's advisers.[36] The rise and fall of absolute certainties moreover historically coincides with the loss of the British empire. The movement's concern to identify true objects as those which can be successfully 'stated' is a remarkably close analogue of British discourse, barring questions related to present experience, and attracting criticism from many Scottish philosophers of the 1950s and '60s, who attempt to reorientate language towards social being rather than absolute validity. More generally, logical positivism dovetails perfectly, as Davie recognised, with the English 'two-tier' educational system which has since the rise of the public school thrived on specialisation.

Russell's project, as Davie describes it, was one in which philosophy would become entirely utilitarian yet would retain the upper hand by 'correcting' the logical mistakes made by science. Davie also compares the logic of the 'guardians' in Plato's ideal republic, an upper tier of professional scholar-legislators who remain apart from the other citizens.[37] Similarly, the primacy of educational quality *itself*, measured in a vacuum, leads to a Platonic class of provider, still often implicit in praise of Enlightenment history which does not take account of imperialism.[38] On a social plane of course a guardian-like meta-language actually existed, in the Standard English guaranteed by the older model of English Literature. This canonical standard was rebranded in Russell's Cambridge by New Criticism, a literary-critical movement coinciding with logical positivism, also standing as representative of Anglo-British recuperation. New Criticism operated until at least the 1960s by relying on cultural authorities outside of and prior to any act of reading or social context; it is in a line of ahistorical metaphors for British gradualism. New Criticism's method, like that of the English Constitution, evaluates given statements relative to previous and ultimately non-textual and unaccountable sources.[39] New Criticism's and the Movement's dogged avoidance of questions of the act of writing helps explain the enthusiasm of the later insistence on text around the time of the demise of English Literature.

The standard meta-language of the Anglo-British Platonic guardians in a sense in turn protects the 'Britishness' of the English constitution, unchanged in 1707 and remaining intact by not being coherently written out at all. Davie points out that the 'nightmare speculations about "meta-languages"' which Russell and Ryle raise could be solved by acknowledging the social function of language, introducing a 'foreign interlocutor'. The importance Russell places on the paradox of the Cretan stating that 'all Cretans are liars' seems to underscore the way knowledge should be set in a context of place:

> whereas the statement 'all Cretans are liars' when said by Epimenides, the Cretan, simultaneously affirms and denies itself or, in other words, says nothing in much the same sense as 'all statements made in English are false' says nothing, the same general assertion as to the untrustworthy character of all Cretans, if Epimenides lets Socrates the Athenian do the talking, not merely becomes intelligently discussable, but also begins to make sense, in much the same way as 'all statements made in English are false' begins to say something and becomes discussable as soon as it is translated into French.[40]

Thus one recurrent and increasingly well-defined theme of the Gifford lectures delivered at Glasgow University in the 1950s was an opposition to British philosophies centred on validity rather than shared experience. In his relatively under-discussed *The Modern Predicament* (1955), H. J. Paton sets himself against the logical positivist ban on ethics beyond truth – as in *Language, Truth, and Logic*. For Paton logical positivism requires a world of observable and separate objects which, however, get 'stuck to' the terminology describing them – 'rather like a dog that glues its nose to the end of the walking stick with which we are trying to point'.[41] Its ideal language would be 'a language that no-one talks'.[42] Put together with the fact that Standard English is a minority dialect with universal aims, this prioritising of ahistorical validity in favour of those already authorised to speak represents a general British malaise – 'British philosophers, as a rule, confine themselves to Standard English'.[43] Deaf to otherness, British philosophy is thus 'false to the nature of language itself'.[44]

Paton instead returns to a Reid-like 'common world' consisting of 'all actual and possible perspectives'.[45] Where for Ayer, only analytic *a priori* statements are possible, Paton regards this 'veto' as an evacuation of values from philosophy and senses that if validity becomes a primary principle, philosophy will have nowhere left to go.[46] As for Davie, for Paton translation skews the possibility of an ideal language as the final court of appeal: '[i]t is always unreasonable for any philosopher to tell others that they must speak his language. This has often been done in the past, sometimes by thinkers who imagined that the language they spoke was ordinary

English'.[47] Recalling Reid and the primacy of agency, Paton suggests that meaning should be sought 'in action and not in thought'.[48] The struggle of action is to reconstitute experience as incorporating otherness, and 'unless I do assume this, I cannot take you to be a person like myself at all, and there would be no possibility of communication between us'.[49] The 'modern predicament' that Paton describes is thus a gulf between solipsistic validity and social faith. This is not an English problem, but a British one: the English have the ability to avoid modern alienation 'by their distrust of philosophy and their love of fair play'.[50]

Macmurray, the Personal and the Postcolonial

Strong likenesses to the largely postcolonial body of thought known as theory are to be found in a figure critical of both existentialism, viewed as the maintenance of the world at the expense of method, but more so of logical positivism, viewed as the maintenance of the method at the expense of the world.[51] John Macmurray takes a strong line against logical positivism's turning its back on the world, yet also refuses (unlike Laing, as we shall see) the existentialist turn inwards. His thinking is postcolonial in as much as it is post-Enlightenment, moving from the Humean sceptical self towards a form of the personal very close to that of the anti-colonial activist Frantz Fanon. Both show how the person is reduced via Hume/Kant to the subjective – a 'positioned selfhood' removed from social action. For Fanon, democratised nationhood points to decolonisation; for Macmurray, personalised society points to a form of experience not limited to the pragmatic state. For both writers, pragmatic, individualistic society is overcome in the first instance by a Hegelian mutuality between persons – recognition. Recognition does not figure in logical positivists like Russell, for whom mutual understanding would be outranked by meta-linguistic truth-tests. Fanon wants the self to go beyond the Humean-Kantian subject via imposition on the other's recognition, so that persons are 'mutually recognizing each other'.[52] Similarly, devolution 'from' one region 'to' another region would not fulfil the condition of recognition, and is not a meaningful action, but rather an unethical 'freeing' into non-being.[53] In this sense, there is a lack of recognition in the older British idea of devolution, which barely begins to address demands for democracy.

For Fanon, dysfunctional societies (or Enlightenment-imperial societies) always block recognition with a preceding moral universalism. This moral sense, since it is overwhelmingly based on assumptions backed up by visual impressions, is also open to racism. Thus in Fanon's colonial Martinique an overdetermined ethnic position – a 'crushing objecthood' – comes prior to any experience – as it had in the British ethnicisation of Scotland, Wales and Ireland.[54] For Fanon, agency, the primacy of action over this objecthood, could only be recovered by an assertion of an *expérience vécue* (lived-experience) demanding recognition. In Fanon's Algeria the lack of recognition was so extreme that violence in the nation's name became a social bond, a duty, an ontology, and even a form of communion. Britain's nations – though not *as* nations – have of course been on the causing rather than the receiving side of the colonial 'nervous disorders' Fanon describes, but still in Macmurray we find that the mutual resistance of persons is a condition of humanity, without which relationships are merely fearful, negative and defensive.[55] For Macmurray as for Fanon, lack of recognition is always mutual,[56] causing an 'impersonal relation', a relation of mere activity rather than action. But the impersonal relation contains its own downfall, being ambivalent (Macmurray's word), and involving an unstable anxiety over the objectification of the Other:[57]

> The relation of a master to his slave . . . is an impersonal one. It is constituted by the intention of the master to treat the other person 'as a means merely' – to use Kant's phrase . . . as an object possessing certain capacities and characteristics which make him useful.[58]

Macmurray points out that the morally universal individual is unreachable by experience, since universalism requires separation from an object-world upon which everyone agrees; the individual always has the same pre-set relation to that object-world.[59] This world cannot be touched by action at all, locking the subject into a 'fortress' of inaction.[60] (A few years later R. D. Laing would use the strikingly similar term 'citadel' to describe the prison-house of the subject).[61] Macmurray stresses action within a British philosophical scene in which he felt that logic's prior authority described an object form perfectly separated from, and not affecting, the world.[62] This is a world in which 'nothing is ever done; in which everything simply happens'.[63]

Macmurray's person rather partakes of *both* subject and object, and is subject only negatively.[64] From birth, learning to differentiate between Others is an ongoing process of movement between poles of need and reflection, an irreducible 'rhythm of withdrawal and return'; individuality arises from this rhythm, but is continuously overridden by action.[65] *You* and *I* are usually only analytical categories, except when the unity of agent and subject is denied in impersonal relationships, and the self splits into controlling and controlled parts – strongly recalling the split self which is state-British in some contexts and national in others.[66] To illustrate the difference between the personal and impersonal relationship, Macmurray, like Fanon and Laing, uses the example of the psychologist who finds himself having to step 'outside of' a personal relationship to diagnose a friend.[67] For Fanon, some societies make this lack of recognition normative: he also finds himself having to 'cure' French *colons* in order to allow them to go back to torturing natives – a perfect example of how, if it is merely institutional, 'civility' can function even when it bypasses the impersonal.[68] Subjects without access to their own lived-experience as agents, like Britons who do not live their national experience, are a source of ethical concern for Macmurray. Where this division is made, aggression is always mutual: '[the subject's] relation to the Other becomes ambivalent. He is divided in himself, fearing and therefore hating what he loves, turned against himself because he is against the Other'.[69]

In Macmurray, personal and impersonal relationships are also productive of different forms of knowledge: of these, Enlightenment thought sees impersonal, subjective knowledge as primary (it is behind, for example, science) and denies its being based on any prior experience or emotion.[70] In a way we would now associate with critical theory, Macmurray attacks the self-established Cartesian *cogito* enabled by knowledge of the world, and left intact by Hume, Kant and Russell.[71] The self should rather be described as a mixture of knower and known.[72] He points out that Enlightenment cognitive categories were themselves limited by terms such as civility or moral law; reason is always already guiding knowledge, meaning that knowledge must also be inherently practical and active, rather than neutral and prior.[73] When Macmurray turns to modern political institutions, he tellingly links Hobbes and Rousseau, figures who both assume 'negative' bases for sovereignty as protection of the individual through submission to either a protective (Hobbes) or ideal (Rousseau) state.[74] The inactive form of state answers general anxieties over security with negative guarantees,[75] and is a pragmatic state which only works as long as each Briton has another nationality reserved for more immediate types of experience,[76] and as long as that alternative nationality never aspires to the qualities of statehood. Macmurray's criticism of inaction strongly connotes criticism of the 'continuant' Britishness which the earlier phase of

Enlightenment helped set up. Indeed Macmurray's line from the Enlightenment to the British logical positivism of his own time shows that both movements block the link between experience and knowledge, even though an against-the-grain reading of Kant suggests that reason is practical. Where Kant, for example, tended to disavow religious experience *qua* experience as simply outside of *a priori* time and space,[77] for Macmurray, Laing and Paton (as, perhaps surprisingly, for Fanon – and recalling the dissenting voices of the Enlightenment such as Thomas Reid), spiritual experience represents the practical and present inclusion of a shared second person.[78] Macmurray even suggests that spiritual experience is not so much universal as 'national'.[79]

Both Macmurray and Fanon are post-Humean in their criticism of authority gained from the division of subject and object in vision. Since vision requires the object to occupy a separate space from a self-enclosed subject, and light to take time to cross that space, visual experience does not share its time, separating off a prior knowledge which always reaches the colonised 'late', in what postcolonial critics have called a 'colonial time-lag' – recalling post-union Scotland's imperative to 'catch up' (or for that matter, the imperative of any of today's less globalised countries to 'catch up'). But for Macmurray, there can be no point at which to stand back and spatially verify objects, since movement and knowledge are not separable, and action's knowledge is oriented towards a world which is alterable and always mid-alteration.[80] And since knowledge is not primarily a knowledge of objects, education is not a process of accumulating particular facts, but remains possible without compulsory specified pre-designated goals, marking out a place for generalist humanities:

> the generalisation of knowledge, as the negative aspect of action, makes possible an activity which intends the accumulation of knowledge, without any defined reference to the practical intentions which makes it possible.[81]

Macmurray then worries about the separation and spatialisation of discrete objects (of study) surveyed by a separate subject. Surveillance, in Macmurray as in psychoanalysis and critical theory, is a source of knowledge forcing the person to traumatically misrecognise herself in the social as object. Macmurray complains that 'the modus of depersonalization is largely visual',[82] structuring power relations in the 'west':[83] '[f]rom the time of the Greeks, and especially through the influence of Plato, "vision" has tended to be the model on which all *knowledge* is construed. Thought is taken to be an inner vision'.[84]

Not only does the metaphor of vision separate subject and object and bind them in a single spatial metaphor, it also requires that the distinction between images and things be mediated *logically*, while seeming natural and universal. Logic can assume primacy in visually construing the object, as in the case of shadows – also a frequent image in postcolonial and modernist literature.[85] Vision for Macmurray is thus more properly described as 'a formation of an image in the self',[86] and 'purely subjective or mental . . . *prima facie* a pure receptivity'.[87] Conversely, touch is perception in action, incurring in the Other a productive resistance. Tactile resistance modifies the will of self and Other in a shared present, and demonstrates that the 'ambiguity of the Other' is both a source of resistance *and* support.[88] For Macmurray, society should not be described as organic – a word often used to describe British gradualism and tradition – but as active and moral.[89] The acting agent generates the past intentionally by actualising one option, and makes history rather than watching history unfold, meaning that '[t]he distinction between right and wrong is inherent [only] in the nature of action'.[90] The organic/active split in thinking traditions, mapped onto the context of sub-British national action within the organic state, is close to that described by Bhabha between 'anterior' ('organic') and 'performative' (active) nations.[91]

Bhabha's important adaptations of Fanon require two modifications: firstly, the context of devolution has been inexplicably underrepresented by stars of British Cultural Studies;[92] secondly and conversely, Scottish history cannot simply escape from anteriority, since it also contains British subjectivity which has been pushed epistemologically prior to national experience. If history is the history of action, the 'recovery' of Scottish, English or Welsh history in a British context demands an active process of interrogating knowledge which always seems to describe who 'we' are. Fanon describes the importance of a move away from ethnocentric appeals to a pre-colonial past, one paradoxically both necessary and impossible without statehood.[93] Where experience does not touch the state, official talk stresses a continuous 'people' re-emerging intact – an image commonly attributed to 'tribal' desires for devolution. For Macmurray such images of the state as prior authority show a 'fear of anarchy' and a 'negative and general anxiety'.[94] Such anxieties have typically been both generated by and answered by the overarching state of Britain, whose status quo ultimately belongs to a Hobbesian tradition of political thought in which 'fear of anarchy' blocks action and supports the idea of constitution as an unimpeachable organic balance. The 'general' of 'general anxiety' here is not the open-ended 'general' of 'general education', but undefined fear of attack recycled with uncanny ease by British political parties in post-war general elections.

Laing, the New Left and the Sartrean Legacy

The critical theory which in the 1980s became central to the discipline formerly known as English Literature grew largely from criticism of the relationship between the French Enlightenment and the French empire, particularly in Algeria. Here I have proposed a similarly deconstructive stance towards the Scottish Enlightenment, whose universalist ideas can be placed behind an empire even wider in scope than the French one. If theory was an effect of the breakdown of universal civility exported in global contexts, it might also be expected to arise from sub-British and post-British cultures after imperialism as much as it did from post-Algerian-war France.

As well as John Macmurray's personalism, a more popular sub-British existentialist reaction to logical positivism's stress on validity had been strongly 'continental'. From the early 1960s R. D. Laing was showing an interest in existentialism; by the end of the 1950s, Macmurray had acknowledged but ultimately rejected both streams (though he dismisses logical positivism much more brutally than existentialism). Macmurray takes being as a primary problem, but unlike Sartre takes the solidity of the dual relationship as an article of faith. As we have seen, personalism also shows strong links to postcolonialism's determination to take back action from mere activity; postcolonialism, for example via Fanon, is in turn concerned about Sartrean questions of ontology in colonial situations in which personhood is disturbed at origin by 'race'. The Sartre who is behind Fanon also influences Scottish thought of the 1960s. For John Macquarrie, the concentration on being was in terms of 'realising what the potentials of human existence are'.[95] Macquarrie wrote perhaps the most authoritative English-language guide to existentialism, the 1972 Penguin book *Existentialism*, summing up interest in the tradition, and citing Macmurray and Laing.[96]

Laing was early influenced by Sartrean existentialism, and aimed after Glasgow not to go to Oxbridge for postgraduate study (as did many ambitious thinkers of the time) but to study in Germany with Karl Jaspers, a plan in which he was finally frustrated.[97] Laing's existentialism was representative of a wave which would later become more visible in the determined attention to moment-to-moment experience in storytellers like James Kelman and Janice Galloway. Laing's concern was not so much (as is still sometimes assumed) to do away with the terms of psychiatry, as to look at how these terms made up a system of exclusion, an almost Foucauldian interrogation of the parameters of discourse on the person. In this sense his method is not simply 'anti-psychiatric' so much as anti-universalist and historical. His debt to Sartrean existentialism, *contra* British thought's reliance on verifiable statements, is most obvious in the influence of *Being and Nothingness* on *The Divided Self* (1963), and in Laing's co-authored study of Sartre, *Reason and Violence* (1964). Laing's work was fairly quickly successful within an emerging field of interdisciplinary thought, and the Sartrean influence was unpacked in two studies both from 1977, M. Howarth-Williams's *R. D. Laing: His Work and its Relevance for Sociology*, and A. Collier's *R. D. Laing: The Philosophy and Politics of Psychotherapy*.[98] Laing established himself as part of a community of thought which was only problematically 'British', which was highly critical of state discourse, and which, unlike the old left, freely mixed imperial and domestic critiques.

Laing's reception however has been chequered. Russell Jacoby had two years before Howarth-Williams and Collier oddly defined him as a 'post-Freudian', giving him a psychoanalytic framework running counter to Laing's own strong denial of the Freudian topology of consciousness.[99] Laing's denial of Freudian 'space' is resonant in a post-imperial environment where spatial models of the mind require the savage to inhabit the 'underneath', as in *Totem and Taboo*. Peter Sedgwick's *Psycho Politics* (1982) offered a fairly harsh but influential division of the early acceptable Laing and the later loony Laing, a division in part responsible for 'depoliticising' Laing's work, despite his very real political commitments even after *The Politics of Experience* (1967).[100] In 1987 Laing featured in Elaine Showalter's *The Female Malady*, in which his Kingsley Hall experiment in non-psychiatric healing was re-cast as a patriarchal exercise in exploitation, somewhat contrary to the data available on patients like Mary Barnes.[101] Showalter's subtitle however shows that her area of study is 'English Culture'; Laing gives 'English anti-psychiatry a powerful spokesman'.[102] She also places a dismal Glasgow within the English context of Alan Sillitoe and John Wain,[103] losing all place specificity, and the specificity of this counter-imperial voice. Zbigniew Kotowicz's more recent *R. D. Laing and the Paths of Anti-Psychiatry* has the advantages firstly of recognising the primacy of mutual recognition (though not its possible connections to a personalist philosophical tradition) and secondly linking Laing's anti-psychiatric politics to patients' union movements such as Sozialistisches Patienten Kollektiv, demonstrating his importance in a post-1968 Europe.[104] Nevertheless, Kotowicz also breezes past any possible sub-British context by noting that '[q]uite unusually for someone educated at that time in Britain Laing felt drawn to the philosophical tradition of the Continent, chiefly phenomenology and existentialism', a set of interests which are in the British context 'almost alien'.[105] The points to be made here are that Glasgow University, site of the Gifford lectures, was by this time hardly typical of a 'British context' of thought, and that for the Scottish New Left continental connections were nothing new – close intellectual connections with France are ancient.

Laing's *The Divided Self* can, of course, be seen as another work in the long Jekyll-and-Hyde tradition of Scottish accounts of personhood split into two. This however is only to point out awareness of identities operating simultaneously on different levels. Laing perceives two splits within the schizoid self (later widened out to 'the person' in general): the first is between the person and the world, the second *within* himself (sic).[106] Laing's patients struggle to become 'embodied', to identify the ontological limits of their selves with those of their bodies. As in Macmurray, the slip from a personal to an impersonal relationship tends to happen with the placement of the person-as-object in the visual field.[107] Although Macmurray is cited only once in *The Divided Self*, and not at all in *The Politics of Experience*, Laing comes close to Macmurray in his reading of Hegel (in this case via Sartre), which makes the personal relationship a basis of human experience, and eclipses sceptcism.[108]

Like Fanon and Macmurray, Laing insists in *The Divided Self* that some levels of depersonalisation are normal for the social functioning of any given society. His examples are, as we might expect, not as horrific as those of Fanon's Algeria; however, as a fellow-psychiatrist his description does strongly recall Fanon's deadly-ironic 'curing' of French colonial torturers: 'social adaptation to a dysfunctional society may be very dangerous. The perfectly adjusted bomber pilot may be a greater threat to species survival than the hospitalised schizophrenic deluded that the Bomb is inside him'.[109]

Depersonalisation can thus be dangerous from a social point of view, and is the root of schizoid reactions ('nervous disorders').[110] This can petrify the person to the extent of making her unable to act – again recalling nations' inactivity *as nations* within the British union. The schizoid, frozen by the choice between agency and subjectivity, comes to fear all action.[111] And like Fanon, Laing insists that depersonalisation is always mutual, and that the subject-object split, once learned, will become automatic; even the analyst – like the Fanonian coloniser – is made into a 'robot'.[112] In Laing's experience, the killing of the self as person becomes a defence mechanism in those who can no longer locate their own humanity.[113] It is easier to lock into continuant activity than to face the trauma of action. But the false-self system which comes to replace the person is only ever structured very precariously, and invites further splits and collapses.[114] It can only maintain a false freedom by being 'transcendent', the dream of the Fanonian native who wishes to be invisible, no longer reducible to the symbolic image. The management of this behaviour as madness, however, relies on the violent naming (in the Derridean sense of violence) of certain persons and actions as mad, and the range of discursive apparatus which goes with this naming.[115] *The Divided Self* thus identifies the subject-object split, demanded by Enlightenment encyclopaedists, as a social sickness.

The false self makes itself the object of the other's gaze, naked and over-compliant with others, over-adapting to become 'a mere mirror of an alien reality' in order to preserve the integrity of the real self, which in turn disappears from view.[116] As in Macmurray, the ground degree zero of the impersonal, subjective relationship is fear and anxiety.[117] The fearful self 'impersonates' the gaze of the other, in a caricature we could readily compare to Homi Bhabha's reading of colonial 'mimicry' in Fanon.[118] Appropriately, the epigram of *The Divided Self*'s Chapter 9 ('Psychotic Developments') is the 'Things fall apart' couplet of Yeats's 'The Second Coming' – also referenced by Chinua Achebe's novel of the same name, and describing the instability of the imperial encounter on both sides.[119] Laing is also in this sense 'personalist': anxiety is the result of not recognising the mutual relationship as coming first in the creation of knowledge.

In strikingly Eliotic-Greater British terms, the false-self system is repeatedly described by Laing as 'sterile', 'empty' and 'dry'.[120] The Eliotic flavour of the schizoid sense of loss is even more noticeable towards the end of *The Divided Self* when, as is typical of Laing, he enters into long semi-quotations of his patients' utterings. Bemoaning dryness and isolation, the speech of this analysand could almost have come directly from *The Waste Land*:

> There is no gentleness, no softness, no warmth in this deep cave . . . Then, I shall be an echo and a shadow, along with the other people, in here, who have become echoes and shadows.[121]

Yet it is in the work where Laing is often suspected of having taken an inner trip too many, *The Politics of Experience*, that some of his most post-imperialist tendencies are to be found. He is here again close to Macmurray, despite a lack of reference – suggesting that the two figures are part of a more general post-British milieu. Right from the opening chapter of *The Politics of Experience*, Laing states even more clearly than in *The Divided Self*, like Macmurray and *contra* logical positivism, that experience should be valued over validity and that scientific approaches to the person fail by ignoring experience altogether: '[n]atural science is concerned only with the observer's experience of things. Never with the way things *experience us*. That is not to say that things do not react to us, and to each other'.[122] As in Macmurray, science has come to have too much authority in assumptions of the nature of experience.[123] Laing notes that any 'science' of persons would have to begin from a relationship rather than a categorisation.[124] In his autobiographical *Wisdom, Madness, and Folly* he even suggests that psychiatry should not even belong to the discipline of medicine, fraught as it is with discursive definitions of madness.[125] Just as Paton asserted that psychiatrists of a rigorously 'scientific' persuasion tend to forget the specificity of their own emotions, in Laing's own words, organic psychiatry is like calling in a TV technician to fix the programme.[126]

Thus the question, lodged materially and historically, is '[c]an human beings be persons today?'[127] Again persons, not subjects, are the origins of actions, and the person 'is a patient-agent'.[128] Like Fanon and Macmurray, Laing stresses that defences can become mechanised, and that an impersonal therapy merely makes a situation worse.[129] In a society underwritten by violence, an over-sane therapist can make a patient mad, and violence, both inside and outside the clinical relationship, can be disguised as love.[130] (Fanon's and Macmurray's reactions to this of course differ: where Fanon, faced every day with colonial torture, felt he could only reclaim the ontology of violence, Macmurray sees aggression as meaningless in human relationships, except as analytical description.) Here Laing draws explicitly on Fanon also to exemplify the way in which colonists must 'mystify' not only natives but also themselves, in a duality of false selves.[131] Mid-twentieth-century British philosophy still tended to place the object in view and admit of no confusion; since this misses mutuality in assuming aggression is emitted from one place, '[v]iolence cannot be seen through the sights of positivism'.[132] Logical positivism mistakes being 'in formation' (truth claims verified through systematic doubt) for being 'on course' (personal ontology).[133]

If *The Politics of Experience* has traditionally been seen as beyond the pale, 'The Bird of Paradise', the short text which ends it, is viewed with special incredulity and generic anxiety (not *real* psychology). But its thematic combination of anti-colonialism, class politics, and popular cultural studies locate it within New Left concerns. Many chapters of *The Politics of Experience* had already been published separately in *New Left Review*, as quite soon after would most of Tom Nairn's *The Break-up of Britain*. *The Politics of Experience* was published two years after the start of Laing's Kingsley Hall experimental treatments, in the same year as the Congress of the Dialectics of Liberation organised by Laing and others in London, involving Stokeley Carmichael, Herbert Marcuse and Allen Ginsberg.[134] This short text makes much more sense if we view it within a longer, colonial, 'counter-modern' aesthetics including Aimé Césaire's *Cahier d'un retour au pays natal* (1939, 1947 in Paris).[135] Surrealism also gets a re-reading from the early 1960s by Edwin Morgan ('Scotland's poet laureate'), who has gone over, localised and re-politicised various forms of early modernism. Laing's 'The Bird of Paradise' in this sense is like a Glaswegian *Cahier*, mixing gory descriptions of urban debris with political rage and confusion – on a city street rather than a beach. Aimé and Suzanne Césaire saw surrealism as a positive technique of disorientation, driving the *gestalt* of subject/object to the depths to 'rise' again in a nation from the ground up – or from the 'I' up: Césaire was as careful in his pronouns as was Laing.[136]

In terms of these models of the person, Britishness is, as Macmurray says of the process of Cartesian doubt, a certainty which only arises from sustained denial of experience.[137] The significance of devolution can be *misrecognised* not only by Britain but also, in the Fanonian sense, even within the person. In Scottish and Welsh contexts, devolution is largely a national process; for the British government, as Nairn argues, it represents the latest attempt to reshuffle local power without constitutional change – actionless activity. The 'self' in 'self-rule' is in British thinking ultimately still rule by individual subjects, rendering action impossible, since action can only be mutual. Given that all of Britain's nations have 'double' identities, a conception of devolution as permission destroys the chances of not only Scottish but also English action, and warns of an English march backwards into tradition and race. In Macmurray's terms societies should enter into agreements 'by common consent',[138] that is, with mutual 'resistance'; the assumption of 'granting devolution to' implies an impossible 'negotiation' between a nation-state and a region, tacitly denying mutual nationhood and thus recognition.[139] 'Devolution to' finds it difficult to conceive of possible outcomes of devolution other than more individual empowerment for British subjects. National experience is still always 'known' before it happens, and sub-British national action eclipsed by the residual Enlightenment images pressed into state service. Paradoxically, no less a figure than Tony Blair has recognised Macmurray's significance in this sense: 'I . . . find him extremely modern . . . in the sense that he confronts what will be the critical political question of the twenty-first century – the relationship between individual and society'.[140]

Despite this, Macmurray reminds us (in the mid-1950s) that politicians cannot be expected to deliver the 'millennium on a platter'.[141] This ironically presages one of the key sales points of post-1997 New Labour multiculturalism, the millennial celebration which saw the building of the unloved London dome, as well as the attempt to re-establish Edinburgh, city of Blair's schooldays, as Britain's second city. Of course, this misrecognition is mutual: Scotland has done more than its share, literally, of *creating* colonial victims, and a 'devolve from' model rejects postcolonial responsibility (in this sense all four nations could simply devolve away from British responsibility and leave no agent of colonial violence). But insofar as Britain represents a form of inaction overlain on other national actions, Scottish colonialism *as Scottish* was not action in the Macmurray sense – it must be grasped to recover action. This recovery is a concretely political thing, but it also requires the kind of appreciation of ambivalence which we find in Macmurray, Laing and Fanon.

Such an ambivalence is to be found in much sub-British writing at the very end of 'English Literature'. The prose of James Kelman, Janice Galloway and others, dating from the inter-referendum years 1979 to 1997, shows not, as is sometimes assumed, a gesture of solidarity with a glamorised proletariat, but a serious attention to the writing out of experience in its full doubleness. Kelman's success particularly represents, relative to English Literature, a taking back of experience from the authority of 'good English', which is always before and always denies links with writing and action. It represents small struggles to locate that action, to write the unwritable, and demonstrates in hesitant and disjointed conversation that the struggle for action and the struggle for enunciation are the same. The straining against the impersonal promise and towards the experiential present should not be seen in isolation, but as having a basis in the previous generation of post-British thinkers of the 1950s and '60s.

Notes

1. Alexander Broadie, *The Scottish Enlightenment* (Edinburgh: Birlinn, 2001), pp. 16, 23.
2. See Henry Louis Gates, Jr, *Figures in Black: Words, Signs, and the 'Racial' Self* (New York and Oxford: Oxford University Press, 1989), pp. 17–18.
3. Marinell Ash, *The Strange Death of Scottish History* (Edinburgh: Ramsay Head Press, 1980); Colin Kidd, *Subverting Scotland's Past: Scottish Whig Historians and the Creation of an Anglo-British Identity, 1689–c. 1830* (Cambridge: Cambridge University Press, 1993), p. 117; cf. Broadie, *The Scottish Enlightenment*, p. 56.
4. Cf. Broadie, *The Scottish Enlightenment*, p. 75.
5. Murray G. H. Pittock, *Inventing and Resisting Britain* (Basingstoke: Palgrave, 1997), p. 141.
6. Cf. G. E. Davie, *The Scottish Enlightenment* (Edinburgh: Birlinn, 1991), pp. 32–3.
7. Cf. Broadie, *The Scottish Enlightenment*, p. 31.
8. Tom Nairn, *The Break-up of Britain: Crisis and Neo-nationalism* (London: NLB, 1977), pp. 140–1.
9. Duncan Forbes, *Hume's Philosophical Politics* (Cambridge: Cambridge University Press, 1975), p. 140.
10. Alexander Broadie, *Why Scottish Philosophy Matters* (Edinburgh: Saltire, 2000), p. 17.
11. Ibid. p. 59.
12. Ibid. p. 68.
13. Thomas Reid, Derek R. Brookes (ed.), *Essays on the Intellectual Powers of Man* (Edinburgh: Edinburgh University Press, 2002), pp. 26–7.
14. Broadie, *The Scottish Enlightenment*, p. 26; cf. Davie, *The Scottish Enlightenment*, p. 20.
15. Broadie, *Why Scottish Philosophy Matters*, p. 91.
16. Cairns Craig, *The Modern Scottish Novel* (Edinburgh: Edinburgh University Press, 1999), p. 23.
17. Edward Said, 'Jane Austin and Empire', in Said, *Culture and Imperialism* (New York: Vintage, 1994), pp. 80–97.
18. Craig, *The Modern Scottish Novel*, p. 78.
19. Michael Foucault, trans. A. M. Sheridan Smith, *The Arachaeology of Knowledge* (London: Tavistock, 1972); Robert Young, *Postcolonialism: An Historical Introduction* (Oxford: Blackwell, 2001), pp. 395–410.
20. See Michael Friedman, *Reconsidering Logical Positivism* (Cambridge: Cambridge University Press, 1999), p. 95.
21. Bertrand Russell, *Our Knowledge of the Outside World* (London: Routledge, 1993), pp. 70–105.
22. Cf. G. E. Davie, *The Crisis of the Democratic Intellect* (Edinburgh: Polygon, 1986), p. 260.
23. A. J. Ayer, *Language, Truth, and Logic* (London: Penguin, 2001), p. 13.
24. See ibid. p. 63.
25. Ibid. p. 10.

26. Ibid. p. 41.
27. Ibid. p. 53.
28. Ibid. p. 26.
29. Ibid. pp. 57, 130.
30. Russell, *Principles of Mathematics* (London: Routledge, 1992), pp. 523–8.
31. Gilbert Ryle, *The Concept of Mind* (London: Penguin, 2000).
32. Ayer, *Language, Truth, and Logic*, p. 127.
33. Ibid. pp. 168, 139.
34. Davie, *The Crisis of the Democratic Intellect*, p. 159.
35. Ibid. p. 191.
36. Raphael Samuel, 'Introduction: Exciting to be English', in Samuel (ed.), *Patriotism: The Making and Unmaking of British National Identity, Vol. I: History and Politics* (London: Routledge, 1989), pp. xviii–lxvii: l–lii.
37. Davie, *The Crisis of the Democratic Intellect*, p. 224.
38. Cf. Lindsay Paterson, *Scottish Education in the Twentieth Century* (Edinburgh: Edinburgh University Press, 2003), p. 166; Broadie, *The Scottish Enlightenment*, p. 47.
39. Cf. Francis Mulhern, *The Moment of Scrutiny* (London: NLB, 1979), pp. 316–18.
40. Davie, *The Crisis of the Democratic Intellect*, p. 201.
41. H. J. Paton, *The Modern Predicament: A Study in the Philosophy of Religion* (London: George Allen and Unwin, 1955), p. 34.
42. Ibid. p. 35.
43. Ibid. p. 35.
44. Ibid. p. 36.
45. Ibid. p. 263.
46. Ibid. p. 39.
47. Ibid. p. 44.
48. Ibid. p. 171.
49. Ibid. p. 265.
50. Ibid. p. 374.
51. John Macmurray, *The Self as Agent* (London: Faber and Faber, 1969), p. 27.
52. Frantz Fanon, *Black Skin, White Masks*, trans. Charles Lam Markmann (London: Pluto, 1986), pp. 216–17.
53. Ibid. p. 10.
54. Ibid. p. 109; Murray Pittock, *Celtic Identity and the British Image* (Manchester: Manchester University Press, 1999), pp. 20–60.
55. Macmurray, *The Self as Agent*, p.123.
56. John Macmurray, *Persons in Relation* (London: Faber and Faber, 1969), pp. 74–5.
57. Ibid. p. 104.
58. Ibid. p. 34.
59. Ibid. p. 127.
60. Macmurray, *The Self as Agent*, p. 55; *Persons in Relation*, p. 208.
61. Laing, *The Divided Self* (New York: Penguin, 1991), p. 80.
62. Macmurray, *The Self as Agent*, pp. 92, 219.
63. Ibid. p. 219.
64. Ibid. p. 12.

65. Macmurray, *Persons in Relation*, p. 91.
66. Macmurray, *The Self as Agent*, p. 98.
67. Macmurray, *Persons in Relation*, p. 29.
68. Frantz Fanon, *The Wretched of the Earth*, trans. Constance Farrington (Harmondsworth: Penguin, 1967), p. 217.
69. Macmurray, *Persons in Relation*, p. 98.
70. Ibid. p. 30–1.
71. Macmurray, *The Self as Agent*, p. 80.
72. Ibid. p. 38.
73. Ibid. p. 54.
74. Macmurray, *Persons in Relation*, pp. 138, 142.
75. Ibid. p. 135.
76. Cf. Nairn, *The Break-up of Britain*, pp. 11–91, 126–95.
77. Macmurray, *The Self as Agent*, p. 70.
78. Ibid. p. 72.
79. Macmurray, *Persons in Relation*, p. 157.
80. Macmurray, *The Self as Agent*, pp. 97, 128, 167.
81. Ibid. p. 182.
82. Macmurray, *Persons in Relation*, p. 83.
83. Ibid. p. 136.
84. Macmurray, *The Self as Agent*, p. 105.
85. Ibid. p. 111.
86. Ibid. p. 112.
87. Ibid. p. 106.
88. Ibid. p. 110.
89. Macmurray, *Persons in Relation*, p. 128.
90. Macmurray, *The Self as Agent*, p. 140.
91. See Homi K. Bhabha, 'DissemiNation: Time, narrative, and the margins of the modern nation', in Bhabha, *The Location of Culture* (London: Routledge, 1994), pp. 139–70.
92. See Robert Crawford, *Devolving English Literature* (Edinburgh: Edinburgh University Press, 2000), p. 309.
93. Fanon, *The Wretched of the Earth*, p. 167.
94. Macmurray, *Persons in Relation*, p. 139.
95. John Macquarrie, *In Search of Humanity* (London: SCM, 1982), p. 2.
96. John Macquarrie, *Existentialism* (Harmondsworth: Penguin, 1972); see Craig Beveridge and Ronald Turnbull, 'Recent Scottish Thought', in Cairns Craig (ed.), *The History of Scottish Literature Vol. 4* (Aberdeen: Aberdeen University Press, 1987), pp. 61–74.
97. See Zbigniew Kotowicz, *R. D. Laing and the Paths of Anti-Psychiatry* (London: Routledge, 1997), p. 2.
98. M. Howarth-Williams, *R. D. Laing: His Work and its Relevance for Sociology* (London: Routledge and Kegan Paul, 1977); A. Collier, *R. D. Laing: The Philosophy and Politics of Psychotherapy* (New York: Pantheon, 1977).
99. Russell Jacoby, *Social Amnesia: A Critique of Conformist Psychology from Adler to Laing* (Boston: Beacon, 1975), pp. 131–51; Sigmund Freud, *Totem and Taboo: Some points of agreement between the mental lives of savages and neurotics*, trans. James Strachey (London: Routledge and Kegan Paul, 1960).

100. Peter Sedgewick, *Psycho Politics* (London: Pluto, 1982); Kotowicz, *R. D. Laing and the Paths of Anti-Psychiatry*, pp. 94–9.
101. Elaine Showalter, *The Female Malady: Women, Madness, and English Culture, 1830–1980* (London: Virago, 1987), pp. 220–47.
102. Ibid. p. 223.
103. Ibid. p. 224.
104. See Kotowicz, *R. D. Laing and the Paths of Anti-Psychiatry*, pp. 15, 29, 71–88; R. D. Laing, *The Politics of Experience* (New York: Pantheon, 1967).
105. Ibid. p. 2.
106. R. D. Laing, *The Divided Self: An Existential Study in Sanity and Madness* (London: Penguin, 1990), p. 17.
107. Ibid. p. 37.
108. For example, ibid. p. 37.
109. R. D. Laing, *The Politics of Experience*, p. 120.
110. Laing, *The Divided Self*, p. 47.
111. Ibid. p. 87.
112. Ibid. p. 49.
113. Ibid. pp. 51, 68.
114. Ibid. pp. 73, 77.
115. For example, ibid. p. 19.
116. Laing, *The Divided Self*, pp. 102, 106, 160.
117. Ibid. pp. 100, 113.
118. Ibid. p. 100; see Homi K. Bhabha, 'Of Mimicry and Man', in *The Location of Culture*, pp. 85–92.
119. Laing, *The Divided Self*, p. 137; Chinua Achebe, *Things Fall Apart* (London: D. Campbell, 1992).
120. Laing, *The Divided Self*, pp. 82, 91.
121. Ibid. pp. 169–70.
122. Laing, *The Politics of Experience*, p. 19.
123. Ibid. p. 54.
124. Laing, *The Divided Self*, p. 21.
125. R. D. Laing, *Wisdom, Madness, and Folly: The Making of a Psychiatrist 1927–1957* (Edinburgh: Canongate, 1998), pp. 1–32.
126. Paton, *The Modern Predicament*, p. 256; R. D. Laing, 'What is the Matter With Mind', in Satish Kumar (ed.), *The Schumacher Lectures* (London: Blond and Briggs, 1980), pp. 1–27.
127. Laing, *The Politics of Experience*, p. 23.
128. Ibid. pp. 23, 30.
129. Ibid. pp. 35, 53.
130. Ibid. pp. 108, 57.
131. Ibid. p. 57.
132. Ibid. p. 61; cf. R. D. Laing, *Reason and Violence* (London: Tavistock, 1964), p. 12.
133. Laing, *The Politics of Experience*, p. 119.
134. Kotowicz, *R. D. Laing and the Paths of Anti-Psychiatry*, p. 55.
135. Aimé Césaire, *Notebook of a Return To My Native Land*, trans. Mirelle Rosello and Annie Pritchard (eds) (Newcastle upon Tyne: Bloodaxe, 1995).

136. See, for example, Suzanne Césaire, editorial material in *Tropiques* 4, in Jacqueline Leiner (ed.), *Tropiques: Collection Complète* (Paris: Jean-Michel Place, 1994), p. 113.
137. Macmurray, *The Self as Agent*, p. 76.
138. Macmurray, *Persons in Relation*, p. 204.
139. Cf. Tom Nairn, *After Britain* (London: Granta, 2000), pp. 182–8.
140. Quoted by Philip Hunt, http://www.ardue.org.uk/jmf/discover.htm. Consulted 2002.
141. Macmurray, *Persons in Relation*, p. 200.

Chapter Five

England Without the Cricket Test

Postcolonial Carnival

We have seen that the late-nineteenth-century split between quasi-federal Greater British culture and local-nationalist culture was underlined by the upheavals of the years 1917 to 1927. 'Celtic' nationalism and decolonisation were linked both indirectly, as part of an anti-imperial movement, and directly by the key colony of Ireland; Scottish nationalism became gradually more separatist from 1917 to 1997 (with unionist bumps in the mid-'30, '50s and mid-'70s). The conditions for post-Britishness would be completed by independence movements which not only destroyed the empire even in its 'softer' culturalist form of Greater Britain but also undermined assumptions which had long attributed constitutional success to the British character.[1] Nor were the fundamentals of the Scottish Renaissance, especially its reliance on a fixed 'people' all speaking the same discrete language, to survive the 1960s unscathed. Ian Hamilton Finlay and Edwin Morgan would often clash with MacDiarmid in print (and in Finlay's case, in person), MacDiarmid increasingly inflexible over 'the kind of Scots in which high poetry can be written'.[2] At the 1962 Edinburgh Book Festival, MacDiarmid laid into an international cast, including Alexander Trocchi and William Burroughs.[3] By the next year Morgan and Finlay were experimenting with concrete poetry. The movement away from Synthetic Scots coincided with a postcolonial reflux of British immigrants. Where during the mid-'50s the number of immigrants was between 12,000 and 15,000 a year, it had risen to 50,000 in 1960, 66,000 in 1961, and 32,000 in the first half of 1962 before the rules were changed.[4] By the time of the 1962 Commonwealth Immigration Act, the official (probably under-estimated) number of 'Colonials' in Britain was 300,000. The vast majority lived in England.

The swinging '60s opened to widespread anxieties over im-migration, concretised in popular fears of being besieged, which found a voice in the Conservative MP Enoch Powell. The year 1958 saw the first of many serious anti-immigration demos in Nottingham and, more seriously, in Notting Hill, though since 1948 and the arrival of immigrants on the *Windrush* there had been scuf-fles at harbours.[5] Powell, not at the time a lone eccentric, held his seat for Wolverhampton South-West from 1950 to 1974, and exerted a decisive influence on the 1970s elections which would eventu-ally enthrone Margaret Thatcher – whose reign is widely accepted as Britain's final breaking point.[6] Zig Layton-Henry has interest-ingly argued that Thatcher played the Powellite race card as a *general* strengthening of executive power.[7] Yasmin Alibhai-Brown notes that Thatcher's anti-immigration stance had become popular in many sectors before her election, given her ability to use an eth-nocentric form of 'patriotism' as a post-imperial sticking-plaster.[8] Raphael Samuel's three-volume *Patriotism* was partly conceived to answer the way in which the right had been gifted patriotism and was using it to re-visit imperialism in the Falklands War (an area tellingly compared to neglected imperial Canada by Richard Gott in Volume I).[9]

Appropriately, race returned just as British national identity was losing the plot, relying on specifically English images to justify British policy. In this sense Powell's Little Englandism was oddly prophetic, though never fully English.[10] Powell's infamous 'rivers of blood' speech, delivered in April 1968, links concerns over the 'national [presumably, British] danger' of immigration to the rank-and-file Englishman imagined to be walking the streets of Wolver-hampton (and the concerned citizen in this speech is more than likely apocryphal).[11] In November of that year in Eastbourne Powell claimed to have captured the hearts of the English people.[12] In a sense Powell was right in his notorious claim that Britain was being 'hollowed out from within by implantation of unassimilated and unassimilable populations'.[13] His topographical image of a Britain centred and in control of a wider scope of peoples – here candidly linked to the colonial image of 'implantation' – is an uncannily ac-curate image of how Greater Britain had lost a central principle it needed to sustain itself. What is left is an ahistorical ethnicity: as Paul Gilroy has noted, the Powellite conception of nationality tended to disingenuously freeze citizenship, since even when immigrants *became British*, for Powell they somehow remained West Indian, African or Asian.[14] This is where Britishness and ethno-cultural ideas of Britain part company: citizenship is no longer sufficient to gain access, and the possibility of being a proper nation-state is lost. In the Powell-Thatcher line too, Britain ceases to have political meaning in terms of rights and representation. From Thatcher's ascendancy to the Conservative leadership in 1975, although the party seemed to take a position which was Anglo-nationalist, its problem was translating its English specificity into anything concrete.[15] This represents not, to borrow the title of Derek Jarman's film, 'the last of England'; nor though was it yet the last of the British state, but the simultaneous maturing of a 1960s English underground and the senility of 'British culture' – a proposition with No Future.[16] Britain is better described as an 'empire state' than a nation-state; nationhood in the integrative sense has passed away to leave state centralisation around a set of default values receding into an imagined past.[17]

This is not to claim that the core feeling in Britain, even amongst people still proud to call themselves British, was Powellite: Powell's own party increasingly viewed him as a liability, and struggled to contain him on the back-benches. (He did however influence the growing National Front, formed a year before the 'rivers of blood' speech. The NF's leader John Tyndall had moved from the 'Greater British Movement' a year before this; their 'National' again, in some highly nebulous sense, still seems to mean British, while claiming ancient traditions.[18] Remarkably, the Greater Britain phrase was revived by Gordon Brown as an ideal near the end of 1998.)[19] Nor was Powell's electoral success in his own seat ever translated into a nationwide public appeal. But while immigrants were increasingly required to take on the *citizenship* meaning of Britishness, the 'Englishing' of Conservative governments continued to accentuate the *ethnicity* sense into the 1990s; the process of Britain becoming its 'outsides' was self-fulfilling. Anthony Barnett has noted from Powell's front-bench days to 1997 a continuity of catastrophe metaphors deployed by the Conservative leadership, which figured each coming general election potentially the last British election ever.[20] Where these panic calls had been aimed at the immigrant threat, by 1999 in Scotland and Wales they were being directed at Yes-Yes votes in the devolution referendums. Such warnings became self-fulfilling: increasingly those experiencing devolution have turned away from British polity, which they regard as not being properly representative.

One of the most fateful misfits of Anglo-British ethnicity with the state during this twilight period is Norman Tebbit's 'cricket test' for immigrants, repainting immigration as English yet without intention towards English statehood. Cricket metaphors are particularly telling: Scotland certainly played cricket at the high point of empire, but even today remains notoriously terrible at the game. A 1969 *Monty Python* sketch lampooned the national cricket team as the worst in the world.[21] But Scotland's hoping for the England team to take a hiding from an ex-colony hardly represents, as some commentators have claimed, a tribal enmity; nor, for that matter, does supporting the West Indies. Sport is not war, and local rivalries abound everywhere; they are only incomprehensible in the light of Tebbit's tendency to equate the England team with the United Kingdom. English cricket's historical civilising overtones, of course, do little to endear it to Greater Britain's others. The late-Victorian public school overtones of the innate civility of the game seemed to be revived as the cultural wing of a general Thatcherite Dickensianism which also saw the return of the deserving poor, TB, the urban slum and the charity ward. Arthur Aughey has recently argued that Anglo-British 'gentility' could be safely parodied in the 1960s, since it had gone underground in the Welfare State – which was of course ruined by the pseudo-nationalist push of the 1980s.[22] Since then, gentility has been pared down to the bones and 'gone the way of RP at the BBC'.[23]

Ironically, the period which saw Tebbit's collapsing of England and the union also saw a series of hopeless cricket defeats of England by the West Indies – as in the 'black wash' of 1986, celebrated by Britain's many residents of Caribbean origins, who thus failed the test and became, by Tebbit's logic, un-British. Cricket metaphors are a *reductio ad absurdum* of Greater Britain, balancing non-English and non-cricketing nations in an Anglo-British civility. It is not coincidental that one of the Caribbean's most important twentieth-century cultural critics, C. L. R. James, a Marxist and anti-colonial activist, was known to many British newspaper readers as a distinguished cricket writer.[24] With New Labour, cricket metaphors have given way to soccer metaphors, in part because of the success of the English Premiership, but also as a last attempt to recognise British diversity: St George's crosses at Euro '96 and World Cup '98 were hailed by some as a revival of Englishness (perhaps those watching with the sound down so they couldn't hear *Rule, Britannia!*). Soccer, with its separate national teams, does not throw a national spanner into Britain as has cricket; indeed it can prove a safe outlet for nationalist sentiment: thus Jim Sillars's comment after the failure of the 1979 devolution referendum that too many

Scots were 'ninety-minute patriots'. Some critics now pointedly ask whether the 'cricket test' could be used on Scottish football fans living in England, making a nonsense of this form of unionist culture.[25] Cricket has been uniquely English yet vaguely inclusive; unable to equate its cultural and national scope, it seems to draw all towards its semi-permeable veil of civility and revel in its own un-pedantic willingness to put off conclusions.[26]

Here I am suggesting more broadly that there is a cultural continuity from the 1960s to 1999 tying together Scotland and Wales, immigrants, and the localism of a re-emerging English society itself. If Scotland is more practised at thinking through questions of stateless nationhood, England has a longer history of direct connection with the land in democratic local systems – a history becoming divergent when images of a countryside home were put into propaganda use in World War I. With the imperial vision of home as the home counties went the nebulously centralising imperial civility of cricket which had been built into the English public school over the last fifty years; this does not however make either the sport or the country undemocratic. Tebbit's cricket may still have been a feature of the English countryside, but that countryside was no longer conceived as the still point of the *British* imperial world. And the ideology of the English countryside *as* Britain from the war underlined how the imperial placement of 'home' within concentric circles of economic and cultural significance, described by Edward Said as being coincident with the rise of the nineteenth-century English novel, never quite fitted for Scots, even during the most unionist phases of British history.[27] Scotland was never any more 'centred' or 'at home', in Said's sense, than were the colonies which Scots helped to conquer.

Significantly, immigrants to the UK have often tended to regard themselves as belonging to the nation in which they live, rather than to their official citizenship. Literary and anecdotal Caribbean stories of coming to England outweigh the dubious political correctness of British national identity. This is surely in part due to the English education made standard in colonies in the nineteenth century; yet it is also a sign that those most cut off from the levers of power of Greater Britishness have tended to act on a local and communitarian basis. Immigrants seeing themselves as English, Scottish or Welsh, moreover do so in the face of great difficulties, since although the UK may grant citizenship and legal protection against racism, Scottish, English or Welsh ethnocentric descriptions of 'our' ancient culture are able to go unchecked. In Scotland there has recently been a tentative movement to re-think this 'our'; in England the ethno-centrism of Englishness remains more or less synonymous with the ethnocentrism of Britishness. But lofty gestures of British multicul-turalism 'from above' are already late for local and postcolonial crossover cultures, for which England is less a default of Greater Britain than as the nation, the place itself, in which they live.

In official 'British culture', the 1960s would become identified with both Britishness itself, especially a form of Britishness briefly going under the 'toe-curlingly embarrassing' term 'Cool Britannia',[28] a du-biously funny pun on the imperialist sentiment of *Rule, Britannia!*. Though these images belong to a moment New Labour would prob-ably like to forget, they were encouraged by the 'rebranding' work of the New Labourite think tank Demos, which attempted to spin old Britishness into a new and saleable diversity.[29] The 'New Britain' slogan was a direct inheritance from the Conservative administra-tion, which had taken it up in 1994. The prefix 'people's' was applied to everything from referendums to the National Lottery, despite the fact that British power was increasingly centralised in the West-minster executive, away from the people. After her death, 'Princess' Diana became, with Blair's implicit blessing, 'the people's princess', although her appeal, and her danger, lay in her being more familiarly *English* than British – as even Elton John realised – and more open to postcolonial foreign liaisons.[30] The official post-1997 celebration of the 'people's' New Britain has been acutely compared by Ken Wor-pole to the Festival of Britain – 'one continuous, interwoven story of British contributions to world civilisation'.[31] In a symptomatic turn of croneyism, Peter Mandelson, chief manager of millennial British-ness, turns out to have been the grandson of Herbert Morrison, chief organiser of the 1951 Festival.[32] By 2000, each 'zone' in the flagship Millennium Dome was privately sponsored, making it hard to see as 'nationally' British at all. A number of possible sites were summarily ignored by the Blair executive, which built the Dome in the extreme south-east of the 'nation', meaning that many, includ-ing the Scots whose support Blair required to maintain Britishness, were unable to visit.[33] The Dome was supposed to be, as Andrew Rawnsley says, '[i]mperially imposing, yet inclusively embracing', recovering the Eliotic lower reaches of the Thames to 'symbolize the regeneration of the creativity and genius of Cool Britannia'.[34] But within a month it was already absorbing Lottery money at a million pounds a day, and being crucified in almost every sector of the press.

The phrase 'Cool Britannia' does not date from the Millennial era, though; it was not (as Murray Pittock has suggested) 'originally' a flavour of ice-cream but was already in existence when it was taken up by Ben & Jerry's in 1996, perhaps as a result of a number of articles in the American magazine *Newsweek* which documented the likelihood of an incumbent New Labo(u)r Party face-lifting London (meaning the United Kingdom).[35] Since images of Britishness are frequently associated in the American media with images of rock music and the swinging '60s (the 'Austin Powers' films are a recent example), it is not surprising to find the phrase in 1967, when it was the title of a song by the British rock/novelty band The Bonzo Dog Doo Dah Band.[36] This stricter dating of 'Cool Britannia' helps show how it indicates a point of reference to the '60s during the late '90s. Cool Britannia peaked in the election and referendum year of 1997, and despite almost immediate disavowal of the term, was over-used to the extent that by March 1998 *The Economist* was complaining that 'many people are already sick of the phrase'.[37] As with the bogey-word 'postmodernism', the history of being sick of 'Cool Britannia' seems somehow longer than the history of use of the term itself, making it easy to brush under the carpet as *passé*. It remains, however, a useful pointer to British culture's last stand.

Perhaps rather than simply becoming tiresome, this phrase *had* to be buried when it was in danger of being identified as the losing side of a cultural struggle against break-off nationalisms and local communities. The Bonzo Dog Doo Dah Band were not unusual in their design-reliance on Union Jacks, Victoriana and British eccentricism; more famous examples include the Beatles' *Sergeant Pepper's Lonely Hearts Club Band* (also 1967), and *Monty Python's Flying Circus* (1969–74) (and one of the cast of Monty Python was the Bonzos' Neil Innes). Raphael Samuel has convincingly shown how in the late stages of British culture, 'retrochic', attracting increasingly recent images, often has the 1960s as a degree zero, and prepares the way for a deranged Anglo-British ethno-nationalism, seen in the growth of the National Trust and Heath's 1971 Immigration legislation.[38] The phrase's doubly retro- or backward-looking mood – 1960s Victoriana in the 1990s – is what concerns us here: as a forward-looking term pointing to a sleek and efficient *future*, 'Cool Britannia' was only taken up by the most ephemerally mercantile of cultural organisations – designers, restaurants and PR firms. In popular culture, Cool Britannia connoted a high Britishness of familiarly 1960s and (therefore) neo-Victorian charm. This is not to say the 1960s can be summed up by state culture: many of today's threads of counterculture, some of which I will discuss below, have their origins in the decade.[39] In the '90s incarnation of 'Cool Britannia', an integrative 'young' Britain was again deployed against more divisive and national ground-level youth culture. But to this ideal of a cool Greater British retro, the reaction of the youth was the most scathing of all. Many had been living a much more local cultural diversity for years, one which had become increasingly detached from Britain as a whole. Youth culture in England had by 1997 largely become more English than British, less based on imperial 'race' than inclusive place.

Reggae's and Punk's 'Ethnicities'

The beginnings of the West London Caribbean music scene, which would become much more widely known in the 1970s, can be traced back to the set-up of sound systems on Ladbroke Grove in 1955.[40] The first Notting Hill Carnival was held in 1959, and took place annually from 1965. Its imported music was frequently percussion-based; its pounding drum and bass, which confirmed some Powellite suspicions about the noisiness of immigrants, has roots in Caribbean traditions of music as repetitive and ritualistic force, transmitted for example via Afro-Jamaican *Kumina* drumming. This is a tactile music, felt as well as listened to – a post-Enlightenment stress on touch as joining persons in a single time of experience. The tactile emphasis contrasts strongly with the European classical stress on melody, which still defined 'tuneful' British pop music as it peaked in the 1960s, and in its Cool Britannic revival. As I have suggested above, colonial and postcolonial culture touch has been set against the Enlightenment association of knowledge with objects remote from the self, allowing for knowledge to precede recognition. Reggae *has* to be loud, since it is based musically and intellectually on vibration. The drum and bass emphasis of reggae and (via New York) disco would also exert a massive influence on music and youth culture in English garages increasingly detached from official British culture.

Thus the Trinidadian steel drum's politics of touch go back to its evolution in the 1940s as a pragmatic way to retain Africanistic drumming after the illegalisation of percussion by the British administration as a dangerous political statement. Trinidadian Carnival's communicative and communitarian significance lay not simply in making noise, not even just in rendering music tactile, but also in gathering a crowd capable of spontaneous celebration and revolt. Under colonialism, it had become an assertion of native agency, first for the slave and then post-1834 for the 'emancipated' worker. Earl Lovelace's novel *The Dragon Can't Dance* (1979) – now a minor classic within English Literature and its spin-offs – describes how, in an increasingly corporate-sponsored neocolonial Port of Spain, people still perceive themselves in lucid bursts of carnival as being part of a collective. Celebration is also a political act; it is unmanageable, its demand for recognition involving the entire person, spiritual and corporeal:

> This is the guts of the people, their blood; this is the self of the people that they screaming out they possess, that they scrimp and save and whore and work and thief to drag out of the hard rockstone and dirt to show the world they is people . . . With a strong, piercing scream, he stepped out into the street, his chains rattling, his arms outflung, his head lolling, in a slow, threatening dance of the Beast, so that the people of the Hill turned to him, recognising him, and said, 'Yes! Yes! That is Dragon!'[41]

Carnival both shakes up the current possibilities of political economy and also destroys the idea of culture as a production of specific great individuals broadcast to masses. For Mikhail Bakhtin, who, significantly, became highly fashionable in Scotland in the 1980s, carnival disrupts the normal cycle of producer–consumer by involving all people in political process. Bakhtin's carnival resists any clear division of subject and object at all: 'Carnival is not a spectacle seen by the people; they live in it, and everyone participates because its very idea embraces all the people. While carnival lasts, there is no other life outside it'.[42] Carnival is not like the official festival/feast, reliant on erudite and media-wise parodies. Unlike millennial Cool Britannia, it represents a semi-articulated mix of ridicule, joy, and anger:

> As opposed to the official feast, one might say that the carnival celebrated temporary liberation from the prevailing truth and from the established order; it marked the suspension of all hierarchical rank, privileges, norms, and prohibitions. Carnival was the true feast of time, the feast of becoming, change and renewal. It was hostile to all that was immortalised and completed.[43]

British ability to manage carnival was tested during this period at Notting Hill Carnivals. Since the nineteenth century, Notting Hill had been occupied by gypsies, Irish labourers and other undesirables and was increasingly known as a working-class neighbourhood used as a holding area for immigrants; it is symptomatic that today it has become one of the most expensive areas of the city, giving its name to a film starring that most marketable Anglo-Briton – Hugh Grant – who brings his own buffoon-like Welsh sidekick.[44] By the time carnival arrived in Britain, it already had a strong class dynamic; West London ghettoisation confirmed the class consciousness of workers in monoculture plantations.[45] Garveyite consciousness movements had become common by the 1960s, though they were discouraged by post-independence governments, at least before the Jamaican government's mid-'70s flirtation with socialism which led to virtual sanctions by the US. Garveyite, maroon and rastafarian impulses against imperialism were imported to Britain via the largely young and largely male immigrant population (the 1962 Immigration Act made it harder for men to bring their families afterwards). The most serious of the Notting Hill disturbances linked vectors of class *and* ethnicity, is linked to the carnivalesque Notting Hill Fayre, and were not really race riots at all.[46] Paul Gilroy shows how the disturbances of 1976–7 came at a time when punk was emerging in the same West London cultural scene amongst white working-class youths. Punk's union flag-burning corresponded to Queen Elizabeth II's Silver Jubilee in 1977, an irony seized on by the Sex Pistols' 'God Save the Queen', the number one single in Jubilee week, and by Derek Jarman's more highbrow 1978 film *Jubilee*.[47] Britishness remained unfashionable into the 1980s, perhaps one reason why later governments felt it was there for the reclaiming.

Gilroy stresses white punks' readiness, in organisations like Rock Against Racism and fanzines like *Temporary Hoarding* and *Sniffin' Glue*, to turn class politics into a challenge on the endemic British racism which was reaching a peak in the mid-'70s.[48] Sarcastic about 'British' heritage, punk also appears as a marker of the postcolonial; as Dick Hebdige famously suggested near the time, white youths increasingly viewed race as a function of social class, and recognised in themselves something like a post-British 'white ethnicity'.[49] As Gilroy puts it:

> the encounter with black culture in general and Rastafari in particular had changed the terms on which black and white young people engaged each other. From now on, 'race' could not longer be dealt with as a matter for private negotiation in the shadows of the ghettos or the inner-city shebeen where a token white presence might be acceptable.[50]

Gilroy rightly goes on to exemplify The Clash's 'White Riot', a classic example of punk's ethnicity/class crossover: 'Black men have got a lotta problems/But they don't mind throwing a brick/But white men have too much school/Where they teach you to be thick'.[51] On other occasions The Clash made equally provocative statements about punk's historical context: 'English Civil War' suggests that at least one white sector of the new English carnivalesque viewed itself as a form of resistant republicanism.[52] The republican parallel represents something of a mini-genre within punk, its most famous expression perhaps Elvis Costello's 'Oliver's Army'.[53] (Seventeenth-century Cromwellian republicanism, though, would probably have swept aside bordering nations, as David Hume recognised when he spoke in favour of monarchism in Britain but not in America.)[54] The Clash were certainly aware of the difference made to England by the immigrant context: their cover version of Junior Marvin's 'Police and Thieves' acknowledges the Jamaican presence in punk, their style a seemingly improbable fusion of garage rock and reggae.[55]

Even the Sex Pistols can be linked to postcolonial and post-British contexts beyond simply defacing flags and safety-pinning the monarch. During the band's late-'70s nascence, John Lydon (Johnny Rotten), the most eloquent as well as the angriest member, made frequent and lengthy pronouncements on the end of Britishness in the popular media. Gilroy quotes '[t]here's no such thing as patriotism any more . . . I'm not asking blacks to like us. That's irrelevant. It's just that we're doing something they'd want to do if they had the chance'.[56] Lydon often visited reggae clubs, and was listening to roots dub about ten years before a dub collection became *de rigeur* for a techno crowd full of ex-punks. When the Sex Pistols broke up, Lydon formed Public Image Limited with college friend Jah Wobble (John Wardle), given the ironic nickname Jah for his own interest in reggae.[57] Public Image Limited massively accentuated the bass guitar, recalling roots reggae, again connoting the postcolonial tactile; as Jah Wobble put it, 'nobody had listened to the bass guitar in white music before'.[58] Jah Wobble has gone on to work with some of the most popular artists associated with the rave and techno movement, including Andy Wetherall and Primal Scream; his label 30 Hertz, referring to a frequency so low that it can be *felt*, now features experimental music with a range of sub-British themes, including Celtic myth and the most Anglo-Israeli of English poets, William Blake. At the time of writing, his latest production connects the English and the postcolonial even more strongly, and is entitled 'English Roots Music'.[59]

Like Jah Wobble, many other ex-punks were quick to see the counter-cultural potential of dub-literate electronica; Cabaret

Voltaire's Richard Kirk helped put the Sheffield label Warp on the map in his reincarnation as Sweet Exorcist; Biting Tongues' Graham Massey, later of 808 State, was a spokesman for rave's ability to surpass the more solitary rebellions of punk.[60] In Manchester the Factory label, which had been known for the English restlessness of Joy Division and then New Order, later ran the Hacienda club, named after a Situationist slogan,[61] probably rave's most famous 'legitimate' club. After post-punk and during the darkest times for ethnic relations around 1981, the 'two-tone' movement recalled Jamaican ska and pointedly featured bands with black and white members who were aware of the history behind the cultural admixture. Two-tone positioned itself between commercial pop music and dub; The Specials' 'Ghost Town' (1981) captures the mood well, lamenting a loss of infrastructure causing the youth to turn in on themselves, then fading into haunting reggae brass, percussion and police sirens.[62]

The mid-1980s, though, saw a partial turn back to an indie rock, some of which would nevertheless cross over to form important links with club dance music. The label Creation, founded by Scottish entrepreneur Alan McGee, began by featuring bands like The Pastels, Jasmine Minks and The Jesus and Mary Chain (whose drummer would break off to form Primal Scream). While one stream of Creation artists pioneered a rock-dance fusion which drew on both black and white musical traditions (perhaps best exemplified by Primal Scream's classic *Screamadelica*, 1991, drawing on soul and gospel), another stream took an increasingly retro-British position. Creation became properly famous in the mid-'90s with the rise of a particularly persistent strain of indie pop eventually known as 'Britpop', exemplified by Oasis. As the name suggests, Britpop packaged the north for the south (unlike the Hacienda, which was resolutely northern) in a '60s British retro style amnesic about punk's anti-Powellite anger. It was an almost exclusively white movement.[63] The movement is sometimes popularly associated with the Union Jack-wearing Spice Girls (one of whom was later suspiciously gifted an ambassadorial position by the Blair government) but better fits bands like Oasis, Blur and Elastica, all of whose images involve self-reliant opportunism and a posturingly 'lazy' disinterest in society. On the back of Oasis's success, McGee became a New Labour donor: both the band and the boss made a well-publicised visit to the Blairs' home in July 1997, by which time the government had already sealed McGee's status as state broker of youth culture by giving him a seat on the Creative Industries Task Force quango.[64] Being groomed as one of the 'ambassadors for the new Britain', the Scot McGee was taking on a familiarly British mantle belonging in the pages of a Linda Colley history.[65] Getting used to success down south, and missing Rangers' home games at Ibrox – perhaps the only place in Britain where mass loyalist hatred is still legal – McGee himself was often portrayed as a latter-day canny Protestant adventurer come south to seek his fortune. Coming to London, this lad o' pairts 'had only £40 in his pocket and a single O-Level', the BBC reminisced when McGee quit Creation in 1999.[66] (Students in Scotland do not sit 'O-Levels'.)

But by the end of the 1990s, various axes of discontent had again risen up against retro-British state-sponsored Britpop as they had against Powellism in the mid-'70s. This time, the discontents co-incided with the common feeling that 'British' no longer worked as a term. Asian Dub Foundation exemplified a counter-British and historically aware fusion of rock, dance and reggae styles also recalling the sentiment of punk. The statement in The Clash's 'London Calling' that 'phoney Beatlemania has bitten the dust' finds a 2000 echo in ADF's anti-Cool Britannia 'Real Great Britain': 'Blairful of Thatcher/stuck on the 45/The suits have changed/But the old ties survive/New Britannia Cool/Who are you trying to fool?/Behind your fashion-tashion I see nothing at all ... /So will the real, the real Great Britain step forward/This is the national Identity Parade/Shoe gazer nation forever looking backwards/Time to reject the sixties charade'.[67] This imperative to 'step forward' should be taken as a post-British demand to re-speak democracy, a demand of the kind described by Tom Nairn (in Scotland) and Anthony Barnett and Will Hutton (in England). (Here though, 'the 45' of course refers not to the 1745 Jacobite uprising but to the song 'Brimful of Asha' by Britannia-friendly band Cornershop).[68] The 'community' of ADF's *Community Music* was now a powerful English underground; ig-noring the official channels of Britpop, many of its participants had met in the English countryside during the rave movement, in un-predictable ways that had less in common with pre-spun Millennial London than the chaos of carnival.

The 808 State

The rave movement, largely rising from the English countryside, mobilised huge numbers around the turn of the 1990s. Its first major summer was 1987; it peaked around 1989, then enjoyed a second wave before shading off into other forms which continued to exert an influence throughout the '90s. Its stress on percussion and bass survived from the immigrant culture of reggae; repetitive percussion takes precedence over any sequential narrative progression of melodic verses and choruses. The tactile was reflected in techno in bass frequencies often lowered as far as possible, and given a new twist by a generation of analogue equipment recalling that used by '70s dub producers. The Roland TB303 gave acid house its characteristic analogue stabs, and allowed for an infinite number of variations controlled by hand; in analogue, unlike digital, there are no discrete and mediated units of sound – each frequency is specific and contingent. Guru producer Aphex Twin has thus spoken of exploring 'in-between' notes, notes never finally corresponding to digital intervals.[69] In the performance of the DJ – brought to England via the Caribbean/black American context – hands-on vinyl mixing and scratching have accentuated the significance of touch in cultural production. Analogue equipment was cheap enough for many young people to afford; comparisons of the Roland 303, 808 and 909 series to punk's second-hand guitar were justifiably common in the music press. Like punk, rave's DIY music was hostile to official forms of British cultural unity; the number who actively dropped out of the traditional channels of production and consumption was even larger. When a Manchester techno band took the name '808 State', the word 'state' sounded not only like a pun on the vaguely druggy 'state of mind' but also a serious indication of new and unpredictable forms of determination not connected to the state already there (somewhat redolent of the Enlightenment 'Republic of Letters'). Rave's inheritance of postcolonial touch shows how, even in the individuating and democratically problematic period of the late 1980s, a challenge was arising from 'below' and refusing meanings which had undergone official categorisation, whether ideological or digital. The only spin doctors some now listened to were DJs.

Dance music culture corresponds to post-British tendencies in literature because it rises from personal relationships with as against the remote universalising authority of English Literature. Throughout the 1990s, the tactile aesthetics of producers, mixers, distributors, DJs and dancers increasingly leaned into and redefined one another. The cycle of production went from 'producer' to remixer to DJ to crowd participation and back to 'producer', and largely gave up specifying a single product, or separating creator and consumer. As Simon Reynolds puts it, even the dancers are 'a cog in a collective "desiring machine"'.[70] Discussions of this form of culture require, as Reynolds points out, a break with 'the dominant English Lit and socialist realist paradigms' used to describe culture as a set of bounded narratives produced by a known *auteur* for limited audiences.[71] Rave is thus a key example of the splitting of Britain into 'two societies: the traditional leisure culture of alcohol and entertainment (spectator sports, TV) versus the more participatory, effusive culture of all-night dancing and Ecstasy'.[72] As I have suggested, the newer half of this divide is not really British at all: it relies on a communications network which bypasses British institutions and fits onto a very English tradition of occupying the land at ground level. Outdoor raves were events at which black and white youth mixed, perhaps for the first time (*contra* the 'nightclub' scenario in which black males were liable to be hailed as bouncers rather than cultural producers).[73] Also present were travellers of various kinds, including the 'tribes' who made the illegal free rave their mission in life,[74] as well as activists and people from the local area. Travellers' groups who often viewed themselves as 'indigenous Englanders' (such as the Dongas) met middle-class suburban kids in an English national dialectic.[75] Events relied on information networks largely unrelated to mass media, and on an economics only rarely driven by profit. Youth disillusionment with politics is thus typically overstated: rather, there was a turn away from party politics in its British form and towards a post-British politics of place.

So while Sarah Thornton's account of 'subcultural capital' in her *Club Cultures* is useful in that it offers a way of understanding how subcultures reorganise themselves to avoid entanglement of their terms in the media ('acid house' is a case in point), it nevertheless makes a mistake in treating subcultural capital in the same way as ordinary financial capital, as a market with a measurable value. Her study overestimates the extent to which rave represented a single 'industry' with measurable 'attendance' and figures for consumption. It also suggests, against the evidence, that white producers stole Jamaican culture and gave it an 'orientalist' spin.[76] It conflates rave, usually free of charge, involving highly unpredictable and post-British mixes of people, outdoors and with no *door*, far less a door policy, with the more general club culture into which some of it inevitably merged. Rave belonged outside the official feast: '[p]aying to go to a club or licensed party was classed as selling out, buying into the system. If it wasn't free it wasn't good'.[77] Ironically also, although Thornton scrupulously dismisses Theodor Adorno's notorious description of popular music as brain-numbing and repetitious, she nevertheless still describes the music as 'escape' – 'the constant pulse of the bass blocks thoughts'.[78]

The idea that subculture is an 'escape' from the social, rather than a constituent part of it, is a familiarly high-British reading. But it was below and beyond this level that rave communities operated. Running counter to the Anglo-Britishing of pre-1997 governments as well as the Cool Britannia of post-1997 governments, the 'ambient' wing of techno was presaged by '70s mystic-hippy English figures like Brian Eno, Pink Floyd and Mike Oldfield; the movement as a whole was strongly drawn to the English (or Welsh) countryside rather than to the Anglo-British rural imagined community painted by the Countryside Rally of 10 July 1997. So much attention has been paid to the countryside lobbies' increasingly corporate version of rural England, at times with help from the New Labour government,[79] that what was happening in the countryside itself has often been overlooked as a constituent of Englishness.[80] The countryside was also characterised by a decreasing agricultural sector replaced by speculative purchase of land by city-dwellers, making for a highly unstable 'tradition'.[81] The rave movement on the other hand was frequently fascinated by sites of specifically English historical importance such as Stonehenge; by the 1990s, this interest was overlapping with a festival circuit taking in Glastonbury and WOMAD.[82]

The reaction of John Major's administration to this failure of governance in the Anglo-British heartland was Sections 61 to 65 of the 1994 Criminal Justice and Public Order Act.[83] The Act is frequently forgotten by Scottish historians in favour of the easier target of the Poll Tax, but is perhaps of even greater significance to the crisis of Britain. Unlike previous Criminal Justice Acts, the 1994 Act dedicates three sections specifically to rave (described, *pace* Adorno, as a music 'wholly or predominantly characterised by the emission of a succession of repetitive beats').[84] Whereas over one hundred people were required to actually constitute a rave, the number who could be suspected of planning to hold a rave was defined as 'two or more persons'.[85] This closely corresponds to the distinction above between the individual nature of British nationality and the communitarian-personal nature of sub-British nationality: even reaching beyond the borders of the self was now a crime. Tellingly, the Act recycled policing techniques first used in the miners' strike, on this new form of combination.[86] As punk had presaged, this was in a sense a new civil war, being contested for the land of England. In the same year, the campaign This Land Is Ours, setting out from the land the Diggers had seized in 1649, attempted a push to take land back from corporate-British interests.[87] The movement was broadbased, and its recommendations have been accepted as policy by the

Green Party –[88] a party represented in the devolved Scottish Parliament but not in a British Parliament six times its size. In his account of the campaign, George Monbiot mentions the Highland Clearances; this is particularly telling, since both moments are part of the same imperial process, addressing a Britain newly culturally established in the 1810s, and looking increasingly shaky in the 1990s. As Monbiot realises, this process is not merely a national phenomenon but is part of an economics which reaches way beyond Britain and involves global ethical questions.

Ironically, the 1994 Criminal Justice Act was followed a year later by the white paper *Rural England: A Nation Committed to a Living Countryside*, which linked England, nationhood and the apparent renaissance of the country. The White Paper talked of the 'enduring character of England' – a speculative re-drawing of tradition based on an interwoven set of myths Patrick Wright has called 'Deep England'.[89] From World War I, a generalised version of the countryside sat uncomfortably with more unapologetically English writers like Wordsworth and Morris, who had been more local, communitarian and inclusive.[90] The green–pub–church English village dredged up by Major's mid-'90s sub-Baldwinesque nonsense had already become unfamiliar early in the century, due to the clash between ideas of urbanisation as contamination and economic pressures from above, such as land development.[91] John Major's leaden repetition of the cricketing image in 'long shadows on county grounds, warm beer, [and] invincible green suburbs' was *already* desperately out of date: 'manna from heaven for the satirists'.[92] Early in the century, national culture had already been replaced by what Stephen Haseler has described as 'theme-park Englishness' (and Haseler notes that cricket, guardian of English gamesmanship in the expanding public schools, it is not much of a team game, unlike, say, football).[93] Jeremy Paxman has also arrestingly illustrated how cricket was until 1914 a close metaphor for war on behalf of an Anglo-Britain increasingly presented as one part of its countryside.[94]

Contrary to what was actually happening there, the English 'countryside' in official Anglo-British discourse had become seen as needing to be 'defended' from incomers, and by implication, immigrants, including gypsies and old-style Irish travellers, who, especially after 1994, could all be arrested 'on suspicion'.[95] Defenders of this anxious ethnicity, the Countryside Alliance denied national experience for an undying, ahistorical countryside, any criticism of which became *de facto* unpatriotic.[96] Major's speech on 'New Age Travellers'

at the Tory Conference in 1992 – 'not in this age, not in any age' –
is a perfect example of this disavowal of historical change (how can
policies reach 'any age'?). The quasi-countryside was, as Ian Baucom puts it, 'a defensive response to the global project of the British
empire',[97] while England struggled via carnival and cultural change
to occupy and rejuvenate its own locales. England was taken back
on a communitarian plane, taking back – as Salman Rushdie has
described it in relation to reaction to the immigration legislation of
1981 – 'a contemporary space of English belonging'.[98]

In this reading, rather than an invasion 'into' Englishness, the
riot is part of England's democratic nature, in somewhat Orwellian
terms. (The underside of this is of course is the football hooligan; perhaps much more significant to post-Britishness than the occasional
St George's cross is the fact that sometime between the devolution
referendums the BBC managed to stop describing the England expe-
ditionary force as 'British'. Britain has no national soccer team.) The
creators of the defensive Anglo-British countryside were increasingly troubled by a rural rave culture which seemed to '"belong"
in the city' away from the early-twentieth-century Anglo-British
'here'.[99] The 1994 Criminal Justice Act and its reactionary 'rural'
contexts pointed up an English battle for a specific kind of community, hamstrung by a British concentration on privatisation and
property. The British reaction was ludicrous: in terminology strikingly recalling John Macmurray, the 1994 Act gave police the 'power
to stop persons from proceeding'.[100] As Raphael Samuel pointed out
(in 1989), there had been a major shift away from the large music
concerts of the 1970s: under 1979–97 administrations, crowds were
gradually illegalised.[101] Since the conflict between the subjective
and the personal came from the over-adjustment of influential Enlightenment thinkers like Adam Smith and David Hume, it is telling
that one of the most popular descriptions of rave culture disruptive
to English Literature's sensibilities should issue from the city which
had taken upon itself so much of the burden of civility – Edinburgh.

Imperial Bad Trips

Partly as a result of a voice which disobeys previous conventions of
'Scots' (but is heir to a legacy travelling through Edwin Morgan, Ian
Hamilton Finlay and James Kelman), partly because of cursory readings, and partly because of bad journalese about a 'chemical generation', Irvine Welsh's post-British carnivalesque has been limited to a

sarcastic aside by much of the Scottish literary elite. This is unfortunate, not to say symptomatic, since his first three books, issuing from the four years immediately prior to the devolution referendum, tie together postcolonial and local themes in a fairly determined move away from remaining Greater British culture and its cultural backbone, English Literature. This is not to argue for the author in terms of the old Eng. Lit. paradigms of defending individual reputations or securing canonical places, but to note that in this popular and often-exported fiction, all of the youth movements discussed above are connected from a perspective of a post-imperial cultural tradition.

The characters of *Trainspotting* (1993) frequently refer to punk's earliest moments, including New York Dolls, Frank Zappa and Iggy Pop (whose music was re-introduced to a new generation, albeit in sanitised form, via the book's film). Various subcultures, of which the drug subculture is only one, draw these characters towards rave, which speaks to their disaffection as punk had. In *Marabou Stork Nightmares* (1996), rave takes up much of the burden of community as such, in the ruins of a British society with no society. Its carnivalesque is nevertheless also frequently horrific – the novel centres on a multiple rape confused by a bad acid trip, and connects gender, colonialism and British loyalism. The book is dedicated being to 'all the punters and posses I've met up with last year at Pure, Yip Yap, Slam, Sativa, Back to Basics, The Ministry, Sabresonic, Desert Storm, The Mazzo, The Roxy, Sunday Social and Rez'.[102] Its next page links two epigrams, the first describing Hume's encouragement of the colonial export of a universal ethics, and the second from Major's extraordinary anti-traveller speech, 'We should condemn more and understand less'.[103] Where Hume and Smith tried to put Scotland in the forefront of a British empire, the confusedly Anglo-British government looked adrift in trying to resurrect ideals of civility in the notoriously nebulous 'back to basics' (which, plus a dose of sarcasm, became the name of the club acknowledged in the preface).[104]

Trainspotting reverses the universalisation of English Literature proceeding from Edinburgh: here Edinburgh is mercilessly localised, its stage housing estates carefully hidden from the 'historical' city of the New Town and the Royal Mile. One example of this localising reversal comes when two of the main characters come across transatlantic opportunity – echoing American colonial trade – in the form of Canadian tourists on a London-bound train. Departing Edinburgh, they perceive their journey as one between important metropolitan centres – 'capital fuckin cities n that'[105] – but are provincialised by the tourists, who fail to understand their Edinburgh accents:

> –Whair's it yis come fae then?
>
> –Sorry, I can't really understand you...These foreign cunts've goat trouble wi the Queen's fuckin English, ken. Ye huv tae speak louder, slower, n likesay mair posh, fir the cunts tae understand ye.[106]

The ironic misjudgement of Edinburgh dialect as 'Queen's fuckin English' flattens the British adaptations the city underwent for access to American colonial riches. Despite attempts to make Edinburgh 'sound aw fuckin posh', the tourists are unconvinced, leaving the protagonists adrift from the Anglophone opportunity which the high-British scenery seems to promise. (And even some of this scenery has duly eroded: the name 'North British Hotel' for example has become 'The Balmoral'.) 'The First Day of the Edinburgh Festival', similarly, takes place away from the 'official feast', down a toilet bowl in a peripheral council estate betting shop trying to recover opium suppositories. The joke here is not so much the toilet humour as that the other punters fail to notice how civil society has collapsed to a life of waiting in the shells of housing schemes. Leaving the toilet, and suspected of ruining the society-less society, Renton is faced with 'Muirhoose's Charles Bronson', emasculated protector of an imaginary Atlantic-imperial home.[107] The book's characters are of two kinds, one identifying itself as local-Irish-Catholic and the other as British unionist-loyalist, a division ignored by the film yet central to the rivalry between the brothers Renton and Billy (the latter a common nickname for the old-fashioned loyalist). This division echoes colonial identity, and is frequently used to contrast British and post-British cultural tendencies. When the Irish-descended Spud and his half-black uncle go for a pint in an ill-chosen pub, they find it full of orangemen; as with any imperialist society, violence is built into the surveillance which precedes contact, in a Fanonian exchange of looks: 'Rents's auld boy's a soap-dodger [Glaswegian] and a Paris Bun [hun], but he's no really intae this sortay gig any mair ... Different story wi Billy though. He's intae aw this Orange stuff, this sortay Jambo [Heart of Midlothian]/Hun gig. He gies us a nod fae the bar, but ah don't think the cat really digs us, but'.[108]

Billy joins the British army and dies on service in Northern Ireland; at the funeral the loyalist side of the family express resentment at his brother's junky connections, connoting a laziness read via a Protestant work ethic closely intertwined with colonial opportunity.

However, *Trainspotting* has become more familiar from the Danny Boyle film version which followed three years later, which connotes Cool Britannia against the plot of the book. In streamlining the story, the film symptomatically cut out most of those sections of the book critical of Britishness. The insights about Scottish loyalism's centrality to empire, for example, are replaced by the crude 'colonised by wankers' speech put into the mouth of Ewan McGregor in the wrong scene, loudly reverting to the nation as 'race' and feeding into New Right English images of Scottish nationalism as 'tribal'. Boyle's *Trainspotting* fitted well into a seemingly endless series of Cool Britannic films showing a retro-leaning British film revival stretching from *Shallow Grave* (1994) through *Brassed Off!* (1997) to *Purely Belter* (2000), *Greenfingers* (2001) and *Blow Dry* (2001).[109] These films recount Alan McGee-type stories of modern lads o' pairts overcoming their own broken communities, usually in the north, to excel on an elite British stage. Thus Billy Elliot in the film of the same name (2000) 'escapes' a community destroyed by the miners' strike, and the embarrassingly provincial attitudes of his family, to dance for the Royal Ballet in a performance only his father can afford to attend.[110] In the film *Trainspotting*, in contrast to the character's highly ambivalent attitude in the book, Renton uses his canniness to leave Leith, ending the film walking alone in the sunshine of London. The connections between colonialism, sectarianism, free trade and unionism, carefully linked in the book, are thus equally carefully excised from the film. Where Renton fits comfortably into Boyle's Cool London, the book's 'London Crawling' section, echoing the song by The Clash noted above, sees the narrator describe his habitual defensiveness on arriving in the state capital.[111] Where the book is in the third person across a number of narrators, the film centres on the individual figure of Renton to the extent that he sometimes has to refer to himself in third person. The other characters do not speak. (In the follow-up, *Porno* (2002), one appropriately has a history of Leith rejected by a posh Edinburgh publishing firm who criticise the English of his 'badly written celebration of yob culture'; the publisher's address is '13 Kailyard Grove').[112] Ewan McGregor, also the plummy younger Alec Guinness in the second series of *Star Wars*, ends Boyle's 1997 film *A Life Less Ordinary* with one of Oasis's most Britpop songs, 'Round Our Way'.[113] This marks the same 'optimistic' note of escape as *Trainspotting*'s entirely interpolated 'choose life' scene.

Marabou Stork Nightmares has an even more explicitly post-British content, linking and parodying a working-class Protestant colonial identity and the colonialism which gave it a worldwide expression. Using the originally English stage of rave, Scotland's colonial aspiration here undergoes ridicule as exaggeratedly upper-class British dialects are piled onto native Scottish ones within the narrator's damaged memory. Working-class loyalist Scots made good front-line imperial infantry, an equation made explicit by Billy's death in *Trainspotting*; they still make good foot soldiers in territory battles as soccer casuals, not only with McGee's Rangers but also with Heart of Midlothian, the Edinburgh club which shares its name with a novel by Walter Scott. The 'Jambola Park PLC' of *Marabou Stork Nightmares* (the etymology is Hearts – Jam Tarts – Jambo – Jambola) functions something like the 'inner station' in Joseph Conrad's *Heart of Darkness*: it is both a loyalist-colonial safe haven and a placeless place where language is standardised away from speech until it breaks down into a nonsensical parody of 'good English' – 'absolutely scrumptious apple crumble absolutely drenched in whipped cream'.[114] The rape in which the narrator has participated becomes mixed up with a nightmare of colonial exploration and hunting, a confusion provoked by a dubious refereeing decision and an LSD experience which creates a slippage of a single letter – the 'Z' of the rave 'Rezurrection' becoming the 'Z' of 'Zero Tolerance', a campaign against domestic violence. We have seen how the analogue ethic of rave encourages slippages by refusing division into discrete units of meaning, and that in England this joined carnivalesque as an unmanageable folk culture. The LSD/analogue connection is also made explicit by a technique in the film version of Welsh's *The Acid House* (1998) which describes the progress of another fateful trip by using vinyl scratching to capture the analogue sense of things slipping out of place.[115] As I have suggested, an 'analogue' chain of contingent meaning can come to signify localism in societies fighting against images of themselves. As well as Edwin Morgan's more overt experiments with 'video scratching', since the mid-1970s Ian Hamilton Finlay has often taken French Enlightenment images and words and forced them to undergo various 'displacements' of context, dropping slabs of marble civility on the borders of the garden and the wild.[116]

The council estates of Edinburgh are removed from Edinburgh's town centre as 'the hill' of Lovelace's *The Dragon Can't Dance* is removed from Port of Spain – albeit at a greater distance, away from all urban infrastructure and from the paths of wandering tourists. Like *The Dragon Can't Dance*, the Edinburgh carnival of *Marabou Stork Nightmares* also ends in a miscarriage of justice and in-fighting;

unlike the official feast/Festival, the carnival does not guarantee a settled conclusion, or even a good time. It is difficult to imagine anything *less* of a celebration than the central rape scene of *Marabou Stork Nightmares*. And although proposals have doubtless crossed the desks of numerous media executives, the novel is unlikely to be filmed, at least with any sense of integrity. (In this sense it preserves its 'subcultural capital', in the sense of Sarah Thornton's Bourdieu). The novel's sexual violence belongs to the phase of the novel *before* the rave which provides terrible insights into past behaviour by loosening gender roles: dance music culture was a movement which rejected the culture of bagging off in pairs, as in High Street nightclubs' heterosexist fit with the nuclear family. As Reynolds powerfully argues, the 1987–9 rave movement revolutionised the aims of youth culture precisely by *not* seeing sex as one of its 'transgressive' functions (anticipated by John *Lydon's bon mot* 'sex is *boring*').[117] Rather, it brought together a huge number of undifferentiated other people (Macmurray's 'eternal Thou'), in an asexual intimacy; Reynolds frequently points out that ecstasy incites both pleasure in touch and disinterest in penetrative sex. The rave scene even loosened gender programming, as Maria Pini has interestingly shown.[118] Moreover, the Detroit house of 1987–9 which kick-started the British rave movement, pioneered by producers like Derrick May and Jeff Mills, was in effect a re-reading of the often gay and often black New York culture of disco, which again set analogue voice and effects on a beat and bass line loud enough to be *felt*. Although house music and the recreational use of ecstasy were both American inventions, they were only put together in the English context.[119]

So from its earliest appreciation of black producers, the key moments of the 'British' rave movement involved extraordinary cross-influences of black and white, straight and gay, 'feminine' disco and 'masculine' Eurobeat. Just before the fateful acid experience which will send him to the hospital, *Marabou Stork Nightmares*'s Roy encounters his gay brother Bernard as if for the first time, confesses to having 'allowed [himself] to feel', and is struck by the amount of hatred and violence he has transmitted through his British loyalist upbringing. For Roy the connection is tactile and tangible but inexpressible:

> . . . what's wrong, Roy? What is it? Yir talkin aboot love, eh?
>
> I thought bitterly about that, –Nah, no love, the reverse ay that, I smiled, then I gave him a tight hug. He reciprocated.[120]

Set in Edinburgh, the tactile, working across black and white culture and undermining the heterosexism which had replaced society with 'individual families', also takes apart the Scottish Enlightenment's conception of Britishness and its later incarnation, Cool Britannia. This environment resembles rave not only in that it has rave in its story but also in that it is post-English Literature, using local/national dialects which neither simply repeat the standard dialect nor follow an artificial language to answer it. As I will argue in the next chapter, if put into historical context, this post-Eng. Lit. emphasis on a previously impossible writing is a key process of a need to find an unBritish voice, no longer centred, as was 1920s and '30s nationalism, on ethnicised images of the nation. One key English response was centred on a rave/festival circuit with long roots in the reclamation of the countryside; the Scottish dance music scene was slower, and too easily slipped into brutal 'hardcore' and drug bingeing (as suggested by the use of LSD).[121] On the other hand, as the idea of a rave-influenced novel itself shows, Scotland has been intimately concerned with questions of language and representation as they rise up through local communities. The dialect novel, as I will suggest in the next chapter in the context of writing and agency, is not only a *response* to a new political confidence but also a *cause* of changing ideas of representation.

Notes

1. See Donald W. Livingstone, 'Hume, English Barbarism and American Independence', in Richard B. Sher and Jeffrey R. Smitten (eds), *Scotland and America in the Age of Enlightenment* (Edinburgh: Edinburgh University Press, 1990), pp. 133–47: 136.
2. Hugh MacDiarmid, *Letters*, ed. Alan Bold (London: Hamish Hamilton, 1984), p. 687.
3. Andrew Murray Scott, 'Mr. MacDairmid and Mr. Trocchi: Where Extremists Meet', *Chapman*, 83, 1996, pp. 36–9; Edwin Morgan, 'The Fold-in Conference', *Edinburgh Review*, 97, spring 1997, pp. 94–102.
4. Zig Layton-Henry, *The Politics of Immigration: Immigration, 'Race' and 'Race' Relations in Post-War Britain* (Oxford: Blackwell, 1992), pp. 13, 71–7; Lloyd Bradley, *This is Reggae Music* (New York: Grove, 2000), pp. 111–32.
5. Bradley, *This is Reggae Music*, p. 113; see also Mike Phillips and Trevor Phillips, *Windrush: The irresistible rise of multi-racial Britain* (London: HarperCollins, 1998); Keith Robbins, *Great Britain: Identities, Institutions, and the Idea of Britishness* (Harlow: Longman, 1998), p. 326; Yasmin Alibhai-Brown, *Who Do We Think We Are?: Imagining the New Britain* (London: Penguin, 2001), p. 86; Layton-Henry, *The Politics of Immigration*, pp. 36–9.
6. Anthony Barnett, *This Time: Our Constitutional Revolution* (London: Vintage, 1997), pp. 43–6; Alibhai-Brown, *Who Do We Think We Are?*, p. 72; Zig Layton-Henry, *The Politics of Immigration in Britain*, pp. 180–214.

7. Layton-Henry, *The Politics of Immigration*, pp. 195–8; David Marquand, 'The Twilight of the British State? Henry Dubb versus Sceptered Awe', *Political Quarterly*, 64, 1993, pp. 210–21.
8. Alibhai-Brown, *Who Do We Think We Are?*, pp. 78–9.
9. Richard Gott, 'Little Englanders', in Raphael Samuel (ed.), *Patriotism: The Making and Unmaking of British National Identity, Vol. 1: History and Politics* (London: Routledge, 1989), pp. 90–102: 95.
10. Enoch Powell, ed. Richard Ritchie, *A Nation or No Nation?: Six Years in British Politics* (London: Batsford, 1978), pp. 160–74; cf. Paul Foot, *The Rise of Enoch Powell: An examination of Enoch Powell's attitude to immigration and race* (London: Cornmarket, 1969), pp. 40–2.
11. *Birmingham Post*, 'Speech that's raising a storm', 22 April 1968.
12. Tom Nairn, *The Break-up of Britain: Crisis and Neo-nationalism* (London: NLB, 1977), p. 275; Zig-Henry, *The Politics of Immigration*, p. 82.
13. Quoted in Paul Gilroy, *There Ain't No Black in the Union Jack* (London: Routledge, 1987), p. 43.
14. Gilroy, *There Ain't No Black*, p. 46.
15. Christopher Harvie, *Scotland and Nationalism: Scottish Society and Politics 1707–1994* (London: Routledge, 1994), pp. 183, 209.
16. Derek Jarman (dir), *The Last of England* (UK: Channel Four Films, 1987); George McKay, *Senseless Acts of Beauty: Cultures of Resistance Since the Sixties* (London: Verso, 1996), pp. 1–9.
17. See David McCrone, 'Scotland and the Union: Changing Identities in the British State', in David Morley and Kevin Robins (eds), *British Cultural Studies: Geography, Nationality, and Identity* (Oxford: Oxford University Press, 2001), pp. 97–108: 100.
18. Layton-Henry, *The Politics of Immigration*, p. 90.
19. Gordon Brown, 'Building a Greater Britain', *The Guardian*, 12 November 1998.
20. See Barnett, *This Time*, pp. 43–5.
21. 'Man Turns Into Scotsman', *Monty Python's Flying Circus*, episode 7, November 1969, BBC TV.
22. Arthur Aughey, *Nationalism, Devolution, and the Challenge to the United Kingdom State* (London: Pluto, 2001), p. 39.
23. Ibid. p. 49.
24. See, as an introduction, C. L. R. James, *Beyond a Boundary* (London: Serpent's Tail, 1994).
25. Alexander Grant and Keith Stringer, 'Introduction' to *Uniting the Kingdom? The Making of British Identity* (London: Routledge, 1995), pp. 3–11: 4.
26. Cf. Robert Young, 'The Procrastinator', *Parallax*, 10, 1999, pp. 7–9.
27. Edward Said, 'Jane Austen and Empire', in Said, *Culture and Imperialism* (New York: Vintage, 1994), pp. 80–97.
28. Morley and Robins, 'Introduction' to *British Cultural Studies*, pp. 1–15: 3.
29. Mark Leonard, *Britain TM: Reviewing Our Identity* (London: Demos, 1997).
30. See Stephen Driver and Luke Martell, 'Blair and "Britishness"', in Morley and Robins (eds), *British Cultural Studies*, pp. 461–72: 464.

31. Ken Worpole, 'Cartels and Lotteries: Heritage and Cultural Policy in Britain', in Morley and Robins (eds), *British Cultural Studies*, pp. 235–48: 241.
32. Ibid. p. 243.
33. Ibid. p. 243.
34. Andrew Rawnsley, *Servants of the People: The Inside Story of New Labour* (London: Hamish Hamilton, 2000), p. 252.
35. Murray G. H. Pittock, *Celtic Identity and the British Image* (Manchester: Manchester University Press, 1999), p. 102.
36. http://bridge.anglia.ac.uk/~systimk/music/bonzos/Tracks/ Cool-B.Htmlx. Consulted 2002.
37. 'Nothing is sadder than trying too hard to be cool', *The Economist*, 14 March 1998.
38. Raphael Samuel, 'Introduction: Exciting to be English', in Samuel (ed.), *Patriotism, Vol. I: History and Politics*, pp. xviii–lxvii: xxxix, xliv–xlv, xxxiii, lv.
39. Cf. George McKay, *Senseless Acts of Beauty*, pp. 1–9.
40. Bradley, *This is Reggae Music*, p. 115.
41. Earl Lovelace, *The Dragon Can't Dance* (Harlow: Longman, 2000), p. 137.
42. Mikhail Bakhtin, selection from *Rabelais and his World*, in Pam Morris (ed.), *The Bakhtin Reader* (London: Arnold, 1994), p. 198.
43. Bakhtin, from *Rabelais and his World*, p. 199.
44. Raphael Samuel, 'Introduction: Little Platoons', in Samuel (ed.), *Patriotism, Vol. II: Minorities and Outsiders*, pp. ix–xxxix: xi; Roger Mitchell (dir), *Notting Hill* (USA: PolyGram, 1999).
45. See, for example, Sam Selvon, *The Lonely Londoners* (London: Longman, 1979).
46. Gilroy, *There Ain't No Black*, pp. 15–42, 114–52; George McKay, *Glastonbury: A Very English Fair* (London: Gollancz, 2000), pp. 6–14, 139–44.
47. Sex Pistols, 'God Save the Queen', on *God Save the Queen* (UK: Virgin, 1977); Derek Jarman and Christopher Hobbs (dirs), *Jubilee* (UK: Megalovision, 1978).
48. Gilroy, *There Ain't No Black*, pp. 72–113.
49. Dick Hebdige, *Subculture: The Meaning of Style* (London: Methuen, 1979).
50. Gilroy, *There Ain't No Black*, p. 123.
51. The Clash, 'White Riot', on *The Clash* (CBS, 1977).
52. The Clash, 'English Civil War', on *Give 'Em Enough Rope* (Epic, 1978).
53. Elvis Costello, 'Oliver's Army', on *Armed Forces* (Radar, 1979).
54. See Livingstone, 'Hume, English Barbarism and American Independence', pp. 136–40.
55. The Clash, 'Police and Thieves', on *The Clash* (EK, CBS, 1977).
56. Quoted in Gilroy, *There Ain't No Black*, pp. 124–5; the original interview is in *Rolling Stone* magazine, 20 October 1977.
57. see http://www.thefilthandthefury.co.uk/F&FODDERSTOMPF/ MEMBERS/wobble.html; also http://www.emusic.com/artist/10559/ 10559278.html. Consulted 2002.
58. Quoted in www.towerhamlets.gov.uk/templates/news/details.cf.m? newsid=712. Consulted 2002.

59. http://www.30hertzrecords.com/. Consulted 2003.
60. Simon Reynolds, *Generation Ecstasy: Into the World of Techno and Rave Culture* (New York: Routledge, 1999), pp. 28, 102.
61. Ibid. p. 93.
62. The Specials, 'Ghost Town' (2-Tone, 1981).
63. See David Hesmondshalgh, 'British Popular Music and National Identity', in Morley and Robins (eds), *British Cultural Studies*, pp. 273–86.
64. 'Stars out again at Downing Street', *The Times*, 31 July 1997.
65. Worpole, 'Cartels and Lotteries', p. 236.
66. BBC News online, 26 November 1999, http://news.bbc.co.uk/2/hi/uk/537881.stm. Consulted 2002.
67. The Clash, 'London Calling', on *London Calling* (Epic, 1979); Asian Dub Foundation, 'Real Great Britain', on *Community Music* (London Records, 2000).
68. Cornershop, 'Brimful of Asha', on *When I Was Born For The 7th Time* (UK: Wiiija, 1997).
69. Reynolds, 'Generation Ecstasy', p. 198.
70. Ibid. p. 5.
71. Ibid. p. 9.
72. Ibid. p. 237.
73. Cf. Mary Anna Wright, 'The Great British Ecstasy Revolution', in George McKay (ed.), *DIY Culture: Party and Protest in Nineties Britain* (London: Verso, 1998), pp. 228–42: 232.
74. Reynolds, 'Generation Ecstasy', pp. 163–78.
75. Sibley, 'The Control of Space: Travellers, Youth, and Drug Cultures', in Morley and Robins (eds), *British Cultural Studies*, pp. 417–30: 420; cf. McKay, *Senseless Acts of Beauty*, pp. 145–8.
76. Sarah Thornton, *Club Cultures: Music, Media, and Subcultural Capital* (Cambridge: Polity, 1995), p. 105.
77. Wright, 'The Great British Ecstasy Revolution', p. 237; cf. Hakim Bey, *The Temporary Autonomous Zone: Ontological Anarchy, Poetic Terrorism* (New York: Autonomedia, 1991), p. 106.
78. Thornton, *Club Cultures*, p. 60.
79. George Monbiot, *Captive State* (London: Pan, 2001), pp. 225–51.
80. Alun Hawkins, 'Rurality and Urban Identity', in Morley and Robins (eds), *British Cultural Studies*, pp. 145–56: 145.
81. Cf. Hawkins, 'Rurality and Urban Identity', p. 146.
82. Reynolds, 'Generation Ecstasy', p. 164; cf. George McKay, *Glastonbury*.
83. Criminal Justice and Public Order Act 1994. Online version: www.hmso.gov.uk/acts.htm#acts. Consulted 2002.
84. Criminal Justice and Public Order Act, 63.1.b.
85. Criminal Justice and Public Order Act, 63.1, 63.2.a.
86. Sibley, 'The Control of Space', p. 426.
87. George Monbiot, 'Reclaim the fields and country lanes!: The Land Is Ours campaign', in McKay (ed.), *DIY Culture*, pp. 174–86: 174.
88. Monbiot, 'Reclaim the fields and country lanes!', p. 174.

89. White Paper quoted in Hawkins, 'Rurality and Urban Identity', p. 148; see Patrick Wright, *On Living in an Old Country* (London: Verso, 1995).
90. Hawkins, 'Rurality and Urban Identity', p. 149; cf. Ian Baucom, *Out of Place: Englishness, Empire, and the Locations of Identity* (Princeton: Princeton University Press, 1999), pp. 3–83.
91. Hawkins, 'Rurality and Urban Identity', pp. 151–2.
92. Jeremy Paxman, *The English* (London: Penguin, 1999), p. 143; Major quoted at http://news.bbc.co.uk/2/hi/uk/1701843.stm. Consulted 2002.
93. Stephen Haseler, *The English Tribe: Identity, Nation and Europe* (London: Macmillan, 1996), pp. 3, 56–9.
94. Paxman, *The English*, pp. 194–206.
95. Raphael Samuel, 'Introduction: Little Platoons', in Samuel (ed.), *Patriotism, Vol. II: Minorities and Outsiders*, pp. ix–xxxix: ix–x; on similar demonisation of Irish, p. xiii, and Welsh, p. xxiv.
96. Hawkins, 'Rurality and Urban Identity', p. 154.
97. Baucom, *Out of Place*, p. 39.
98. Quoted in ibid. p. 39.
99. Sibley, 'The Control of Space', p. 421.
100. Criminal Justice and Public Order Act, 65.
101. Samuel, 'Introduction: Little Platoons', pp. xxiii–xxxiii.
102. Irvine Welsh, *Marabou Stork Nightmares* (London: Vintage, 1996).
103. Ibid.
104. Cf. Will Hutton, *The State We're In* (London: Vintage, 1996), p. 323.
105. Welsh, *Trainspotting* (London: Minerva, 1994), p. 113; the word 'cunt' rarely has a gender bias in Scottish English.
106. Ibid. pp. 114–15.
107. Ibid. p. 24.
108. Ibid. p. 127.
109. Danny Boyle (dir), *Shallow Grave* (UK: Channel Four Films, Figment Films, PolyGram, Glasgow Film Fund, 1994); Mark Herman (dir), *Brassed Off!* (UK: Prominent Features and Channel Four Films, 1997); Mark Herman (dir), *Purely Belter* (UK: Film Four, 2000); Joel Hershman (dir), *Greenfingers* (UK: Boneyard Entertainment, Xingu Films, Travis Swords Productions, Fireworks Pictures, 2001); Paddy Breathnach (dir), *Blow Dry* (UK: Mirage Enterprises, West Eleven Productions, IMF Productions, Intermedia Films, Miramax, 2000).
110. Stephen Daldry (dir), *Billy Elliot* (UK: Working Title Films, 2000).
111. Welsh, *Trainspotting*, pp. 227–39.
112. Irvine Welsh, *Porno* (London: Jonathan Cape, 2002), pp. 377–81: 381.
113. Danny Boyle (dir), *A Life Less Ordinary* (Twentieth Century Fox, 1997).
114. Welsh, *Marabou Stork Nightmares*, p. 37.
115. Paul McGuigan (dir), *The Acid House* (UK: Picture Palace North and Umbrella, 1999).
116. Edwin Morgan, *Emergent Poems* (Stuttgart: Harsjörg Meyer, 1967); see, for example, Ian Hamilton Finlay, with Ron Costley and Stephen Bann, *Heroic Emblems* (Vermont: Z Press, 1977).

117. Reynolds, *Generation Ecstasy*, pp. 63–7.
118. Maria Pini, *Club Cultures and Female Subjectivity: The Move From Home to House* (Basingstoke: Palgrave, 2001).
119. Cf. Wright, 'The Great British Ecstasy Revolution', p. 230.
120. Welsh, *Marabou Stork Nightmares*, p. 250.
121. Reynolds, *Generation Ecstasy*, pp. 288–91.

Chapter Six

Can the Sub-Briton Speak?

Iconic Texts

I have suggested above how in the pre-devolutionary years, post-British cultural movements can be associated with a re-negotiation of sovereignty which often bypassed party politics. This has been noticeable not only in a divergence of images of England but also in other parts of Britain whose political representation became even more dissociated from state government after 1979. In the 1997 British general election in Scotland, the traditionally unionist party, the Conservative and Unionist Party then in government, returned no MPs at all; New Labour, largely thanks to the late John Smith, had to promise a referendum on devolution, about which the incumbent Prime Minister was rightly increasingly anxious – 'it wasn't my idea'.[1] Around this time changes in the shape of Britain were being associated with longer-term constitutional movements in both England and Scotland. In empiricist tradition, the status quo of political representation seemed simply always already there and, as I will show, was often presented as a case of luck. But in a situation in which proposals for splitting the state would always be outnumbered by all the major Westminster parties, and where the constitution consists of parliamentary custom and statutory precedents rather than a written contract, the action of writing itself becomes a political process. By the time of devolution, theory had become central to the once more securely British field of English Literature; increasingly senile in its older function of guarding a canon of Anglo-British national consciousness, English but not properly so, Eng. Lit. became fascinated by the effects of the 'traces' or excesses of writing over speech – a reversal of the adaptation of speech to a standard writing. But the English constitution, the one still used by the

UK today, is built to *fail to* adapt voice to writing, and did so even when the English Parliament was dissolved in 1707. This chapter contends that the recovery of possible written Englishes other than the authoritative one has enabled a 'writerly' rebellion against the silence embodied in the English constitution.

Writing out of a double nation/state language is not new to peripheral Britons. In the story most often associated with Scots' split personality, their 'strandedness' between nation and state,[2] Robert Louis Stevenson's Jekyll/Hyde reveals his true identity in a signature. Hearing Hyde apparently butchering the doctor behind a locked door, the rest of the cast listens outside anxiously before breaking in and realising by looking at a letter handwritten by Jekyll that his signature and that of the monster are inexplicably the same.[3] Later confirmation of this unsupportable doubleness comes from hearing Jekyll/Hyde's voice, but the first indication is written. This reversal of the Platonic hierarchy of speech and writing is also a striking early reversal of English Literature, for which writing had been a model for the raw medium of speech throughout the empire (and Stevenson was far from nationalist; he often addressed, Greater British style, the 'English reader'). 'Jekyll and Hyde', generically set in London, totally lacks London-like detail, and is simply 'the most ordinary and respectable quarters'.[4] Its primary interlocutor, Mr Utterson, immediately recognisable as a caricature of an Edinburgh lawyer, is ironically unable to 'utter' in his own dialect. In this *unheimlich* Edinburgh, the crazed Hyde's barbarity is exaggerated by his murdering a British MP, and Jekyll increasingly views Hyde's barbarity, proto-Freudian style, as a sign of his own suppressed and inexpressible wishes.[5]

Stevenson's story was in its time viewed by much of the Scottish elite as sub-literary druggy shock-horror as was Welsh's *Trainspotting*; the second story, however, attempts to write out of the local dialect, showing a significant turnaround in Edinburgh's tradition of British obedience. The first story locates a debilitating doubleness within Victorian British life so accurately that mention of it is a cliché in Scottish Studies – one recent edition's cover portrays a picture of a bust of Stevenson himself on fire, denoting both aesthetic schism and a new aggression towards its debilitating effects.[6] It uses Standard English while gnawing away at the problem of representing locality, especially to a London audience. For the second form of writing there was no orthographic precedent at all, no rules of spelling and punctuation; to write an English influenced by speech was to leave the paths of linguistic sanity altogether. The recent form of the dialect novel, with roots in the 1980s work of James Kelman, returns us to a time before Adam Smith's *Lectures on Rhetoric* in a way that Synthetic Scots had not quite managed; problematising linguistic over-adjustment, it raises questions about the legitimacy of representations which are not written, but taken as read.[7] These questions of representation belong to the immediately pre-devolutionary period.

One of the most sophisticated accounts of British nations' relation to the silence of the English constitution is Neil MacCormick's 1999 *Questioning Sovereignty*.[8] Here the UK is described as an 'evolved state', a state based on adaptations to tradition rather than having started anew at any one point. The evolved, unwritten state, Burke's state over Paine's, is nevertheless highly unstable, since the English government in 1707 made very little political adjustment to it. Any absorption of Scottish representation under the name of England, as implied by the failure to rewrite the constitution, may be in contravention of Article 25 of the Articles of Union, which seems to render null and void the final sovereignty of the English government in favour of a new state:

> [a]ll laws and statutes in either kingdom, so far as they are contrary to or inconsistent with the terms of these articles, or any one of them, shall, from and after the Union, cease and become void, and shall be so declared to be by the respective parliaments of the said kingdoms.[9]

This, of course, is not what happened; the British Parliament instead maintained precedent and common law, and a popular Britain/England conflation 'stems from the tendency for high politics in Britain to flow from English constitutional history' in historians running through Hume, Macauley and Bagehot.[10] Thus for Richard Law in 1947, the House of Commons was still 'the most typically English of our institutions'.[11] Again, the Scottish Enlightenment is complicitous; most early North British intellectuals viewed the English constitution as natural advancement. As Colin Kidd says, 'The modern British achievement of a system of genuine liberty was explained by the Scottish sociological Whigs within the broad framework of a history of progress – of commercialism, defeudalisation, and refinement'.[12] Under the influence of British Whiggery, a separate Scottish past became 'an ideologically insignificant saga of events which lacked the backbone of a successful story of legal, institutional or economic development'.[13] Scotland (like England) stopped writing itself. By the end of the nineteenth century, the constitutional guru A. V. Dicey could casually state that, even if

Scotland had had a constitutional part to play in 1707, (British) Parliament, in its gradualist and unwritten fashion, had the authority to overturn the results of any foundational moment of union.[14] Since there was no founding moment, MacCormick stresses the ongoing negotiations implied by the plural term 'Acts of Union' – a point also made by the title of Leith Davis's book of a year before, a book primarily concerned with written or 'literary negotiations'.[15]

In other words there was *no* union except as held up by standards of writing. More fundamentally, we might ask why, if the aim was to create a new state, the English Parliament and apparatus of government was simply allowed to remain on the same site using the same staff, instead of moving to a neutral city. No one would expect a future EU government to move to the Reichstag and adopt the German constitution because Germany is its largest member. The 'flexible' absorption is paradoxical, its binding status dubious:

> The United Kingdom's constitutional laws neither permit nor preclude Scottish independence … [t]he constitutional principle of parliamentary sovereignty … states that a subsequent parliament can undo the decision of a previous parliament. In fact, the Act of Union itself has been frequently amended by Parliament … [16]

Irish 'union' also came and went without invalidating the constitution, showing how the range of the state can be completely changed without any corresponding action of rewriting. Without an eternity clause (more precisely, with an eternity clause which was simply superseded Dicey-style), the Articles of Union were adaptable even beyond the point of apparently invalidating themselves; union can be seen as representing a purely silent centre of gravity amidst the statute and precedent. As Jo Eric Murkens describes, the contradiction of a constitution able to amend itself out of all recognition even against the wishes of its member nations makes important the UK government's pledge 'in principle' to respect expressions of national sovereignty, like those which grew in the 1980s.[17] When 'in principle' takes the place of definite rules, many of the constitutional blind alleys come down to political voice in a very literal sense: the Scottish Parliament has become more 'the voice of the Scottish electorate' than Westminster, and the only requirement for reform is a will to write, 'setting out the terms of independence … [with] a draft constitution'.[18]

Moreover in constitutional terms, the argument that Scotland was 'colonised' is not as far-fetched as it seems. If the remainder of the UK becomes a continuant state, Scotland will have to have a 'clean slate' of the kind given to the Irish Free State after 1922. Continuant status, as laid down by the Vienna convention, was intended to allow colonies to break away and leave the coloniser intact; Scotland, if it left a rest-of-the-UK which became continuant, would retrospectively have been a colony to the same extent as was the Republic of Ireland.[19] This is of course only true if England insists on continuant status for whatever is left of the UK, rather than writing its own constitution and taking on statehood. One indication that this is a good idea is that it avoids the absurdity that Scotland has suffered colonial violence; such a retrospective status would be an accident of England's unwillingness to let go of a British idea it didn't invent and its people don't care about. England thus has a chance to identify the *real* colonies and strengthen its own nationhood in the process, rather than letting Scottish vulgar nationalists get away with oppressed-Scotland claims which do no one any good.

So within the seemingly cohesive Britain described by Linda Colley and others, the absence of coherently written rules has masked a fundamental opposition of views as to who holds final legal control, and whether the English constitution is even valid in a British state. Looking at Scottish political tradition, taking into account its constitution in 1707 would have probably made for a more inclusive and community-based polity for the new Britain, and possibly less of the British imperialism to which Scots nevertheless contributed. As MacCormick puts it:

> The old Scottish constitution, as Scots authorities like George Buchanan were very insistent, was never a constitution based on conquest. Hence the *Ius Regni*, the law of the kingdom, could never be interpreted as constituting an absolute monarchy whether in or out of Parliament, but only as authorizing a limited one depending on popular assent. From this, and from such other iconic texts as the Declaration of Arbroath, has derived the thesis that in Scottish constitutional tradition, sovereignty belonged to the people, to the community of the realm, rather than to Parliament, or, strictly, King or Queen in Parliament.[20]

But union was soon broadly perceived by both 'partners' as part of the development of the English constitution as a grand narrative: 'it is easy to interpret the constitution as a continuing evolution of the old English customary constitution as a patchwork of convention, common law, and statute'.[21] Postcolonial critics have often noted how the Victorian novel grounded this narrative in a shared folk tale which packages and arranges Greater British civility; few have described how Scotland's quiescence is a requirement of this – or how writing back over that quiescence troubles Britain as a national idea. In this sense, polity is up for the writing.

Thus the impasse between constitutional assumptions north and south in an unstable Britain can be extrapolated forward to the 1988 Claim of Right for Scotland, intended as an official request that those resident in Scotland be able to choose their own representation. The full effects of the claim's writing over constitutional silence were perhaps not fully understood by some of its signatories: as MacCormick points out, it was signed by a number of New Labour MPs who then went on to have a hand in devolution legislation insisting on Westminster as a final authority.[22] But since the nature of British sovereignty is contradictory and open for textual contestation, the form of the Claim is important – a broad community of agreement concretised in signatures. In MacCormick's account of the early 1700s, as in that of T. M. Devine, union was preceded by a storm of rhetoric and theoretical manoeuvres; we might well speculate the same about the run-up to the *end* of the union, in the context of pre-devolutionary concern to recover a post-British writing. And if the question of political representation boils down to the cultural confidence to *write* constitutional documents, then speculations on post-British sovereignty belong as much to literary theory as to constitutional law.

Claims of Right

The Claim of Right for Scotland was produced by a wide-based Constitutional Steering Committee in 1988, and provided one early sign that in the 1990s any prospective New Labour government would be required to make a serious referendum pledge to get the Scottish support it needed. The Committee was taken from a cross-section of figures from public life, education and the arts; they were not professional politicians, nor were they chosen for nationalist leanings.[23] The Claim acknowledges in its prologue similar documents dating from 1689 and 1842;[24] a more recent antecedent, however, was the Scottish Covenant conceived by SNP Secretary John MacCormick in 1949, after the failure of his attempts to establish a convention, almost a *de facto* parliament, in 1948.[25] (One of MacCormick's other wheezes was to challenge the title of Elizabeth 'the second' – the first of Britain – on her coronation, a completely serious exposure of how misdirected PC-speak about calling England Britain fails to address deep contradictions in the scope of the British government.) The Scottish Covenant had demanded constitutional reform, and, like the Claim of Right, directly connected writing to political process by asking for personal signatures. By the middle of the next year it had attracted over a million, and finally exceeded two million. From a high-British point of view, this new form of iconic text, a virtual plebiscite, fits uncomfortably onto the union's constitutional silence. Directed at the constitution, it does not make 'territorial' claims for any given region or nation, far less ethnicity, even asking for a par-liament 'in all loyalty to the Crown and within the framework of the United Kingdom'.[26] The Claim of Right similarly begins by stating that the question is not of any one British region or nation, but of the lack of adjustment made to the English constitution after the Acts of Union – a 'fundamental truth' in the colloquial mistake of referring to British government as English government.[27] The 1989 edition of the Claim which reprints the text with various commentaries was also among the first volumes in the influential series *Determinations*, reflecting an extraordinarily interdisciplinary range of concerns; laid end to end, the series reads like a consolidated account of the Third Scottish Renaissance.

In England, questions of democracy have rarely been accompa-nied by specific investigation into the nation's place in the UK as they were in the Claim, and have issued from isolated, if eloquent, voices. Pre-devolution, Will Hutton frequently argued against the unwrit-ten constitution, noting as a precedent Lord Radcliffe's Reith Lec-tures of 1951 (the year of the first, pre-millennial British Festival).[28] Hutton also puzzles over the lack of apparent 'catastrophic' change coming, and can imagine only a gradualist Labour swing to Social Democratic good sense.[29] Not taken into account of course is the possible significance of devolution, its political inflection in Britain's fringes, its long context, and the depth of the democratic questions it raises. In its millennial form devolution *is* catastrophic for Britain: it is the apparently impossible spontaneous break which forces us to start writing, and which is to some extent presaged by Hutton. Early constitutional claims mostly came from areas which created Britain by adapting to it; they had become almost inevitable in those areas, whereas they remain difficult to imagine in the heart of gradualist Britain. The pro-constitution movement Charter 88 numbers its sig-natures in tens of thousands, in contrast to the Scottish Covenant's millions. Anthony Barnett, founding director of Charter 88, accounts for influential criticisms of constitutional silence from the English side in 1997 in *This Time*, written soon after the New Labour victory, at a time of what he later regarded as partly misguided hope.[30] The book fed into Tom Nairn's withering critique of the 'power retained' attitude of the pro-British devolvers, *After Britain* (2000), which frequently mentions Barnett – indeed the two authors seem to have dedicated their books to one another. Nairn's position is one of democracy all round: a primary aim of Scottish, or English, nation-level thinking is accountability not yet possible in the British system. Where Barnett's critique departs from Nairn's is in seeing any account of the failure of Britain to 'keep the multinational state' as a 'pessimistic' account (somewhat against Barnett's own logic of releasing sovereignty).[31]

Inflected through the Greater Britain Barnett appropriately calls the 'Empire State', the English problem here is complacency about the export of English identity in a British state.[32] For Barnett, this complacency has resulted from an unwillingness to shift from the Hobbesian idea that power is a 'zero-sum', that moving power is also 'giving it away' – an idea we have seen described by John Macmurray as bound to the 'pragmatic' state.[33] English national sentiment within Britain has thus come to feel 'besieged'.[34] This tendency to avoid power-sharing, as in British attitudes to the European Union as threatening and invasive, Barnett sees as being contrary to England's democracy and as requiring a written constitution. Since 'democracy is inconceivable without nationalism', he calls for a 'civic nationalism'.[35] Taking apart this Anglophone empire from the inside, he attacks the received wisdom that a coherent written constitution is not part of our tradition, tellingly linking democratic process to 'speaking in one's own voice'.[36] Where the current voice of the English people was still 'self-mocking' and even 'self-colonising' in its tendency to view the constitution as immobile – and increasingly centred on the super-constitutional figure of the Prime Minister – Barnett proposes a democratic action which requires the constitution to be codified in writing.

The dangers of the increased power of the Executive and the Prime Minister in the British Parliament – Thatcher's 'conviction politics' inherited by Blair's spin doctors – had been stressed by the Claim of Right in 1988: 'we have now reached the point where the Prime Minister has in practice a degree of arbitrary power few, if any, English and no Scottish monarchs have rivalled'.[37] The problem as Barnett sees it, as had David Hume, is that since the Westminster government has never adjusted to union, it has become inured to shifts in power and has come to react by protecting at all costs an increasingly unrepresentative system propped up by quangos.[38] That 'Scotland had led the way' in criticising a strong unconstitutional executive is by now a received wisdom.[39] The discernment of non-English models leading English ones goes back before the 1979 devolution vote, when the diplomat and nationalist P. H. Scott was stressing that after the disappearance of the British bonds of Protestantism, monarchy and empire, only Scotland could 'take the lead' as a model of post-British society.[40] But what makes Barnett's account of constitutional change in Scotland unusual is his appreciation of the link between national action and the act of writing democracy. Here I have argued that Scottish constitutional claims arose in part from a rising awareness that eighteenth-century Scotland had silenced itself via adjustment to an imperial linguistic standard. As Barnett notes, the Scottish White Paper on devolution was carefully drafted: the connections between speaking, writing and democracy had already been grasped in culture. Scotland's will to write its way out of the British constitutional 'balance' had behind it, as he says, 'calm', a long culture of working to reclaim 'voice'.

Even more than Barnett realised in 1997, the far-from-perfect Scottish and Welsh assemblies have taken on a responsibility for parliamentary accountability beyond their own jurisdictions. To an extent which is easy to underestimate if viewed as PC humbug or measured in terms of the failures of politicians, written parliamentary guidelines, simply by being written, have bypassed many of the vested interests which have regulated the function of the British Parliament in terms of 'race', class and gender. In 1999 the Scottish Parliament decreed that any Bill presented by the Scottish Executive must be accompanied by, amongst other documents, a Policy Memorandum accounting for:

  (i) the policy objectives of the Bill;

 (ii) whether alternative ways of meeting those objectives were considered and, if so, why the approach taken in the Bill was adopted;

(iii) the consultation, if any, which was undertaken on those objectives and the ways of meeting them or on the detail of the Bill and a summary of the outcome of that consultation; and

(iv) an assessment of the effects, if any, of the Bill on equal opportunities, human rights, island communities, local government, sustainable development and any other matter which the Scottish Ministers consider relevant.[41]

The innocuous-looking roll-call of rights in section (iv) exemplifies an accountability of the type called for by Barnett. It has not been entirely successful: while the Scottish Parliament immediately elected a 37 per cent proportion of women (almost 50 per cent if we discount the Conservative Party), and the Welsh Assembly almost equal men and women, there are no non-white MSPs whatsoever. But Barnett is right in suggesting that the overall constitutional change that is occurring is in the growth of accountable 'voice'; the challenge remaining is to let that voice develop in a dialectical relationship with the older image of each nation under the union, rather than assuming those images will simply fall away – as a look round Holyrood's white faces shows they have not. In Scotland, the reclamation of voice dovetails perfectly with the end of the authority of a Standard English centred in London since Chaucer and Caxton and riding on the back of English Literature, but once canonised largely by Scots themselves.

Voice, Action and 'Luck': A Literary Analogue

Although there has since the Middle Ages been a literature in Scots, or a revived artificial Scots, only very recently has there grown a literature in spoken Scottish dialects. This growth has been part of a Third Renaissance, peaking in the two decades somewhere soon after the 1979 devolution failure, and differing in important respects from the earlier, more prescriptive forms. Cairns Craig dates the growth of the current 'dialect novel' in the 1990s back to James Kelman's *The Busconductor Hines* (1984).[42] Scottish English is grammatically and lexically highly discrete (and is thus often still mistakenly referred to as Scots language). The relative stability of this generic dialect represents a deliberate identification towards a sameness of expression within a wider language; the process has largely been driven by a national desire to share a non-Standard form of English.[43] But despite notable early individual exceptions like Lewis Grassic Gibbon, there was still no common practice of using non-Standard dialects for literary diegesis (primary description) as opposed to merely dialogue. The recent dialect novel represents an altogether different cultural form to the Synthetic Scots of the First Renaissance, which, although conceived as an anti-unionist movement, nevertheless tended to amplify the assumptions of 'good English' by leaving it intact. Kelman's writing, for example, mixes Scots and English as a normal mode of narration; it enacts a search for recognition (in the sense of the term used by Macmurray and Fanon) and, in writing out this search, attempts to inscribe the very possibility of social action. This process of writing out experience reverses the tradition of adjustment to given standards and opens the door for similar methods in Irvine Welsh, Janice Galloway and others. What Kelman is concerned with is the possibility that, if writing is separate from social action, then the person's sovereignty is merely presented to her as a matter of fate, custom or luck. Many of his earlier stories are thus saturated by luck, set in betting shops and pubs ('waiting rooms'), replacing the traditional stages of the Scottish working-class novel, factories and working men's clubs, as does the betting shop non-society in *Trainspotting*.[44] They feature characters stuck in *activities*, struggling to find *action*.

Presenting 'luck' as social fate has been endemic to post-1979 British governments. The National Lottery, the world's biggest, began in 1994, and was enthusiastically taken up by the post-1997 Labour government, its vacant hopefulness well suited to Cool Britannia. The White Paper 'The People's Lottery' was published in July 1997, underlining the New Labour conviction that anything could be made to seem democratic by prefixing it with 'people's'.[45] The 1997 New Labour victory came at a peak of Lottery ticket sales: of the ten top weeks of sales between 1994 and 2001, four were in 1997 between May and December.[46] As a form of taxation, the Lottery outranks every other method for sheer classism: only between 16 and 17 per cent of ticket sales are accounted for by the 'AB' social group, yet the Lottery funds *both* public projects which would previously have used means-tested direct taxation *and* high-profile arts projects which have almost exclusively AB audiences.[47] In other words, the high-profile metropolitan and 'millennial' arts events which were used to shore up the idea of Britain as a nation were paid for largely by Britain's poorest, who then had it sold back to them.[48] National Lottery TV programmes are filled out with the banalities of 'boy bands' and the drawing of numbers is accompanied by a prole-friendly pseudo-science of numbers which is truly Orwellian ('[i]t was their delight, their folly, their anodyne, their intellectual stimulant').[49] And as if parodying the disjunction of cause and effect enabled by pre-writing taxation as luck, the Lottery's beneficiaries are known as 'good causes'. When we look more closely at the 'good causes', we find that from the inception of the Lottery to 2002, London was awarded 4.45 times more funding than Scotland for 'Arts' projects and 4.22 times more for 'Millennium' projects, yet only 1.81 times more for 'Heritage'.[50] This means that Scotland has been allotted relatively more money according to what it *was*, or what it is seen as having been: 'heritage'. The word *heritage*, used to connote a nostalgic and flattened-out version of history, became a subject of serious criticism in the 1990s;[51] most people no longer view their history as 'heritage'. Yet under the logic of Cool Britannia, the Lottery heritage bolsters a multicultural British 'nation'; the slogan of the Lottery is 'you played, the nation won'.

To some observers, James Kelman seemed to offer a fashionable flavour of Britishness when the Booker Prize of 1994 came around, and to become a beneficiary of multicultural British luck. But the Prize, which he accepted with a fitting lack of grace, came from a long struggle from the bottom up against two-and-a-half centuries of English Literature. Those writing in non-Standard dialects remain outside of the standards of comprehension, the standards of mass marketing, and the standards of canonisation. The 1994 award excited strong counter-passions amongst those troubled by the book's misfit with English Literature; one judge, Rabbi Julia Neuberger, famously described the winning work as 'crap'.[52] Her objections seem to have arisen from a mixture of simply not understanding the book – of being a native speaker of a dialect of English which she regarded as unimpeachable – and of regarding its content as correspondingly trivial. One line of objection – like the 'content analysis' which used to be common in philology – simply enumerated the number of times Kelman's narrator used the word 'fuck'. The issue in these objections about 'bad language' is not merely a question of the specific validation of some swear words ('crap') but not others ('fuck'); the intervention of the dialect novel goes beyond Adam Smith's extrinsic appeals for the self-repression of all that is not properly 'English'.

Kelman's story *My Eldest*, from his 1998 collection *The Good Times*, is one of the clearest attempts so far to impose recognition on an environment which seems determined by luck. It squeezes into a mere three pages the struggle of a narrator to connect with his wife and children on a day out at the seaside near a nuclear submarine base. The surrounding environment seems at times to be 'just happening', and the narrator struggles to take control. *My Eldest* gives the search for action a political twist by having the family picnicking near a base whose influence in terms of environment, international politics and economics is largely unknown to them: the narrator is mystified by his inability to control his relationship to these two intersecting types of 'nuclear' family. The beach has often imaged a site of cultural crossover or ambivalence, where the unknown washes up onto the known; it also places an imperial economy of vision and knowledge – the native seen as different and therefore primitive. The context was recognised by MacDiarmid's *On a Raised Beach* (1934), whose speaker speculates upon an ancient arrangement of stones, aware that they in some sense 'contain' history connected beyond human comprehension – but unable to get at this 'locked in' history. His problem on the beach is to get hold of human action in the company of these 'historical' stones:

> Detached intellectuals, not one stone will move,
> Not the least of them, not a fraction of an inch. It is not
> The reality of life that is hard to know.
> It is nearest of all and easiest to grasp,
> But you must participate in it to proclaim it.[53]

MacDiarmid was aware of the urgency of breaking down the stones' objectivity with participation – 'I must get into this stone world now'[54] – yet he never solved the problem, and his poetic voice continues to synthesise objects in the same way as had the British encyclopaedic tradition which arranges pre-existing objects around a discrete subject. In societies in which individuals are separated by their placedness in visual, subjective space, history as a mutual experience becomes unreachable, and political decisions seem to become detached from effects. It is in this context that Kelman's protagonist struggles to break down the objecthood of what he 'observes', and to recognise a co-existence:

> This observing the sea; waves breaking, the little boat with
> its blue cockpit; the seabirds. These might be the elements,
> not the central elements...Of course I knew things would
> co-exist. Their very presence, a relationship, the living. Also
> when ye returned a freedom.[55]

This particular beach is appropriately chosen: Scottish resistance to the establishment of nuclear bases was strong, and marked a point at which Scottish participants in the British Labour movement began to have to think more 'nationally', particularly via the Campaign for Nuclear Disarmament.[56] The nuclear question would also return to plague any continuant UK government after Scottish independence: due to nuclear non-proliferation, Scotland could not become a nuclear power even if it wanted to, yet the UK strike force, the future rest-of-the-UK or England strike force, is based in Scotland. British administrations of the 1980s which drew British defence policy close to the cold war US were overwhelmingly opposed in Scotland, but returned on the basis of the votes of 20 per cent of the Scottish electorate in 1983, 18 per cent in 1987, and 19 per cent in 1992, and were only shifted in the 1997 general election with a 12 per cent wipe-out. Ironically, when the Conservative Party failed to return any MPs in Scotland it was only the semi-PR system of voting used in the Scottish Parliament which gave them any national recognition in Scotland at all. But if this started as an anti-Tory tide, ethical questions raised made it into an anti-British one: a survey by *The Economist* in 1999 found that a staggeringly low 8 per cent of Scots believed in the continuing influence of Westminster.[57] Action against nuclear bases had been one of the concretising moments.

Outside of the nation then, representation had come to seem to be simply handed down, and political fate mere luck. An irony of the 'nuclear' family in Kelman is that any genetic mutations which arise as a result of pollution also seem a matter of luck to the protagonists. The relationship between father and son is always already disturbed in ways unknown. Nor is the 'uncertainty theory' of genetic disturbance new: from the 1950s, Britain secretly tested atomic weapons' effects, genetic and otherwise, on its own front-line soldiers, a disproportionate number of whom were Scottish.[58] More recently the Blair government attempted to use its presidency of the EU to steer through legislation allowing companies to conceal information on genetic modification.[59] Kelman's characters are used to being handed down such state 'luck' which is not really luck. They are painfully aware of the need to change it, yet struggle to find anything to *say* which can transform luck into social action: 'Everybody carries a certain amount of luck: it is the kind of luck, this is what matters. I knew about my luck, the kind I carried. What could be said about that'.[60]

This type of relationship with society, as we have seen, was described by John Macmurray in terms of Hobbesian 'pragmatic' states.[61] For Macmurray as for Kelman, such a state is only 'at best an aspect of society',[62] and 'objective' societies are to be rejected; history should be enacted, rather than simply watched.[63] Kelman's prose does not 'portray' any character as entirely third-person. His narrator's most impersonal moments surround him being placed spatially, in a field of vision: 'the things I was seeing, everything was just so distant. It had nothing to do with me. It really did not have anything to do with me'.[64] Touch however is perception *in action*, short-circuiting rational mediation and combining action and resistance in a shared present.[65] Where the viewing subject maintains separateness in vision, the agent inhabits time as distinctions generated by doing.[66] Although MacDiarmid's speaker picks up a stone, he is baffled by its ahistorical nature – 'I grasp one of them and I have in my grip/The beginning and the end of the world'.[67] Kelman's speaker can grasp locality over time in non-visual ways:

as he surveys the coast, he feels 'the sense too of history, the old graveyard was not in view but I knew precisely where it was, the clump of trees that led to it'.[68]

The authoritative suppression of the irrational and of linguistic wandering is here suspended, and the narration moves between first, second and third persons. Kelman's prose enacts a continuous process of 'translating' back and forth between 'high' English and local dialect, powerfully described by Cairns Criag as an ongoing negotiation, a 'dialect and dialectics', within the self.[69] In this sense, Kelman as representative of the Third Scottish Renaissance forces questions of representation not forced by MacDiarmid in the First. In Kelman the reader has to think as agent in negotiating the narration. The process is one of inviting mutual action:

> The standard written forms of language and the represen-
> tation of oral pronunciation are so mixed in Kelman's lan-
> guage that there is no distinction between the narrative voice
> and the character's speech or thoughts: no hierarchy of lan-
> guage is established which orders the value to be put on the
> characters' language in relation to any other mode of speech
> or writing within the text. The text is designed visually to
> resist the moment of arrest in which the reader switches be-
> tween the narrative voice of the text and the represented
> speech of a character, and what this does is to create a lin-
> guistic equality between speech and narration which allows
> the narrator to adopt the speech idioms of his characters, or
> the characters to think or speak in 'standard English', with
> equal status.[70]

The Sound of England

Most commentators on British culture and politics, Scottish and English, left and right, agree that Scotland's finding a voice is the most likely reason for the break-up of the union.[71] Where England has tended to export culture without much regard for national borders, Britain's others have become increasingly sensitised to the effects of laying the state over the nation.[72] In part due to the nation's cultural success in export, there have been few sensible voices on England's 'separation' from the UK. Even Eric Hobsbawm's seminal account of *Nations and Nationalism* (1982) ignores the possibility of English nationalism.[73] Neither in 1979 nor 1997 was England given the opportunity to vote on devolution, nor is such an opportunity commonly suggested, a fact that betrays widespread assumptions about what does and does not constitute a nation.[74] Yet in recent years, the 'English problem' has received intense attention, some studies more serious than others, but all broadly aiming for the expression of something which previously seemed inexpressible, a national 'voice' not subsumed in the UK.

As Krishan Kumar points out at the outset of his *The Making of English National Identity*, a real intention can be diagnosed in the *faux pas* 'England, I mean Britain'. For Kumar, 'England, I mean Britain' really means England, but the inability to speak English-ness itself is symptomatic of England's difficulty in thinking its way out of union and empire. And by now, as Arthur Aughey notes, '[i]t is too late to save Britain by the proper use of nomenclature'.[75] Tellingly, although Kumar's suasive account represents a step forward in English Studies, at times it is itself more about Anglocentrism than England; the substantial qualities of England after its default position in union and empire for 300 years remain difficult to pick out. Writers primarily concerned with Scotland have often stressed the need for an appreciation of English expression (Tom Nairn is a case in point), though have seldom suggested what qualities that Englishness might have. Even Kumar, three decades after *The Break-Up of Britain*, is struggling to point out what Englishness is; he does, however, point up some key metaphors. Post-British Englishness has to negotiate materials as far back as far as the free-born Anglo-Saxon.[76] Though problematic in both 'ethnic' (the ruling classes remained Anglo-Norman, or even Anglo-Norman-Welsh-Scottish)[77] and cultural senses (that most English of writers, Shakespeare, relied on an interplay of Germanic and Romance vocabularies), the survival of the free-born Anglo-Saxon became a principle of continuity during the high-British and Francophobe context of the late-eighteenth- and early-nineteenth-century wars.[78]

Given the difficulty of defining England, the when of English nationalism is debatable. For Alan Macfarlane a distinct market economy was established by the thirteenth century; for Gerald Newman English nationalism begins with the Gallophobia of the 1740s (a timing worryingly close to that of Britishness); for Robert Colls and Philip Dodd, the school study of English and History are a starting point.[79] In most accounts England is gradualist, sceptical and liberty-loving; France is theoretical, revolutionary and systematic. England is fair play, France philosophy.[80] England is a global standard; nationalism is something fanatical, semi-pathological, and foreign, '[h]ence the unwillingness to accept that there is or can be such a thing as English nationalism'.[81] We have seen this tradition of 'continuity' and gradualism in attitudes about the constitution; for Kumar, Anglo-Britain has created a polity which also corresponds to a continuing 'national' destiny: 'it has over the centuries developed a set of institutions, symbols and traditions that can lead to a form of emotional identification remarkably similar to that evoked by ethnic nationhood'.[82]

In recent times, the English constitutional 'balance' has increasingly relied on the powerlessness of the monarch, and re-brandings of Britishness have not so much emerged from cultural grass roots as been engineered by central policy. Many have pointed out how accents on television throughout the 1990s became notably more 'regional' (as if Standard English is not itself regional), in a strained attempt to maintain British multiculturalism. This risks forcing a specific Englishness out the back end, if only by a process of elimination. In this sense, while Scotland and Wales (albeit as 'regions') are becoming increasingly audible, Anglo-Britishness becomes increasingly voiceless. As Andrew Marr puts it, '[o]nce, [Boris] Johnson [RP speaker] had the voice of Reith's BBC, the voice of the empire, the voice of monarchy and order. Today, it has become embarrassing. There is no British voice. Britishness is becoming steadily harder to hear'.[83] The point about the 'regionalisation' of the BBC should be carefully qualified: as Murray Pittock points out (writing in 1997), only about 2 per cent of BBC TV programmes are made in Scotland.[84] But the BBC has increasingly blocked prestige English speech, pressing for English *regionalism* as a potential equivalent to Scottish *national* independence. There is as yet, in Colley's terms, no 'counterweight nationality' to British England; English national *expérience vécue* has not yet been identified.[85] There are very few English civic institutions speaking with a specifically English national voice.

Kumar has related the disappearance of national voice to the habit of perpetual outwards push, battles kept remote while a nebulously bordered 'home' remained safe. If not given strict borders, the 'first empire' (the unification of England, the annexation of Wales, Anglo-Scottish union) can be seen as pushing outwards since medieval times, especially if the post-1066 period is seen as one of Anglo-Norman aristocratic rule rather than as suffering under the 'Norman yoke'.[86] England only accepted the term 'Britain' as late as the sixteenth century, and from medieval times until the British-imperial phase, Scotland was commonly seen as a dissident county of England; until the end of the nineteenth century, 'England' was a catch-all term for Britishness accepted by ambitious Scots.[87] As Kumar recognises, English voice got lost in its global purpose – though the connection of first and second empires only partly explains why Kumar feels able to draw an 'English' continuity from the first to second empires when there was so much of Scotland in the second.[88]

England is drawing back from a double process of absorption in which it played the ventriloquist; it is looking for a stable speaking place, while its cultural, if not its geographical, borders continue to slip.[89] Although Kumar notes the tendency of England to define itself against others,[90] to some extent he falls victim to the same typology, waiting until Chapter 7 – 'The moment of Englishness' – to pick out some of the specific qualities of Englishness. Kumar also, perhaps somewhat ahistorically, and despite acknowledging writers like David McCrone and Colin Kidd,[91] still describes Britain as having a shared culture and Colley-like 'organic attachments'.[92] His point though is that refusing, at least until the last decade, to attempt to define itself, England has refused to speak: 'despite constantly confusing the two terms, the English have kept some part of themselves of themselves aloof from Britain'.[93] Thus, as for Nairn, the growth of Greater Britain eclipsed the possibility of English nationalism.[94] English nationalism is too small for 'England' in its Greater British sense;[95] England may still have generations of overcoming the imperial agoraphobia Colley dates back to the empire which appeared after the Seven Years' War.[96] Where, in the process of retreat, 'England's gracious ceding of empire' is seen by some writers as proof of tolerance and strength,[97] the seamless progression from Greater British to sub-British makes it hard for England to find a voice in the way that Scotland was able to in the 1980s and '90s.

One property that Kumar suggests is a revival of Anglo-Saxonisms and ruralisms in late Victorian and Edwardian English culture from Morris and Ruskin to Vaughan Williams and folk song. The folk song revival of the 1900s was still exerting an influence on classical music in the 1940s, and had entered into mainstream pedagogy.[98] The inter-war quasi-nationalist moment also sees a new interest in Anglican church-going; Simon Jenkins' recent plaintive claim that '[m]y beloved churches seem to wave despairingly as they sink under a sea of vivid red roofs and concrete drives' is remarkably close to Orwell's 1939 Oxfordshire disappearing under suburbs in *Coming Up For Air*.[99] This Anglo-revivalist tendency does find a voice, from Arthur Quiller-Couch's *Oxford Book of English Verse* (1900) and poetic Georgianism (Nairn's 'abstract upper-class kitsch')[100] to the desperate rearguard Anglo-Britishness of T. S. Eliot. Rambling and the 'rediscovery' of the English countryside also emerged at this time, exemplified by the radio programme *The Archers*.[101] In painterly images of England there is a revival of Constable's villages, perhaps in response to the need to provide an idyllic 'home' for World War I soldiers to imagine themselves returning to – and suggesting that Scotland was increasingly not 'at home' in twentieth-century Anglo-Britain.[102] In 1933 Herbert Read nevertheless imagined that 'Irishmen, Welshmen and Scotsmen have identified themselves' with this image.[103] F. R. Leavis's 'organic community' was derived in part from George Stuart's *Change in the Village* (1912) and *The Wheelwright's Shop* (1923); his journal *Scrunity* continued, against the teaching of 'civics', to advocate the use of publications by the Council for the Preservation of Rural England for serious pedagogical use.[104] The idea of 'organic' bonds in *Britain* would of course surface amidst some cultural desperation in John Major; it also appears, though, in Linda Colley's history of Britain 'forging' its 'national' bonds.

These English national voices are almost all white,[105] and, in the absence of any form of citizenship or state, are perpetually backward-facing, prevented by tradition from catching up to the actual experience of English people.[106] In other words, if this is English nationalism speaking, it is, like Nairn's Scottish nationalist culture, late and stunted compared to its European counterparts – perhaps even more so, since the nation was prone to bungling. Or as Nairn puts it: 'in Edinburgh people are at least ashamed of *The Sunday Post* and *STV*; in England their folklore equivalents are taken seriously'.[107] Without a proper nationalist thinking in terms of citizenship, Englishness has been able to revert to instinct and tradition.[108] Yet in Morris's hands, country life was inherently communitarian;[109] in Ruskin's, the aura of a countryside attempting to resist the ravages of the industrial revolution has a definite politics of place which should save it from countryside lobbies. Such accounts of the country, which we might anachronistically call cultural critiques, pass from Morris and Orwell to Raymond Williams and 'British Cultural Studies'. This tradition is not reliant on 'racial' continuity, and is not closed to admixture and immigration. For the most influential English writers of the inter-war and early Cultural Studies period, England is not a 'race' at all: such additions belong to immigration panics of the Powellite moment.[110]

The divorce of nation and experience, whether in England/Wales or Scotland, is interestingly linked by Andrew Marr to the increase in rates of depression.[111] These effects have also been recognised by the English filmmaker Ken Loach, who, in films like *My Name is Joe* – tellingly, set in Glasgow – attempts to show the ways in which facing insoluble problems in a highly privatised British society leaves people with a sense of having no choice.[112] Lying underneath the more individualistic have-a-go mentality of the likes of *Billy Elliot*, this naturalism seems a mirror image of the propaganda role of the inter-war British film industry (and the BBC): the integrative Anglo-British identity is here un-created.[113] *Pace* Nairn, Marr also identifies the 1979 devolution referendum, the point before the Scottish revival and the English naturalism of Ken Loach, as the last point at which the British government could have controlled the fate of Britain.[114] The '79 referendum, to put it another way, was the last point at which Scots were liable to think that they still somehow had a stake in the welfare state they had helped to create. Even so, 'apathy' can be overstated unless we notice that (as James Mitchell has pointed out) funding for the 'No' campaign was out of scale with that for the 'Yes' campaign,[115] and bear in mind that rules for counting the votes were changed at the last moment by George Cunningham's notorious '40 per cent of the electorate' amendment.

As it is, an increasingly Englished Conservative and Unionist Party, in failing to account properly for their Englishness, have left any *apologia* for Britain to New Labour, which has had to whip its own nationalist wing. (In Scotland, 'Unionist' was rapidly dropped from the Conservative Party name after devolution.) Because of the shrinking of its power base to the south-east of England, the Conservative Party became *de facto* the spokesperson for English national sentiment; this is ironic given the tradition of Englishness *as* liberalism. Merely getting the nation's name right during the Thatcher and Major administrations would perhaps have given the Conservative Party a chance to occupy the centre of a post-British English state, even despite the retreat of support from the north. As it is, English voices have come later and, at least until the early 2000s, have had to struggle against an Anglo-British 'thousand years' narrative reheated by the New Right.[116] Meanwhile, some Scots have been calling for a 'restoration of English political identity' for at least a couple of decades.[117] Recently however, English voice has been more properly connected to the recovery of English *place*, and the final chapter will place some accounts of emergent Englishness and Scottishness alongside accounts of devolution.

Notes

1. Andrew Rawnsley, *Servants of the People: The Inside Story of New Labour* (London: Hamish Hamilton, 2000), p. 243.
2. Cf. Tom Nairn, *The Break-up of Britain: Crisis and Neo-nationalism* (London: NLB, 1977), p. 146.
3. Robert Louis Stevenson, 'The Strange Case of Dr. Jekyll and Mr. Hyde', in Jenni Calder (ed.), *The Strange Case of Dr. Jekyll and Mr. Hyde, and other stories* (London: Penguin, 1979), pp. 27–97: 65–7.
4. Andrew Lang, review in *Saturday Review*, January 1886, in Paul Maixner (ed.), *Robert Louis Stevenson: The Critical Heritage* (London: Routledge and Kegan Paul, 1971), pp. 199–201: 200.
5. Stevenson, ed. Calder, 'Jekyll and Hyde', pp. 46–50, 88–97.
6. Robert Louis Stevenson, *The Strange Tale of Dr. Jekyll and Mr. Hyde* (Edinburgh: Canongate Classics, 2001).
7. Here 'UK' is used, as it was on the original document, to refer to the state created in 1707; 'the United Kingdom' did not, as is widely believed, begin with union with Ireland.
8. Neil MacCormick, *Questioning Sovereignty* (Oxford: Oxford University Press, 1999).
9. Quoted in ibid. p. 53.
10. Graham Morton, *Unionist Nationalism: Governing Urban Scotland 1830–1860* (East Linton: Tuckwell, 1999), p. 2.
11. Quoted in Raphael Samuel, 'Introduction: Exciting to be English', in Samuel (ed.), *Patriotism: The Making and Unmaking of British National Identity, Vol. I: History and Politics* (London: Routledge, 1989), p. xxv.
12. Colin Kidd, *Subverting Scotland's Past: Scottish Whig Historians and the Creation of an Anglo-British Identity, 1689–c.1830* (Cambridge: Cambridge University Press, 1993), p. 119.
13. Ibid. pp. 6–7, 207; cf. David Craig, *Scottish Literature and the Scottish People 1680–1830* (London: Chatto and Windus, 1961), pp. 273–93; Duncan Glen, *Whither Scotland?: A prejudiced look at the future of a nation* (London: Gollancz, 1971).
14. A. V. Dicey, *An Introduction to the Study of the Law of the Constitution* (Basingstoke: Macmillan Education, 1959), pp. 64–5; on the lack of a foundational moment, cf. Keith Robbins, *Great Britain: Identities, Institutions, and the Idea of Britishness* (Harlow: Longman, 1998), p. 4.
15. Leith Davis, *Acts of Union: Scotland and the Literary Negotiation of the British Nation, 1707–1830* (Stanford: Stanford University Press, 1998).
16. Jo Eric Murkens, *Scottish Independence: A Practical Guide* (Edinburgh: Edinburgh University Press, 2003), p. 11.
17. Ibid. pp. 12–19.
18. Ibid. pp. 29, 31.
19. Cf. ibid. pp. 114–28.
20. MacCormick, *Questioning Sovereignty*, p. 55.
21. Ibid. p. 57.
22. Ibid. p. 60.

23. Owen Dudley Edwards (ed.), *A Claim of Right For Scotland* (Edinburgh: Polygon, 1989), pp. 1–2.
24. Ibid. p. 10.
25. Christopher Harvie and Peter Jones, *The Road to Home Rule: Images of Scotland's Cause* (Edinburgh: Polygon, 2000), p. 59.
26. Reproduced in ibid. p. 61.
27. Edwards (ed.), *A Claim of Right*, p. 13.
28. Will Sutton, *The State We're In* (London: Vintage, 1996), pp. 286–7.
29. Ibid. p. 319.
30. Anthony Barnett, *This Time: Our Constitutional Revolution* (London: Vintage, 1997).
31. Nairn, *After Britain* (London: Granta, 2000), p. 324.
32. Barnett, *This Time*, p. 295; David Marquand, *The New Reckoning* (Cambridge: Cambridge University Press, 1997).
33. Cf. Neil MacCormick, 'Sovereignty: Myth and Reality', *Scottish Affairs*, 11, 1995, pp. 1–13; Stephen Haseler, *The English Tribe: Identity, Nation and Europe* (London: Macmillan, 1996), p. 185.
34. Cf. Anthony Barnett, 'After Nationalism', in Raphael Samuel (ed.), *Patriotism, Vol. 1: History and Politics*, pp. 140–55: 143; 'Introduction: Little Platoons', in Samuel (ed.) *Patriotism, Vol. II: Minorities and Outsiders*, pp. ix–xxxix: xxiii.
35. Barnett, *This Time*, p. 153.
36. Ibid. p. 3.
37. Edwards (ed.), *A Claim of Right*, p. 18.
38. Cf. Will Hutton, *The State We're In* (London: Vintage, 1996), p. 287.
39. Barnett, *This Time*, p. 186.
40. For example, P. H. Scott, 'The End of Britishness', *Cencrastus*, 46, autumn 1993, pp. 7–10; cf. David McCrone, 'Scotland and the Union: Changing Identities in the British State', in David Morley and Kevin Robins (eds), *British Cultural Studies: Geography, Nationality, and Identity* (Oxford: Oxford University Press, 2001), pp. 97–108: 97.
41. Online guide to the Scottish Parliament: http://www.scottishparliament.uk/parl.bus/bills-guide:/gpb-1.htm#P179.23768.
42. James Kelman, *The Busconductor Hines* (Edinburgh: Polygon, 1984).
43. Peter Trudgill, *Sociolinguistics: An Introduction to Language and Society* (London: Penguin, 2000), pp. 94–5.
44. Irvine Welsh, *Trainspotting* (London: Minerva, 1994), pp. 24–7.
45. Ken Worpole, 'Cartels and Lotteries: Heritage and Cultural Policy in Britain', in Morley and Robins (eds), *British Cultural Studies*, pp. 235–48: 236.
46. *The National Lottery: Facts and Figures* (Liverpool: The National Lottery, 2002), p. 8.
47. Ibid. p. 9.
48. See Warpole, 'Cartels and Lotteries', p. 239.
49. George Orwell, ed. Peter Davison, *Complete Works Vol. 9: Nineteen Eighty-Four* (London: Secker and Warburg, 1997), p. 89.
50. http://www.lottery.culture.gov.uk/summary/area.htlm. Consulted 2002.

51. David McCrone, Angela Morris and Richard Kiely, *Scotland the Brand: The Making of Scottish Heritage* (Edinburgh: Edinburgh University Press, 1995).
52. BBC News online: http://news.bbc.co.uk/2/hi/uk/179131/stm. Consulted 2002.
53. Hugh MacDiarmid, 'On a Raised Beach', in Michael Grieve and W. R. Aitken (eds), *Collected Poems Vol. I* (Manchester: Carcanet, 1992), pp. 422–33: 432.
54. MacDiarmid, 'On a Raised Beach', p. 426.
55. James Kelman, 'My Eldest', in *The Good Times* (New York: Anchor, 1999), pp. 47–50: 47.
56. Harvie and Jones, *The Road to Home Rule*, pp. 70–2.
57. Quoted in Murray G. H. Pittock, *A New History of Scotland* (Stroud: Sutton, 2003), p. 286.
58. See Ken McGinley, *No Risk Involved* (Edinburgh: Mainstream, 1991).
59. See George Monbiot, *Captive State* (London: Pan, 2001).
60. Kelman, *The Good Times*, p. 48.
61. John Macmurray, *Persons in Relation* (London: Faber and Faber, 1969), pp. 138, 142.
62. Ibid. pp. 132, 144.
63. Ibid. pp. 97, 128.
64. Kelman, 'My Eldest', p. 48.
65. John Macmurray, *The Self as Agent* (London: Faber and Faber, 1969), pp. 108, 177.
66. Ibid. pp. 132–3.
67. MacDiarmid, 'On a Raised Beach', p. 428.
68. Kelman, 'My Eldest', p. 47.
69. Cairns Craig, *The Modern Scottish Novel* (Edinburgh: Edinburgh University Press, 1999), pp. 15–116.
70. Ibid. p. 101.
71. See Krishan Kumar, *The Making of English National Identity* (Cambridge: Cambridge University Press, 2003), p. 64.
72. See ibid. p. 1.
73. Eric Hobsbawm, *Nations and Nationalism Since 1780* (Cambridge: Cambridge University Press, 1990), especially pp. 163–92; Kumar, *The Making of English National Identity*, p. 18.
74. Cf. Marquand, 'How United is the United Kingdom?', in Alexander Grant and Keith Stringer (eds), *Uniting the Kingdom?: The Making of British History* (London: Routledge, 1995), pp. 277–91: 280.
75. Arthur Aughey, *Nationalism, Devolution, and the Challenge to the United Kingdom State* (London: Pluto, 2001), p. 7.
76. Cf. Andrew Marr, *The Day Britain Died* (London: Profile, 2000), p. 100; Kumar, *The Making of English National Identity*, pp. 202–17.
77. See Kumar, *The Making of English National Identity*, pp. 9, 77–85.
78. Colley, *Britons: Forging the Nation 1707–1837* (London: Pimlico, 2003), p. 90.
79. Alan Macfarlane, *Origins of English Individualism: The Family, Property, and Social Transition*, pp. 165–8 (Oxford: Blackwell, 1978); Robert Colls and Philip Dodd (eds), *Englishness, Politics and Culture 1880–1920*

(London: Croom Helm, 1986); Gerald Newman, *The Rise of English Nationalism: A Cultural History* (New York: St Martin's Press, 1997), pp. 87–120.

80. Cf. Marr, *The Day Britain Died*, p. 102.
81. Kumar, *The Making of English National Identity*, p. 20.
82. Ibid. p. 239.
83. Marr, *The Day Britain Died*, p. 22.
84. Murray G. H. Pittock, *Inventing and Resisting Britain: Cultural Identities in Britain and Ireland, 1685–1789* (Basingstoke: Penguin, 1997), p. 6.
85. Cf. Kumar, *The Making of English National Identity*, p. 187; Ian Baucom, *Out of Place: Englishness, Empire, and the Locations of Identity* (Princeton: Princeton University Press, 1999), pp. 194–222.
86. See Kumar, *The Making of English National Identity*, p. 9; Cf. Michael Hechter, *Internal Colonialism: The Celtic Fringe in British National Development* (London: Routledge and Kegan Paul, 1975).
87. Kumar, *The Making of English National Identity*, pp. 63–4, 81.
88. Cf. ibid. pp. 32, 191.
89. Ibid. p. 2.
90. Ibid. p. 62.
91. See David McCrone, 'Unmasking Britannia: The Rise and Fall of British National Identity', *Nations and Nationalism*, 3–4, 1997, pp. 579–96; Colin Kidd, *Subverting Scotland's Past*.
92. Kumar, *The Making of English National Identity*, p. 147; he uses the alternative phrase 'emotional attachments' on p. 239; see also Kidd, *Subverting Scotland's Past*, pp. 310–40.
93. Marr, *The Day Britain Died*, p. 131.
94. Nairn, *The Break-up of Britain*, pp. 21–35; Kumar, *The Making of English National Identity*, p. 176.
95. Kumar, *The Making of English National Identity*, pp. 185–6.
96. Colley, *Britons*, pp. 98–100.
97. For example, Roger Scruton, *England: An Elegy* (London: Chatto and Windus, 2000), p. 195.
98. Alun Hawkins, 'Rurality and Urban Identity', in Morley and Robins (eds), *British Cultural Studies*, pp. 145–56: 150.
99. George Orwell, *Coming Up For Air* (London: Penguin, 2001). p. 000; Jenkins quoted in Marr, *The Day Britain Died*, p. 112, see also p. 54.
100. Nairn, *The Break-up of Britain*, p. 261.
101. Hawkins, 'Rurality and Urban Identity', p. 152.
102. Cf. Alex Potts, 'Constable Country Between the Wars', in Samuel (ed.), *Patriotism, Vol. III: National Fictions* (London: Routledge, 1989), pp. 160–86: 166.
103. Quoted in Potts, 'Constable Country Between the Wars', p. 175.
104. Ken Worpole, 'Village School or Blackboard Jungle?', in Samuel (ed.), *Patriotism, Vol. III: National Fictions*, pp. 130–2; Francis Mulhern, *The Moment of Scrunity* (London: NLB, 1979), p. 101.
105. Cf. Yasmin Alibhai-Brown, *Who Do We Think We Are?: Imagining the New Britain* (London: Penguin, 2001), p. 25; Paul Gilroy, *Black Atlantic: Modernity and Double Consciousness* (London: Verso, 1993), pp. 1–40.
106. Cf. Hutton, *The State We're In*, p. 335.
107. Nairn, *The Break-up of Britain*, p. 178.

108. See also Ernest Barker, *National Character and the Factors in its Formation* (London: Methuen, 1927); Arthur Bryant, *The National Character* (London: Longmans, 1934); J. B. Priestley, *English Journey* (Harmondsworth: Penguin, 1977).
109. See Kumar, *The Making of English National Identity*, p. 215.
110. Baucom, *Out of Place*, pp. 12–13.
111. Marr, *The Day Britain Died*, pp. 10–11.
112. Ken Loach (dir), *My Name is Joe* (Germany, UK, France, Spain: Westdeutscher Rundfunk, Tornasol Films, Degato Film, Channel Four Films, 1999).
113. Stephen Daldry (dir), *Billy Elliot* (UK: Working Title Films, 2000); Marr, *The Day Britain Died*, pp. 32–3.
114. Marr, *The Day Britain Died*, p. 65.
115. James Mitchell, *Strategies for Self-Government: The Campaigns for a Scottish Parliament* (Edinburgh: Polygon, 1986), pp. 100–01.
116. For example, Simon Heffer, *Nor Shall My Sword: The Reinvention of England* (London: Weidenfeld and Nicolson, 1999), pp. 40–8.
117. Quoted in Kumar, *The Making of English National Identity*, p. 269.

Chapter Seven

Reading the Empire State

British History in Post-British Perspective

The preceding chapters have attempted to chart a path amongst powerful recent post-British perspectives, including Tom Nairn's *After Britain* (2000), Robert Crawford's *Devolving English Literature* (1992/2000), Cairns Craig's *Out of History* (1996), and Murray G. H. Pittock's *Inventing and Resisting Britain* (1997), all of which connect to wider debates over the union going back a couple of decades. *After Britain* may seem an odd mode given Nairn's related subject matter in *Faces of Nationalism* (1997) and this study's debt to *The Break-up of Britain* (1977). But it is in *After Britain* that Nairn nails the idea of post-British citizenship as democratic renewal, opening up a general theory of sub-British nationhood without imperialism. Nairn has long been prone to inane accusations of anti-Englishness; as he recognises, what has happened is that the parameters of the break-up of Britain have remained unclear on the English side, while the specifics of Scotland's emergence from Britain are much more obvious. Like most books on devolution and culture, above I have also used a disproportionate number of Scottish examples to illustrate a process so far more significant there than in England – although England will form the vast majority of (and perhaps the entire) continuant state.

The recent explosion of post-British analysis has established the importance all round of at least accounting for the representation of sub-British nations. Before this, a culture of lopsided regionalism still blocked accounts of each nation's place in British history, particularly imperial history. This is still true of some accounts, such as Michael Fry's *The Scottish Empire*, in which British Scotland is congenitally unionist, calculating, 'enterprising' and 'individual'.[1] Fry does not address the question of how Scotland *as nation* stands in relation to British colonialism, seeing rather a set of individual negotiations with extant power – itself a very British interpretation. The real question of Scotland's, and England's, national responsibility within British imperialism is tricky, and is a question candidly dodged by most Scottish nationalists, who prefer to concentrate on Scotland's repression. Thus *The Scottish Empire*, in some ways a groundbreaking account, comes from a Unionist Tory, and meanwhile the Scottish Parliament has little more to say than Westminster about imperialism; it is only parties outwith the British mainstream, elected via a more democratic system, that force any debate at all. But two related processes that force the question of national place are the growing desire for a more democratic form of citizenship *throughout* the UK, and the multiplying and connecting of perspectives throughout the former empire.[2] In these senses, Fry's deeply-researched and interesting history also appears something of a red herring, without much to say about Scottish action except when it disappears under an individualist British historiography of development, and thus stops being action at all. In Fry's account, the innocuous-sounding 'encounter' with a 'diversity of cultures among mankind' in an atmosphere of 'temperance and tolerance' even made Scotland more like Scotland; he argues quite convincingly that post-imperial Scottish nationalism arose from a re-reading of imperialism's 'progress'.[3] This, though, does not tell us much about how sub-British national emergence relates to empire. Here I have suggested that Scotland should be proactive in working with England to find national cultures stuck at quasi-ethnic status within the union. Correspondingly, devolutionary comment which states that Scots are now quite comfortable in their own identity[4] should be clear about this: Scotland *is* ethnocentric, since it lacks citizenship or any other satisfactory marker of continuity except ancestry. Scottish, or English, independence would have to pass through an ethnocentric moment, and the speed of its passing can be read as a marker of democracy.

Similarly, against the infuriatingly smug presentation of Gaelic as 'our' national language, we could instead suggest that a generalised will to undo standard English is a Scottish national 'language'. Gaelic certainly is an anti-British language *par excellence*; on the other hand, if the UK Government had had half-way humanitarian asylum rules since 1990, and if Scotland had taken a proportion of these immigrants commensurate with its population, then there would now be many more Scots speaking African and mid-Eastern languages than native Gaelic-speaking Scots – assuming that they were allowed to 'become' Scots. Nor did Scots make a major effort to change British policy on Iraq via the Parliament: perhaps too many were busy learning 'our' language.

One stopper for non-ethnocentric cultural histories has been the division of culture and politics as such. Despite occasional acknowledgement that political devolution has been a response to growing cultural identity (at times overestimating the growth of the SNP as a cultural cipher), political scientists and historians have only recently cited culture seriously in the same breath as citizenship. Conversely, cultural analysts, especially Scottish ones, frequently push individual artists rather than looking at the politics of cultural movements. In *Devolving English Literature*, Robert Crawford powerfully shows how the cultural spine of British identity was established by the margins, but does not address the specificity of the nation rather than the region, or the 'province'. (Similarly, Alexander Broadie's important 2001 study of the Scottish Enlightenment carefully pitches 'patriotism' at unspecific moments in the writing of Hume, Smith and Ferguson, lingering between Scotland and Britain, so as not to have to address the lack of specific reference to the Scottish nation.)[5] Crawford's study enthusiastically explicates many of MacDiarmid's poems, but mentions Marxism only once, making it hard to get a sense of the First Renaissance's ideal of a national community kept alive by dialectic – or that dialectic's failures. Also puzzling is the way the book neatly historicises English Literature yet still uses its methods: biography, canon massaging, individual greatness, tending to fear death by water when approaching the coastline of the discipline. This is despite its own pioneering insight that Scotland has been the lynchpin of the culture of the empire state, and that once the Scottish literary imagination is withdrawn, the British game is up.

Such an understanding of how apparently natural national qualities can bleed from one nation to another remains rare in accounts of English nationality. Ironically, given that England is the home of Cultural Studies, English national culture is often summarily separated from the political, in the sense of representation and citizenship (to some extent reflecting the distinction that used to be made in International Relations between the 'historical'/'primordial'/ethnic nation and the 'modern', inclusive nation).[6] Even Krishan Kumar's subtle account casually cites Scotland – and so, logically, England – as a 'cultural nation', though he is surely aware of the connection of the cultural and the political over the last twenty years, and the importance of citizenship to non-ethnocentric civic rights.[7] A 'cultural nation' without recourse to political process is always ethnocentric – this remains a good reason in itself to stress national citizenship. David Marquand has described the uncultural UK as an 'exit state' rather than a 'voice state', allowing only for withdrawal rather than re-negotiation, and so failing to generate the loyalty required for a national identity.[8] For Marquand, Britain is thus the last unbroken *ancien régime*, with a New Right which has grown as a reaction to cracks in the old 'national' tradition.[9] (This would certainly explain the reactive pulling to the right of the Labour Party in the 1990s). Similarly for Arthur Aughey, Britain has not survived the move from class politics to identity politics.[10]

Marquand elsewhere agrees that the loss of empire leaves Britain no *raison d'état*: 'British identity as such was imperialist, and is incapable of remaking itself'.[11] For Arthur Aughey, '[t]he fragments of its [Britain's] world-view can be expressed in a few simple lines: London at the centre, local patriotism, membership of a major power with global responsibilities and kinship connections throughout the empire or Commonwealth'.[12] This model though 'now appears morally questionable, politically wasteful and historically moribund'.[13] For Bernard Crick, England, especially in the 1980s, has failed to appreciate the duality that was central to Britishness.[14] Or, as Nairn puts it in an *NLR* article of 2000, the British remains temporally frozen while the spirit of the age moves on – recalling the distinction between the continuant and the active in Macmurray.[15] Macmurray also illuminates the links between the continuant and the pragmatic, and should serve as a warning against descriptions of nations' participation in Britain as pragmatic, organic and commercial. Raphael Samuels's extraordinary three-volume collection of essays, *Patriotism*, carefully restates the loss of the organic nation, yet we are never quite sure where this nation is: in the same introduction, about 'be[ing] English', Priestley, Orwell and English soccer fans are adduced to British nationalism, and British foreign policy is described as Anglocentric.[16]

Graham Morton has more recently taken up the theme of historicising the pragmatic reaction to Britishness, specifically in the mid-nineteenth century. Morton's 'unionist nationalism' was settled by Scottish middle classes who held on to empire and continued to negotiate their civic values within the state.[17] Probably baffling to many Britons, the concept of unionist nationalism nevertheless perfectly describes a tendency of Scottish cultural compromise, from the Enlightenment but particularly after the rapid expansion following the Napoleonic wars. Indeed Walter Scott blazed the trail in the period immediately preceding Morton's field; after Scott comes an extraordinarily bleak half-century for Scottish literature, during which cultural identity is rarely linked to political representation. For Morton, a unionist nationalist tendency is reflected in contemporary historical commentators including N. T. Phillipson, R. J. Morris and Donald Dewar;[18] we might even suggest a similar 'pragmatic' tendency even leading from David McCrone's 'stateless nation' model and Michael Keating's sophisticated 'post-national' negotiations.[19] These thinkers' negotiation of citizenship could be seen as a Fanonian critique of state-happy national emergence; it could also however be seen as an heir of unionist nationalism, rarely noting that more general ethical problems – like imperialism – still have to be sorted out in the negotiation of state and nation.

For Murray Pittock in *Inventing and Resisting Britain* (1997), Protestant-imperialist identities of the eighteenth century had already allowed not only for Scottish political incorporation but also for the maintenance of post-1689 ideas of England's natural centrality, an absorption dating back to England's 'first empire'.[20] Both Scotland and Anglo-Ireland were active in the British empire, and Pittock agrees that empire has been Britain's only preserving quality.[21] Both colonising and destructive of its own national experience, Britishness represents a wider assimilative tendency which is not necessarily on behalf of any one region, and contains the seeds of its own downfall. For Nairn, British assimilation was thus 'simply a function of the unique imperialism in the wider world, and of the state-form which corresponds to it internally'.[22] Deprived of an imperial mission, the empire state is now forced to remember that it no longer represents *any* of its nationalities. And every Briton has a sub-British nationality: English tourists abroad do not always, despite the assertions of some commentators, describe themselves as British.[23] Tom Nairn, Lindsay Paterson, Bernard Crick and others have discussed the consequences of Britain's historical failure to address primary identity – that it has not acted as a nation; or in the personalist terms above, it does not involve national action.[24] The imperialist habit, lacking in action as such, has been behind both the form of the British state and British behaviour. Kumar notes that until at least the 1960s, the imperial reaction was so strong that British governments still expressed automatic preferences for the Commonwealth (and then Anglophone Atlanticism) over Europe.[25] The fear of not preserving Greater Britain written into Britishness helps explain why a tradition of 'warnings' still exists (see below), much to the bemusement of most other Europeans, three decades after the UK under Heath accepted the primacy of European law. For some people, as Will Hutton has pointedly noted, Brussels became the new Moscow.[26] As Kumar points out, the North American press helps keep Britain Eurosceptic, and much of the political culture of Cool Britannic New Labour – the culture of 'spin' – was imported from Washington.[27] For Samuel, even 1960s British socialism lost its 'national' tradition and became beholden to American individualism .[28]

Standing intimidatingly behind all accounts is Colley's *Britons: Forging the Nation 1707–1837* (1992), which sews Britain together into a fabric of Protestant and then imperial interests after the Union. Where Colley employs a range of historical texts in the course of her assessment, Howard Weinbrot's *Britannia's Issue* (1993) celebrates the specific achievement of British literature as a *'concordia discors'*, a melting pot that 'stimulates literary greatness' as it successfully incorporates difference.[29] Both can be bracketed together as seeing British history as a series of pragmatic calculations that led to a more or less united identity.[30] Kumar thus makes an interesting comparison between Colley's study and Daniel Defoe's 1709 pro-Union propaganda piece *History of the Union*; Colley is (although loath to accept it) basing her argument on a 'Defoe hypothesis' of calculation and gain.[31] Kumar agrees with Colley that the 1745 uprising was largely ignored in lowland Scotland, and that Scotland was central to early-nineteenth-century Francophobia.[32] But he also makes the Barnett-like argument that an 'expansive' borderless Englishness concretised in Britain produced an unresolved anxiety over European sovereignty 'coming in', a unitary conception of sovereignty as a zero-sum game.[33]

Colley's account of happily pragmatic Britons is indeed not far from Michael Fry's: 'if Great Britain fissures in the future into autonomous Welsh, Scottish and English nations – and it may – this will in part be because its different peoples have decided that they can get ahead better without it'.[34] That the self-interest model remains in Tories who celebrate the individualist, mercantile past is unsurprising; when it is also taken for granted by liberals there is something odd about it. A look at the journalism on devolution at the turn of the 2000s shows that even the liberal-left press takes the self-interest model for granted, usually combined with a quasi-tribal terminology. Although liberal journalists would take for granted an ethical viewpoint as primary in, for example, the question of bombing Iraq, ethical questions of dissolving the state government which makes these decisions, frequently against the wishes of its people, rarely appears. Even the most suasive commentators tend to measure the efficacy of independence negotiations in terms of national self-interest. This is true even from the Scottish side: Michael Keating, using a Quebec-influenced 'regional state' model, often prioritises attaining the best negotiating position; David McCrone measures the worth of the Scottish Parliament in terms of 'efficiency'.[35]

In Colley, the assumption of self-interest is backed up by stressing the Whiggishness of the British peripheries; journalists and landowners were instrumental in turning the Whigs' image into that of the party of freedom by the early nineteenth century, especially when they opposed slavery and bolstered British imperialism's moral mission.[36] Whig reform led at home to the 'people's power' of the period 1815–37 (a phrase oddly recalling 'people's' in New Labour), a period littered with petitions; it also led to bitter disappointment over the 1832 Reform Act, and an English rage still audible in Barnett's *This Time*.[37] But since the period was also one of massive post-Napoleonic expansion, it is unsurprising that Britishness was then at its strongest. Colley exhaustively demonstrates that Scots were enthusiastic participants in the Francophobia and Protestantism which lay at the heart of emerging Britishness, even finding a distinctive identity in the persecution of Catholics (Unionist Nationalism indeed).[38] She stresses, like Kidd, that successful individual Scots adapted their past to an Anglo-British present, and that they were to be found in great numbers in India and the 'rawest frontiers'.[39] Over-participation in colonial expansion and government indeed allowed for a feeling of redress of the lack of direct representation at home.[40] Scottish participation in Britishness (or even the Scottish invention of Britishness) allowed a move from the raw idea of the divine right of kings to a mediated and 'balanced' model of monarch-in-parliament, from the early eighteenth century.[41] In other words, for Colley this constitutional 'balance' was not merely an invention of nineteenth-century Whig historians, as Kidd and others have argued.[42] This is one reason why Colley's account of the new Britishness, with its relative absence of coercion, resistance and class conflict, is open to accusations of Whiggishness itself. As Leith Davis puts it, 'both Colley and Weinbrot employ a narrative that repeats, despite the authors' best intentions, the Whig interpretation of British history as a series of events that eventually lead to a united identity for Scots and English as Britons'.[43] In 1999, Norman Davies's celebrated *The Isles* further tried to answer people's lack of stress on statehood, and more generally historical process, in part generated by Whiggish histories.[44]

One aspect of Colley's account well-suited to post-Britishness is her description of how early British traders required stability and colonialism, and how this pairing required a state of constant war, financed by speculators, joining new maritime power with old land power in the building of Britishness.[45] A dramatic over-expansion led to worries about infection of the Anglo-British way of life by Asiatic decay, the now-familiar sense of postcolonial ambivalence and Anglo-British 'beseigedness'.[46] (Thus, as Orwell sardonically observed, after Waterloo all battles were *lost* on the playing fields of Eton.)[47] Colley expands on this sense of being trapped 'at home' in her more recent *Captives* (2002), portraying Robinson Crusoe as the ultimate Protestant maritime conqueror, nevertheless a slave on his own land.[48] *Captives* is also more vocal about imperial violence, carefully stressing that today's situation is post-colonial but not post-imperial, and that an understanding of empire is 'vital for a proper understanding of our...world'.[49] And this is the real issue of the break-up of Britain: the nation has become unsustainable without empire, over-investing power in a strong Westminster executive, an imperial habit whose *mission civilisatrice* is now no longer even made in Britain anyway.

Un-Modern Modernisation

In 1977, Nairn brought the red/black context back into a popular focus, bemoaning 'habitual class remedies to nationalist ailments', here referring specifically to the Scotland and Wales Bill 1976, conceived as a British 'graduated response' to placate constitutional change (though it was eventually defeated).[50] The year 1976 is now sometimes seen as the last chance for the British government to fully control the process of devolution; yet fear of change of any kind remained strong in a British society 'too anchored in archaism ever to free itself by spontaneous effort or reform'.[51] Devolution, conceived in its constitutional sense, was such a spontaneous reform, and halfway between the publication of the first and second editions of *The Break-up of Britain* it was duly gerrymandered off the agenda. Statesmen (and here we can adduce Thatcher as an honorary bloke) have remained stuck in the backward-facing 'modern' role of holding Britain together, one which holds that nationalism is simply not one of our traditions – an extraordinary claim given the flag-waving that accompanied empire.[52] In response, and as we have seen, especially in the post-World War I period '[t]he deformation of England by her [British] state-history . . . generated a late but unmistakable variety of left-nationalist popular culture'.[53] However, since Britain lacks any 1789-style moment of rethinking itself, for Nairn the crisis of the assimilative state is 'the extremely long-delayed crisis of *the* original bourgeois state-form'.[54] The UK in this sense has been an exemplar of the dangers of stretching the state to cover non-existent identities; it has been, in David McCrone's more recent words, a 'state-nation masquerading as a nation-state'.[55]

Nairn's *After Britain* takes the story forward to 1999, amidst New Labour's puzzlement at losing their grip on what should have been a mere re-shuffling of the regions. The government's willingness to believe, or at least to appear to believe, that Britons still *felt* British was shown by the loose movement of Cool Britannic culture that marked its first term. Major's 'back to basics' metamorphosed into Blair's 'core values'; both are implicitly British characteristics known instinctively. As with all post-war Labour policy, Blair's challenge was to present maintained respect for precedent as increased democracy. At some point the process had become one of *not* responding to cultural change as it came from below. Even when in June 1997, the Department of National Heritage became the Department of Culture, Media and Sport, a rebranded, re-culturalised Britain remained far removed from culture as understood by, for example, Cultural Studies.[56] The think-tank Demos redefined culture as varied inflections of the status quo, and squared the Thatcherite circle. The Thatcher years had seen a largely spurious struggle between 'enterprise' and 'heritage', leaving a 'heritage culture' which the Blair government, so to speak, inherited.[57] As Stuart Hall has pointed out, Blair's modernised Britain was thus strikingly un-modern on just about every social issue, remaining nuclear-family-based, conservative with a small c, and Anglican.[58] Its 'newness' inheres not in increased cultural possibilities but in a strategy of multiple address which can be seen to give everyone the Britain they want, 'a series of audiences that require different messages'.[59] This was the remit of Cool Britannia, Demos, Lottery money and the various millennial projects intended to usher in a New Labour era (itself vaguely imaged as another thousand years of 'unbroken history'). Keith Robbins draws attention to parallels between the millennial celebration of a Labour win in 2000 and that of 1951; the Festival of Britain's imperial theme of the elect nation was then already strained, after the recent loss of India/Pakistan.

But at the end of the millennium, Anglo-Britain was still somehow the New Israel, and prosperity still arose from free trade, grand design and providence.[60] Situated in the extreme south of the 'nation', the Dome was an enormous drain on one of the most deviously classist taxes ever levied, the National Lottery, and undermined its own status as national culture by having each 'zone' sponsored by private corporations. The 'tawdry shell' of the Dome was not strong enough 'to carry so many expectations as the symbol of Labour's "New Britain"'.[61]

But the 'New Britain' sits low-down on the shoulders of the 'old', and by association, white, Britain, in a way that an independent England or Scotland would have the chance to avoid. New Labour Home Secretaries have maintained the immigration policies of Tory governments of 1962, 1971 and 1981, and asylum processes have actually tightened since 1997. Two years after the failure of the first devolution referendum, the 1981 Patriality Act marked a move from *ius soli*, the primacy of residence, to *ius sanguinus*, the primacy of blood – another radical change in the nature of the state.[62] The British executive has become more and more able to take such actions without consultation; in 1998, Blair was still speaking of 'enlightened patriotism', in praise of the super-centralised state inherited from a Thatcherite centralisation described by David Marquand as 'more Jacobin than Tory'.[63] Yasmin Alibhai-Brown's 2000 book *Who Do We Think We Are?* is one passionate attempt to account for anti-immigration panics, convincingly demonstrating how Thatcher's acceleration of post-war immigration rules created a 'twin-track' Britishness – and thus a terminal split in British identity.[64] The book, though, shifts between 'England' and 'Britain' compounding the 'English problem'; as far as we can work out, Englishness is ethnic, and 'the British nation' is multicultural.[65] Like Andrew Marr, her stance is reforming-New British,[66] and her only problem with the 'bright...young' think-tank Demos their clinging on to a 'four-nations' model of Britishness, where there should only be a single Britain with endless diversity.[67] The problem with this thinking is that it *guarantees* racism by keeping Englishness ethno-cultural, blocking muliculturalism within England itself; immigrants become British, but not English. This leads to confusions such as the analysis of the Diana phenomenon which sees Diana as moving beyond Englishness, where Andrew Marr and Neal Ascherson recognise that her radicalism was in her championing Englishness as against a super-national British aristocratic mafia.[68] Nevertheless Britain itself sometimes poses as an ethnicity, as in the phrase 'indigenous Britons'.[69] The ethnicisation is disingenuously Powellite, assuming that immigrants bring their home nations with them, chipping away at Englishness rather than becoming part of it. As historical research has confirmed over the last decade or so, the British 'nation' itself went hand-in-hand with imperial and racial purposes. So the answer to Alibhai-Brown's question of why terms like 'black British' seem so difficult is simply that the idea of 'Britain' doesn't work that way. A more significant question would concern the challenge of being 'black English', or 'black Scottish'. In Scotland at least, immigrants and non-white people are overwhelmingly likely to describe themselves as Scottish rather than British, especially as they are often concentrated in working-class urban environments where being 'British' would mark anyone out for suspicion. The tendency to call this anti-British suspicion 'anti-English' is itself a classically British reaction (and we could ask if it is acceptable to call black Scots 'tribal' if they are pro-devolution). If Alibhai-Brown sounds – as she quotes Marr saying of her own writing – 'lonely',[70] this is not surprising: all Britons are lonely. All Britons, *as* Britons, inhabit the remains of an imperium with the gusts of economic globalisation blowing through it, where every civic body is up for sale for short-term profit,[71] and the sponsoring of political parties by multinational corporations is viewed as democratic. This is normal for pragmatic, mercantile Britain, preserving its traditions in a paradoxically un-modern modernism.

Elegies (Warnings)

Although devolution has been oddly viewed as a kind of betrayal by much of the British liberal press, a more extreme reaction, and in some ways a more telling one, has arisen from certain sectors of the right, who take umbrage at a perceived threat to their own tradition. These elegies for Britain, speaking of loss and break-up, are actually warnings, since they feel that break-up is still avoidable. Most of these commentaries claim to be recovering Englishness; somewhere in their early stages they typically make a claim to accuracy along the lines of 'most Scotsmen these days wouldn't thank you for being called English', yet inevitably go on to describe England as a collapsed Britain.

Studies like Simon Heffer's *Nor Shall My Sword* repeat the 'self-interest' theory of devolution, noting that the Scots used their 'grievance', a delusion of being 'ripped off' by England, to get themselves 'offered ... goodies' in the form of a parliament:[72] no wider ethical point is imaginable. Heffer's now-familiar response is to speak for the put-upon English, who, out of an innate kindness, feel that they 'owe the other peoples in these islands a living'.[73] Like other outraged pseudo-nationalist writers reacting to devolution, Heffer recalls a Wilkesite eighteenth-century tradition of complaint about over-inflated Scottish economic and political power in Anglo-Britain (a tradition which actually had a more serious point than do these writers).[74] Wilkes was an eighteenth-century English radical – some say an early English nationalist – often expelled from Parliament, and known for his criticism of Scottish influence in London. Heffer accepts an anecdotal report in the *Daily Telegraph* as 'clear evidence' of an Anglophobic Scottish racism,[75] and mutual ethnic enmity is assumed whatever the actual circumstances: the Scots 'simply loathe the English, and do so on largely tribal grounds'.[76] Again Heffer sees the primary role of the 'modern' Prime Minister as keeping the union together despite his apparent English nationalism. More tellingly he charts the beginning of the rot back to Gladstone's inability to push through 'Home Rule All Round', when the Home-Rulers had still not become properly nationalist (a backwards extension of the '1976-as-last-chance' theory).[77] Heffer's Englishness is backed up with Powellite hints about the *ius sanguinus*: 'Something stirs deep in the blood of the English'.[78] Perceiving Scotland as ethnic, he is then also bound to perceive England as ethnic.

Jeremy Paxman's better-informed account of 1998 also falls into line with the assumption of Scottish Anglophobia – '[f]or every Scots and Welsh nationalist leader working out a coherent relationship with the rest of Europe, there are a thousand who simply harbour a sullen resentment of the English'.[79] Given this image of a thousand racial malcontents for every one 'coherent' speaker, it is difficult to believe that Paxman inhabits the same island – or works for Reith's BBC. Here devolutionary tribalism is backed up by slim pickings from popular culture, as in the 'colonised by wankers' speech by 'Irving' Welsh, said by one 'smackhead ... to another' (in fact, this is narrative comment, not speech, by a narrator struggling with heroin withdrawal, and painfully over-sensitised to violence. The speech was hugely overplayed in Danny Boyle's film, which stays in the memory of the elegist more than the original text).[80] Again present is the English taxpayer suffering through his (sic) own 'charming' nihilism, and the 'tribal' Celtic regions, whose 'every self-respecting adult considers themselves to belong to an unbroken tradition stretching back to the wearing of woad'.[81] Present too is the football metaphor, which seems here to be taken seriously as an expression of political allegiance.[82] Again, despite early protestations of specific Englishness, Paxman uses 'British' more or less interchangeably – England contested World War II, and the rebranding of Britain from 1997 made a tactical mistake in not playing to England's strengths.[83] Paxman also refuses to call those more recently arrived to his nation English, as in the peculiar statement that 'in Spittalfields 60 per cent of the population are now Bangladeshi', suggesting, again in Powellite vein, that no-one can ever *become* English – making a present-tense England an impossibility at the same time as seeming to stand up for it.[84] In Greater British style, this race-nation seems to 'possess' English language; Paxman echoes another familiar Powellite worry in '[w]hat happens to a people if they lose their own language?'[85] This is not to say the account's individual case studies are not entertaining and insightful; he sees through, for example, Major's calculatedly retro creation of besiegedness relative to the EU after the Catholic and socialist threats had gone.[86]

More straightforwardly New Right is John Redwood's account from the next year, which claims in elegiac mode to describe *The Death of Britain* while representing a rearguard warning against it. Again mixing his terms under a general Anglo-British tradition, Redwood sympathises with Powell's midlander who has experienced the 'sense that somehow England was in danger, that Britain was threatened, that our whole way of life was on the cusp'.[87] As the Thatcherite royal 'we' suggests, 'England' is not easy to pick out from the British government of which Redwood was a member; how Britain's being on the cusp endangers England is not clear. Redwood's Britain is 'at peace with its past' – despite hanging on to neocolonial economics, and despite the fact that half of the population of the northern signatory are trying to pull out.[88] Again Scotland is a potential rogue state, merely using the UK as 'something to rebel against'.[89] Redwood's main aim here, *contra* devolutionary and neo-Chartist movements, is to argue against any kind of constitutional change, stating that since the present constitution is capable of being rewritten, this means it must be more responsive to public demand.[90] This shows a peculiar lack of faith in people's ability to understand their own representation, as seen in the complaint that New Labour 'think the public want a government that listens more and explains more' (echoing John Major's classic 'we should understand less and condemn more').[91] The Euro-sceptical fantasy that the

EU is behind devolution also automatically implies devolution of the English regions – again bypassing the English nation altogether, although the book seems to be about Englishness.[92] Again Scottish self-interest is *the* devolutionary process – an Edinburgh Parliament 'will constantly be demanding more money'.[93] 'True devolution', though, should be to 'people, companies, and families', Redwood argues in Thatcherite vein, carefully avoiding any loose talk of society. Devolution should be exemplified by council house sales and other expressions of the 'individuality of the family'.[94] Here Britain is again individualist and pragmatic, but the UK nation 'a fact of history'.[95] More shrewdly, Redwood recognises the morbid continuity in images of Britain projected by *both* Conservative and New Labour governments: '[t]here are many people who feel unhappy in Mr. Blair's back-to-the-sixties Britain, just as there are [sic] people who felt unhappy with John Major's warm beer and cricket on the village green, with its images of a cosy 1950s'.[96]

Perhaps the most hardline in the elegies/warnings tradition is Roger Scruton's *England: An Elegy*. If Paxman's engaging account sometimes allows itself to bend the terminology, Scruton's is so jam-packed with mistakes that it is difficult to see how it got past a publisher: on the first page he claims that the English 'began to call themselves British and the most popular of their songs affirms that "Britons never never never shall be slaves!"'; he goes on to adduce to an exclusively English tradition John Carlyle, J. S. Mill, the BBC (now perverting everything except the Proms into 'anti-English satire'), *The Oxford English Dictionary*, *The Golden Bough*, David Hume, David Livingstone, and the settling of America.[97] Inexplicably, he brings in Seeley's *The Expansion of England* to underscore the Britishness of the empire, where Seeley stressed the benefits of implantation of English language and culture. Everywhere Scruton struggles against himself to define an un-British England, only relieved by the interpolated hatred of the Scots. Nairn for example is 'writing as an enemy', taking advantage of England's endearing habit of apology.[98] Also approvingly cited is Baldwin's *The Englishman* since it 'emphasises self-government', though both Baldwin and his follower Major were British unionist.[99] For Scruton a sense of tradition carried by the constitutional 'balance' is the core of what he imagines to be England's imperial foreign policy: 'the real achievement of the English is their attempt at world government'.[100] Postcolonial racial anxiety remains in fulminations against the unreined sexual desire of those who 'litter the country with their illegitimate, uncared-for and state-subsidised offspring'.[101] This is an England not looking bravely into the future but one anxious about dilution of its people. Yet the English are to be known as instinctively non-conflictual, reasonable, mercantile, mystical and gentlemanly; England also seems to possess a class harmony which is simply destroyed by being mentioned.[102] As in the other elegaic accounts, England needs to become proactive – something Scottish analysts had been saying for at least three decades.[103]

All the reactive accounts of the post-British moment have certain points in common: they all agree, albeit grudgingly, that Scotland has had to lead the way in terms of political/constitutional change. They all fail to see that the English constitution was compromised in 1707 beyond any bounds of 'flexibility', and that England is involved in a union from which it cannot extract itself merely by refusing to take any more nonsense. They fail to grasp that England has had no foreign policy for three centuries, and that England was not a major imperial power. They are all 'unbroken thousand-year history' accounts, disavowing the fundamental changes in constitution since the Norman Conquest (when, ironically, a foreign language was imposed as that of government, leading to a thousand years of popular Francophobia). The 'thousand years of unbroken history' trope in Prime Ministerial speeches running from Baldwin to Gaitskell to Thatcher to Major ignores the status of the union as well as of immigration, and ignores both the importance of the northern part of England itself to national tradition and the redistribution of wealth to the nation's well-being.[104] These accounts offer at least three related right-wing conspiracy theories about the connection between devolution and Europe: firstly, that both are attempts to entangle the docile English character in rules and theory; secondly, that Europe is all dangerously socialist except England; and thirdly, that both are a Catholic plot by underground Jacobites aiming to depose the Hanoverian monarchy.[105] They all show a Wilkesite concern over how many Scots have insinuated themselves into 'English' government and culture, and all lack Wilkes's actual concern for England. They all link English constitution and English character in a Seeleyesque trope which was itself finally made impossible by the warped Anglo-British nationalism of the 1980s. They all argue that England eventually did the decent thing by its colonies; they all assume that an independent England would 'maintain' its place in organisations like the EU, the UN and the G8, without question of renegotiation – where Scottish analysts tend to wonder about the fate of every former member of the UK.[106] They all portray England as the put-upon benefactor aggressively attacked on many fronts – a tradition with links to Enoch Powell's 1968 speech, combining fear of invasion, pollution and linguistic degeneration.[107] Finally, they all imagine an England which can be post-British without describing, or even adequately understanding, the British context.

The reactive English moment of the warning (elegy) is revealing about the disavowal of Britishness and the misunderstanding of the origins of devolution; but it was also short-lived, its anxiety not representative. Most English people do not think of themselves as racially exclusive; most, mercifully, do not believe everything printed in the *Daily Telegraph*. During the same period there were much more considered accounts of Englishness, from Stephen Haseler's *The English Tribe* (1996) to Ian Baucom's 1999 *Out of Place*, and then Krishan Kumar's *The Making of English National Character* (2003). In *In Search of England* (1999), Michael Wood also neatly set the tone for a possible rediscovery of English history by using 'myth' somewhat in the way of Alisdair MacIntyre: myth prevents the reduction of history to questions of validity, being something from which the stuff of identity is formed. Thus, for example, the myth of the 'Norman yoke' strengthens during times of fear of occupation, such as World War II, in a contingent geography of place, rather than any racial quality.[108] In *The English Tribe*, Stephen Haseler describes how we are 'coming to the end of the British story' (despite which, he tends to repeat the 'thousand years' fallacy).[109] Recognising the difficulty of pinning down England to any set of rules or origin, Haseler is able to usefully describe English thinking, as does Kumar later, as being based on 'themes rather than on ideologies'.[110] Haseler's own republicanism resembles that of Jonathan Freedland in seeing the American revolution as a form of republican democracy England has missed out on (though, as we have seen, Scots were amongst the states' prime spokespeople, giving Scotland more of a sense of a republic *manqué*).[111] In the run-up to the 1997 election, Will Hutton was a major spokesman for a republican social responsibility, constitutionalism, and a (Keynesian) mixed economy, again resembling the liberal republican Adam Smith (though not the incumbent New Labour government, whose economy was scarcely 'mixed').[112] And *contra* Scruton, it *is* possible to feel the sense of sadness at accounts of the decay of England even without 'being' English (whatever that means). For those who have lived in England, each return reveals its countryside to be a bit more knackered and its representatives a bit more compromised. Yet commenting from outside, or as someone who is 'not English' (whatever that means), commentary on this seems unallowable, or in the case of those who 'are Scottish'

(whatever that means), aggressive and 'tribal'. In this sense one begins to sense what non-white Britons must feel like when they hear
that they are the ruin of the country.

The English 'Problem'?

Of course, proactive Englishness need not also be *reactive*. Above I
have tried to argue that devolution should be placed within the
wider context of the ethical breakdown of Greater Britain and the
release of each nation: a number of (mostly Scottish) scholars have
been doing this for some time. At the head of these is Nairn's *The
Break-up of Britain*. Inexplicably described as racial enmity by Scruton, who appears not to have read the book, it argues that the motive
behind separatist devolution movements is not ethnocentric at all:
'the key to these [1970s] neo-nationalist renaissances lies in the slow
foundering of the British state, not in the Celtic bloodstream'.[113] For
Nairn, Scottish separatism has been 'overwhelmingly a politically-
oriented separatism . . . frequently indifferent to the themes of race
and cultural ancestry'.[114] Here Nairn anticipates a widespread
1990s British misreading of devolution across the political board:
'[i]f one does not realise that [the British state] is moribund, like
most of the English left, then naturally Scottish and Welsh nationalism will appear as destructive forces'.[115] George Orwell had
over three decades before this made similar complaints about the
English left's confusion over nationhood, a 'divorce between patriotism and intelligence'.[116] And Orwell is an unflinchingly English
writer, understanding English tradition as inherently democratic
and noting that 'the 'Rule Britannia' stuff . . . is done by small
minorities'.[117]

In Freedland's sense of the republicanism gone underground in
the Enlightenment, the Thatcherite/Majorite/Blairite '80s and '90s
only prolonged and embittered an English adjustment – for some an
embittered 'backlash' – which had already been set out by Nairn in
1977: '[i]n reality, that "backlash" is the frustrated political potency
of the English people'.[118] Nairn's terminology here, carefully placed
inside quotation marks, is telling: the breakdown of Anglo-British
identity has long been brewing, and indeed arises through fundamental problems in the empire state itself. Englishness was, in other
words, displaced by British imperialism, and appears *unheimlich* after imperialism unless reconstructed properly as nationality rather
than ethnicity – thus the anxiety of the elegies (warnings). In his 1999

book *Out of Place*, Ian Baucom describes how the New Right have turned auratic (possessing an aura or spiritual uniqueness) English 'place' into 'race'. The place-specific, inclusive English Romanticism of Wordsworth led to the localism of Ruskin and Morris, nevertheless ending in the Powellite paradox of race without empire.[119] Two years into her Powell-influenced reign, Margaret Thatcher discarded the *ius soli* for the *ius sanguinus*, against the English tradition of democratic communities tied to the soil, *soli*, denying citizenship to Commonwealth citizens, a move debated, insofar as her administration ever debated anything, in the week of the Brixton riots. As Baucom argues, this shifting of the ground of citizenship represented a substantive change which should have contravened the constitution – a 'disavowal of the prescriptive authority which had stood, for so many centuries, at the heart of English law'.[120] Its racialisation signals an ahistorical and insubstantial nationhood, England's Britain rather than England's England, and, in a last echo of Greater Britain, the repudiation of place.[121] Thatcher's abandonment of place for race thus 'discarded the peculiarly English tradition of tradition', and destroyed 'a thousand years' of default-level England without replacing it with an actual England.[122] Paradoxically, under the 'Englishing' Tory governments, the English people were decreasingly represented – an attack made on England not by tribal Celts but by attempts to plaster over the crevice between Greater Britain and English experience. Baucom's aim is to critically move England towards the *ius soli* by showing how English nationalist, quasi- or proto-nationalist writing was associated with local specificity, growing through *contact with* the soil and the auratic places, the Tintern Abbeys of English tradition.[123] In the twentieth century, 'racial' memory became the enemy of English tradition rather than its saviour; '[t]his refusal to believe that nonwhite immigrants could ever become English amounts, of course, to race prejudice, but it also implies a historic repudiation of the aura of the English place'.[124]

Baucom moreover demonstrates how the English space of belonging is also that described by Salman Rushdie, a space inflected by the urban riot (or, put less pejoratively, the carnivalesque gathering of a crowd capable of spontaneous rebellion).[125] Coffee-table accounts like Paxman's hint jocularly at an English tendency to be 'unruly', but do not go the full Orwellian extent of showing how disrespect for order has driven evolving English experience and at times kept it democratic, latterly *contra* Britain. Noting (somewhat in the manner of Paul Virilio) that the televising of the Brixton riots sealed them into a glassy *terra incognita*, 'less the *vanishing* of Englishness than the *dispersal* of its locations of identity',[126] Baucom quotes Rushdie's eloquent rage at England's unwillingness to defend the *ius soli*: 'you sat back and did nothing as Mrs. Thatcher stole the birthright of every one of us, black and white, and of our children and grandchildren for ever'.[127] This is where 'traditional' English identity really inheres, and:

> [w]hile Rushdie's Victorian and Edwardian predecessors did not phrase the problem exactly as he does, they also understand that the nation's uneasy commitment to its empire had massively complicated the task of defining what it meant to be English in large part by making it so difficult simply to determine what kind of place England was.[128]

Rushdie's commitment to the place of experience can in turn be related both backwards to the Chartists' reformulation of the myth of the free-born Anglo-Saxon, and laterally to the concept of the 'performative' in Homi Bhabha, in which the nation is continuously remade against its own ahistorical anteriority. In this sense the rioter can actually save the nation.[129] Similarly, Rushdie's characters, like those of Cairns Craig's James Kelman, 'resist arrest', battering on and remaining active against the retro-constitutional habit of insisting that things don't change because they don't change.[130] David Marquand has also similarly described the struggle as one against a Britain characterised by 'arrested development'.[131]

Conversely the English traditions of democracy, decency and respect for the sovereignty of ever-changing community, passing through Wordsworth, Morris, Orwell and Rushdie, would only be missed by the most obtuse Scot. Tales of general anti-English 'racism' in Scotland were invented by unscrupulous journalists to sell newspapers; no-one with at least one eye open to Anglo-Scottish relations believes them. Most recognise on some level that England has not had a worldwide empire, and there are only a very few enthusiasts for the rebranded Greater Britain left, particularly those reliant on British power, notably the Johnson–Boswell-like partnership of Gordon Brown and Tony Blair. Given its native national traditions of decency, privacy and freedom, it is hard to believe that the former Ukanian republic of England, with a PR-based, constitutional system of representation, would support, for example, the terror campaign behind radioactive conventional and economic attacks on Iraqi civilians since 1990. Or that it would pursue an aggressive policy of rationalisation of public sector services when this policy is destructive of English communities.[132] Would England struggle to think of new ways to re-jig British class identity, from the National Lottery to university fees, setting it apart from Europe, even though large-scale Europhobia only really kicks in with the high-British Seven Years' War? And how much more convincing would James Bond films be if Bond was really spying for England, now that 007 is no longer Sean Connery wearing a Scottish nationalist tattoo? Could England do better than a recent Bond film of Cool Britannic vintage, which opened with a boat chase up the Eliotic, millennial Thames (Dome in view), featuring Timothy Dalton (English gentleman) handled by Judi Dench (English dame) in pursuit of Robert Carlyle (Russo-Scottish psycho)?[133]

It is difficult also to see an independent England fully conversant with its own tradition of localism, rather than the British one of besiegedness, continuing to strengthen immigration rules, or to criminalise and lock up asylum-seekers. Kosovans who have come to seek shelter after Britain has bombed all infrastructure out of their homelands have been seen as 'gypsies', drawing new fears of magic and travellers' arts, and more surveillance.[134] British towns now routinely place security cameras in their high streets. These are British, not English, habits of thought; they can be historicised, compensated for, and gradually de-commissioned. Reaching that phase takes a post-British history: while commentators of various persuasions talk of today's 'post-imperial' phase with abandon, the British government continues, via an Anglophone bond and much as it did in the nineteenth century, to conduct attacks on various parts of the world for strategic economic reasons, while shoring up its own borders. 'Race' should have died almost a century ago, and the weaker English use of 'race' as shared heritage is not systematic in the same way; as Orwell pointed out, only the English saw fascism as incomprehensibly comic, rather than threatening.[135] Going on Nairn's thesis that Scottish Romantic nationalism was submerged by the Anglo-British state variety to reappear as kitsch and kailyard, the emergence of an English neo-Romantic national identity from the Anglo-British form can be seen as the final stage of the process of drawing back to England's borders from the universalism of Greater Britain. For Tony Benn thus, Britain's last colony is England, requiring a post-British liberation struggle against the imperial idea as did the colonies.[136] This is part of a long roll-back beyond and within the borders, and the peak of English frustration comes not when threatened with devolution but when devolution as a sensibly-defined nation is blocked to them, via the cricket test, and the idiotic equation of warm beer and cricket with union. The

Powellite account of Englishness, and his hopes for strict repatriation rules are paradoxically un-English.[137]

Orwell's 'England, Your England' – often rifled by the New Right for quotations – had thus stressed the English tradition of 'privacy' rather than privatisation. Orwell was, of course, behind Bevan's post-1945 Welfare State, though it went much less far than he would have wanted, to judge from his 1941 tract.[138] His basis is an English communitarian sense of trust, which even extends to the 'English [sic] electoral system . . . [even though it is] all but an open fraud'. Reclaiming patriotism, democrats should be pushing for constitutional shake-up – or revolt: Orwell also had the quixotic idea of turning the wartime Home Guard into a revolutionary vanguard.[139] In the candidly titled 'The English Revolution', he maintains the link between English specificity and democratisation: '[p]atriotism has nothing to do with Conservatism. It is actually the opposite of Conservatism, since it is a devotion to something that is always changing and yet is felt to be mystically the same'.[140] This sentence is about as good an anti-racist twist as can be found on the early twentieth-century divergence of views on English land. Orwell adds, as if Powellite debates on immigration were already squarely in view, 'we must add to our heritage or lose it'.[141] This is buried deep in English tradition: the idea that the last to arrive are the most important to the whole community goes back as far as medieval English Christianity. In the medieval English vernacular poem *Pearl* we find a recounting of Matthew 20's Parable of the Vineyard, in which for Christ 'the last [workers] schal be the fyrst that strykez'.[142] This is even related to the embryonic Anglo-Israeli tradition of the elect nation: 'Vchon in scrypture a name con plye/Of Israel barnez'.[143] Since the earliest days of its vernacular literature, England has known that inclusiveness strengthens rather than weakens, that those attached to the land (*ius soli*) should have priority over those who use titles to the land for economic rationalisation (*ius sanguinus*).

Scottish or English history thus cannot be 'introduced' to those who come to their vineyards 'later'; national history cannot be explained to them because they *are* national history. The question of how to circumscribe post-British citizenship is a tricky one, which England has so far virtually ignored. One suggestion would be having been born in Scotland/England *or* having been resident in Scotland/England in 1997 *or* resident at the time of independence with a UK passport. When residency qualifications are thought out like this, 'race' goes out the window. This is, as I have tried to argue, a prime reason for the euthanasia of the British state. Similarly, images of England in mainstream culture have, perhaps since the First

World War, needed to image a striking 'home', and become decreasingly English, against an actual continuity of English contact with the land which has passed through rambling, festivals, traveller routes, 'low-impact communities' and rave. The land was still being lived on while John Major was insisting it be 'recovered' (in the Fanonian sense of recovery as fetishistic longing). Educationally, we could pay more attention to Englishness itself; this might also involve the conversion of departments of 'English Studies' and 'English Literature' into ones which really do study England and English literature, leaving to its own designation the Irish, Scottish and colonial literature which now forms a staple of Eng. Lit. As it stands, in Susan Condor's phrase, England remains an 'unimagined community';[144] in my own terms, reversing the thesis of Craig Beveridge and Ronald Turnbull, and taking seriously the role of vision in the Scottish Enlightenment, we have witnessed an 'eclipse of English culture'.[145]

England has nothing to be afraid of. There is no great gradualist democratic tradition to be protected. Any nation-state which emerges from Britain can scarcely fail to be more democratic than one with no proper constitution, an outmoded first-past-the-post voting system, an executive with a power Saddam Hussein would have envied, a reluctance to reconsider its Anglopone-imperial 'special' position, chronically lazy 'consensus politics', an established church, an upper chamber half-hereditary and half-quango, and a token head of state. A good-humoured stance of procrastination is one response, and this might be acceptable were it not that the habit we call Britain has effects which stretch far beyond British shores. Imperialism could not have happened on the scale it did without state unification; imperial habits are difficult to get rid of via the same state. As many Britons now realise, this is the real point of devolution and similar constitutional movements. The separation of two or three small, relatively unimportant Western European nations is small compared to their behaviour towards the rest of the world; for this reason, and not for any imagined rising ethnic tide, these nations are moving towards what Frantz Fanon called a 'national consciousness, which is not nationalism'.

Notes

1. Michael Fry, *The Scottish Empire* (Edinburgh: Birlinn, 2002).
2. For an attempt to account theoretically for the colonial responsibility of sub-British nations, see Michael Gardiner, 'A Light to the World: British

Devolution and Colonial Vision', in *Interventions: International Journal of Postcolonial Studies*, 6.2, forthcoming.

3. Fry, *The Scottish Empire*, pp. 491–6.
4. For example, Brian Taylor, *Scotland's Parliament: Triumph and Disaster* (Edinburgh: Edinburgh University Press, 2002), pp. 106–22.
5. Alexander Broadie, *The Scottish Enlightenment: The Historical Age of an Historical Nation* (Edinburgh: Birlinn, 2001), for example, pp. 43–77, 94–100.
6. See, for example, Anthony D. Smith, *The Ethnic Origins of Nations* (Oxford: Blackwell, 1988), pp. 6–18.
7. Krishan Kumar, *The Making of English National Identity* (Cambridge: Cambridge University Press, 2003), p. 245.
8. David Marquand, 'How United is the United Kingdom?', in Alexander Grant and Keith Stringer (eds), *Uniting the Kingdom?: The Making of British History* (London: Routledge, 1995), pp. 277–91: 278–88.
9. Marquand, 'How United is the United Kingdom?', p. 286.
10. Arthur Aughey, *Nationalism, Devolution, and the Challenge to the United Kingdom State* (London: Pluto, 2001), p. 16.
11. Marquand, 'How United is the United Kingdom?', pp. 287–8; Marquand, *The New Reckoning: Capitalism, States, and Citizens* (Malden, MA: Polity, 1997); cf. Hopkins, 'Back to the future: from national history to imperial history', *Past and Present*, 164, 1999, pp. 198–243.
12. Aughey, *Nationalism, Devolution, and the Challenge to the United Kingdom State*, p. 39.
13. Ibid. p. 40.
14. Cf. Bernard Crick, *Labour and Scotland's Right* (Edinburgh: East Linton Constituency Labour Party, 1989).
15. Tom Nairn, 'Ukania Under Blair', *New Left Review*, 1, January–February 2000, pp. 69–103.
16. Raphael Samuel, 'Introduction: Exciting to be English', in Samuel (ed.), *Patriotism: The Making and Unmaking of British National Identity, Vol. 1: History and Politics* (London: Routledge, 1989), pp. xviii–lxvii: xx, xxiii, xxvi–xxvii, xxxiv; on a recent *apologia* for British organicism, see Margaret Canovan, *Nationalism and Political Theory* (Cheltenham: Edward Elgar, 1996).
17. Graham Morton, *Unionist Nationalism: Governing Urban Scotland 1830–1860* (East Linton: Tuckwell, 1999), p. 8.
18. Ibid. pp. 9–10.
19. David McCrone, *Understanding Scotland: Sociology of a Stateless Nation* (London: Routledge, 1992); Michael Keating, *Nations Without States* (London: Palgrave, 2001); Keating, 'The Realities and the Limits of Independence', in Eric Jo Murkens, *Scottish Independence: A Practical Guide* (Edinburgh: Edinburgh University Press, 2002), pp. 273–300.
20. Murray G. H. Pittock, *Inventing and Resisting Britain: Cultural Identities in Britain and Ireland 1685–1789* (Basingstoke: Macmillan, 1997).
21. Ibid. p. 135.
22. Tom Nairn, *The Break-up of Britain: Crisis and Neo-nationalism* (London: NLB, 1977), p. 65.

23. Cf. John Redwood, *The Death of Britain: The UK's Constitutional Crisis* (Basingstoke: Macmillan, 1999), p. 190.
24. See Nairn, *After Britain* (London: Granta, 2000); Lindsay Paterson, *The Autonomy of Modern Scotland* (Edinburgh: Edinburgh University Press, 1994); Bernard Crick (ed.), *National Identities: The Constitution of the United Kingdom* (Oxford: Blackwell, 1991).
25. Kumar, *The Making of English National Identity*, p. 176.
26. Hutton, *The State We're In* (London: Vintage, 1996), p. 335.
27. Kumar, *The Making of English National Identity*, p. 199.
28. Samuel, 'Introduction: Exciting to be English', p. xxxi.
29. Howard Weinbrot, *Britannia's Issue: The Rise of British Literature from Dryden to Ossian* (Cambridge: Cambridge University Press, 1993), p. 1.
30. Leith Davis, *Acts of Union: Scotland and the Literary Negotiation of the British Nation, 1707–1830* (Stanford: Stanford University Press, 1998), p. 6.
31. Kumar, *The Making of English National Identity*, pp. 150–1.
32. Ibid. pp. 162–4.
33. Ibid. pp. 272–3.
34. Colley, *Britons: Forging the Nation 1707–1837* (London: Pimlico, 2003), p. xv.
35. For example, Michael Keating, 'Independence in an Interdependent World', in Jo Eric Murkens, *Scottish Independence: A Practical Guide* (Edinburgh: Edinburgh University Press, 2003), pp. 273–84; Keating, *Nations Against the State: The New Politics of Nationalism in Quebec, Catalonia and Scotland* (London: Palgrave, 2001); David McCrone, 'Marking the Card: The Scottish Parliament at 1000 days', paper given at the Institute for British–Irish Studies, University College Dublin, 3 April 2002, online version: file:///Macintosh%20HD/Desktop%20Folder/Online%20Article%20-%20McCrone%2C%20Scott. Consulted 2002.
36. Colley, *Britons*, pp. 344–5, 359–60.
37. Ibid. p. 367; Anthony Barnett, *This Time: Our Constitutional Revolution* (London: Vintage, 1997).
38. Colley, *Britons*, pp. 11–54, 325–31.
39. Ibid. pp. 125–8, 374–5.
40. Ibid. pp. 129–32.
41. Ibid. p. 48.
42. Ibid. p. 52; see Colin Kidd, *Subverting Scotland's Past: Scottish Whig Historians and the Creation of an Anglo-British Identity, 1689–c. 1830* (Cambridge: Cambridge University Press, 1993).
43. Leith Davis, *Acts of Union: Scotland and the Literary Negotiation of the British Nation, 1707–1830* (Stanford: Stanford University Press, 2001).
44. Norman Davies, *The Isles: A History* (London: Macmillan, 1999); cf. J. G. A. Pocock, 'British History: A Plea for a New Subject', *New Zealand Journal of History*, 18.1, 1974, pp. 3–21.
45. Colley, *Britons*, pp. 66, 85–100.
46. Ibid. pp. 101–5; cf. Paul Langford, *A Polite and Mercantile People: England 1727–1783* (Oxford: Oxford University Press, 1989), p. 171; Catherine Hall, 'British Cultural Identities and the Legacy of Empire', in David

Morley and Kevin Robins (eds), *British Cultural Studies: Geography, Nationality, and Identity* (Oxford: Oxford University Press, 2001), pp. 27–39: 28–9.

47. George Orwell, *The Lion and the Unicorn: Socialism and the English Genius* (Harmondsworth: Penguin, 1982), p. 55.
48. Linda Colley, *Captives: Britain, Empire and the World 1600–1825* (London: Jonathan Cape, 2002), p. 1; on the Seven Years' War cf. pp. 5–6, 10–11.
49. Ibid. pp. 374–9.
50. Nairn, *The Break-up of Britain*, pp. 61–3.
51. Ibid. p. 300.
52. Ibid. p. 293.
53. Ibid. p. 304.
54. Ibid. p. 19.
55. David McCrone, 'Scotland and the Union: Changing Identities in the British State', in Morley and Robins (eds), *British Cultural Studies*, pp. 97–108.
56. For example, Ken Warpole, 'Cartels and Lotteries: Heritage and Cultural Policy in Britain', in Morley and Robins (eds), *British Cultural Studies*, pp. 235–48: 242; cf. Stephen Driver and Luke Martell, 'Blair and "Britishness"', in Morley and Robins, *British Cultural Studies*, pp. 461–72: 466.
57. See Patrick Wright, *On Living in an Old Country* (London: Verso, 1985); Alison Light (ed.), *Island Stories: Unravelling Britain* (London: Verso, 1999).
58. Quoted in Driver and Martell, 'Blair and "Britishness"', p. 469.
59. Driver and Martell, 'Blair and Britishness', p. 468.
60. Keith Robbins, *Great Britain: Identities, Institutions, and the Idea of Britishness* (Harlow: Longman, 1998), p. 329.
61. 'Introduction', Morley and Robins (eds), *British Cultural Studies*, pp. 1–26: 9; see also Iain Sinclair, *Sorry Meniscus: Excursions to the Millennium Dome* (London: Profile, 1998).
62. McCrone, 'Scotland and the Union', p. 101; cf. Zig Layton-Henry, *The Politics of Immigration: Immigration, 'Race' and 'Race' Relations in Post-war Britain* (Oxford: Blackwell, 1992), pp. 192–3.
63. Quoted in Driver and Martell, 'Blair and Britishness', p. 462; David Marquand, 'How United is the United Kingdom?', p. 281.
64. Alibhai-Brown, *Who Do We Think We Are?: Imagining the New Britain* (London: Penguin, 2001), p. 80
65. Ibid. p. 21.
66. Ibid. p. 36.
67. Ibid. p. 11.
68. Ibid. pp. 36–9; Andrew Marr, *The Day Britain Died* (London: Profile, 2000); Neal Ascherson, 'Put Out More Flags', *New York Review of Books*, XCVI, 1999, pp. 46–9; cf. Barnett, *This Time*, pp. 80–1, 127–30.
69. Alibhai-Brown, *Who Do We Think We Are?*, p. 1.
70. Ibid. p. xix.
71. Cf. Hutton, *The State We're In*, pp. 321–2.
72. Simon Heffer, *Nor Shall My Sword: The Reinvention of England* (London: Weidenfeld and Nicolson, 1999), pp. 3, 10, 19.
73. Ibid. pp. 3, 36, 31.

74. For example, ibid. p. 26.
75. Ibid. p. 35.
76. Ibid. p. 34; cf., surprisingly, Haseler, *The English Tribe*, p. 156.
77. Heffer, *Nor Shall My Sword*, p. 5.
78. Ibid. pp. 46, 10.
79. Jeremy Paxman, *The English: A Portrait of a People* (London: Penguin, 1999), p. 49.
80. Ibid. p. 52; Irvine Welsh, *Trainspotting* (London: Minerva, 1994), p. 78.
81. Paxman, *The English*, pp. 52–3, 261, 264.
82. Ibid. pp. 246–50.
83. Ibid. pp. 87, 238–9.
84. Ibid. p. 73.
85. Ibid. p. 235.
86. Ibid. pp. 144, 171; see also Raymond Williams, *The Country and the City* (Oxford: Oxford University Press, 1973).
87. Redwood, *The Death of Britain?*, p. 4.
88. Ibid. p. 6.
89. Ibid. p. 190.
90. Ibid. p. 12.
91. Ibid. p. 15.
92. Ibid. pp. 118–19, 142.
93. Ibid. p. 123.
94. Ibid. p. 137.
95. Ibid. p. 190.
96. Ibid. p. 190.
97. Roger Scruton, *England: An Elegy* (London: Chatto and Windus, 2000), pp. 1, 225.
98. Ibid. pp. 252–4.
99. Ibid. p. 44; see Stanley Baldwin, *The Englishman* (London: Longmans, 1940).
100. Scruton, *England*, p. 195.
101. Ibid. p. 246.
102. Ibid. pp. 54–65, 145–6, 161, 172–4, 193.
103. Ibid. p. 67.
104. Andrew Marr, *The Day Britain Died*, p. 20; see David Cannadine, 'British history as a "new subject": politics, perspectives, and prospects', in Grant and Stringer (eds), *Uniting the Kingdom?*, pp. 12–28; John Major as quoted in *The Guardian*, 10 October 1992; see also 'England at sea', *Independent on Sunday*, 20 August 2000; Marr, *The Day Britain Died*, pp. 125–7.
105. See, for example, Kumar, *The Making of English National Identity*, pp. 63, 173.
106. See, for example, Heffer, *Nor Shall My Sword*, p. 12; Murkens, *Scottish Independence*, pp. 141–57.
107. See Ian Baucom, *Out of Place: Englishness, Empire, and the Locations of Identity* (Princeton: Princeton University Press, 1999), p. 15.
108. Michael Wood, *In Search of England* (London: Viking, 1999), especially pp. 1–106.
109. Stephen Haseler, *The English Tribe: Identity, Nation and Europe* (London: Macmillan, 1996), p. 3.

110. Ibid. p. 21.
111. Jonathan Freedland, *Bring Home the Revolution: How Britain can live the American dream* (London: Fourth Estate, 1998); cf. Liah Greenfield, *Nationalism: Five Roads to Modernity* (Cambridge, MA: Harvard University Press, 1992); Robert Colls and Philip Dodd (eds), *Englishness, Politics, and Culture 1880–1920* (London: Croom Helm, 1986).
112. Will Hutton, *The State We're In* (London: Vintage, 1996).
113. Nairn, *The Break-up of Britain*, p. 71.
114. Ibid. p. 71.
115. Ibid. p. 73.
116. Orwell, 'England, Your England', pp. 64–5.
117. Ibid. p. 42.
118. Nairn, *The Break-up of Britain*, p. 81.
119. Cf. Baucom, *Out of Place*, pp. 19–20, 41–74; see also E. P. Thompson, *The Making of the English Working Class* (London: Victor Gollancz, 1964); William Morris, *News From Nowhere* (Cambridge: Cambridge University Press, 1995).
120. Baucom, *Out of Place*, p. 12.
121. Ibid. pp. 13, 30; on postcolonial ignorance, cf. Orwell, 'England, Your England', p. 43; David Marquand, 'How United is the United Kingdom?', p. 289; Bernard Crick, 'The Sense of Identity of the Indigenous British', *New Community*, April 1995, pp. 21–2.
122. Baucom, *Out of Place*, p. 13.
123. Cf. Orwell's stress on the feel of the land in 'England, Your England', p. 36.
124. Baucom, *Out of Place*, p. 21.
125. Ibid. p. 195.
126. Ibid. pp. 214, 220; see Paul Virilio, trans. Michael Degener, *Desert Screen: War at the Speed of Light* (London: Continuum, 2002), pp. 107–39.
127. Quoted in Baucom, *Out of Place*, p. 197.
128. Ibid. p. 37.
129. Ibid. pp. 198–99.
130. Cairns Craig, 'Resisting Arrest; James Kelman', in Gavin Wallace and Rendall Stevenson (eds), *The Scottish Novel Since the Seventies: New Visions, Old Dreams* (Edinburgh: Edinburgh University Press, 1993), pp. 99–114; on Walter Bagehot's praise of the absorptive powers of the constitution, see Scruton, *The English*, p. 177.
131. David Marquand, *The Unprincipled Society* (London: Fontana, 1998); see also McCrone, 'Scotland and the Union'.
132. In *Faces of Nationalism* and *After Britain* Tom Nairn used the epithet 'Ukanian' sarcastically to connote the break-up of the senile Hapsburg empire.
133. Lee Tamahori (dir), *Die Another Day* (USA: Eon Productions, 2002).
134. See David Sibley, 'The Control of Space: Travellers, Youth, and Drug Cultures', in Morley and Robins (eds), *British Cultural Studies*, pp. 417–430: 418–19, 423.
135. See Bill Ashcroft, Gareth Griffiths and Helen Tiffin, *Postcolonial Studies: The Key Concepts* (London: Routledge, 2000), pp. 198–206; Orwell,

'England, Your England', pp. 41–2; cf. Samuel, 'Introduction: Exciting to be English', p. xxiii; Haseler, *The English Tribe*, pp. 43–4.

136. Quoted in Stephen Howe, 'Labour Patriotism, 1939–83', in Samuel (ed.), *Patriotism, Vol. I*, pp. 127–39: 136.

137. Nairn, *The Break-up of Britain*, pp. 259, 272; see Enoch Powell, *Biography of a Nation: A Short History of Britain* (London: Phoenix House, 1955); on England's mistrust of binding systems, see George Orwell, 'England, Your England', p. 43.

138. Orwell, 'England, Your England', p. 40.

139. Ibid. p. 45.

140. Ibid. p. 115.

141. Ibid. p. 123.

142. Malcolm Andrew and Ronald Waldron (eds), *The Poems of the Pearl Manuscript* (Exeter: Exeter University Press, 1987), line 70, orthography modernised.

143. Andrew and Waldron (eds), *The Poems of the Pearl Manuscript*, lines 1039–1040.

144. Susan Condor, 'Unimagined Community? Some Social Psychological Issues Concerning English National Identity', in Glynis M. Breakwell and Evanthia Lyons (eds), *Changing European Identities: Social Psychological Analyses of Social Change* (Oxford: Butterworth-Heinemann, 1996), pp. 41–68.

145. Craig Beveridge and Ronald Turnbull, *The Eclipse of Scottish Culture: Inferiorism and the Intellectuals* (Edinburgh: Polygon, 1989); Gardiner, 'A Light to the World'.

Index

EU Authorised Representative:

Easy Access System Europe Mustamäe tee 50, 10621 Tallinn, Estonia

gpsr.requests@easproject.com

Printed and bound by CPI Group (UK) Ltd, Croydon, CR0 4YY

22/04/2026

02095383-0004